179W

one seven nine west

179W
one seven nine west
by Andrew Taylor

WWW.179W.CO.UK

First published 2015

This paperback edition is first published in
Great Britain in 2015 by Andrew Taylor

WWW.179W.CO.UK

Copyright © 2015 Andrew Taylor
ISBN 978 1 291 99728 6

Dedication

This book is dedicated to the many thousands of people around the world who sent messages of support to myself, my family and all of the race crews across the whole fleet during some dark times; and to those whom have since continued to support & wish us all well. I am truly humbled by the response and the genuine personal interest in this story around the world, which is my motivation for this publication.

I published this book to share my version of the story to those interested. Many people close to the race have their own stories to tell, this however is my version.

I make no personal gain from doing this. In fact it has been extremely hard work to put this together and get it published. I am donating all of the book sale proceeds after costs equally between these charities. So don't please share your book, get your friends to buy their own copy, it's all for a good cause!

'The Ellen MacArthur Cancer Trust'

'Newmarket Day Centre'
In my home town of Newmarket, Suffolk

Introduction

23:32UTC. Sunday 30th March 2014. Andrew Taylor, an amateur sailor, taking part in the 9th Clipper round the world yacht race, aboard the 70' ocean racing yacht CV30 'Derry LondonDerry Doire', fell overboard during horrific weather conditions and was lost at sea for 1hour and 40minutes in the middle of the icy cold North Pacific. In the midst of a violent storm, almost 2,000 miles from the nearest land. With the exception of other racing yachts taking part in the same race, all of whom were over an hour away, no other vessels were within 1,000 miles.

The crew of the yacht were totally alone in their search and the eventual, dramatic recovery of Andrew, who was deeply hypothermic when recovered. Suffering badly from shock with a suspected broken leg sustained during his fall, he was treated and cared for continuously until they reached land some ten days later, by the on board medical team & other members of the crew.

The Derry race crew, the race office teams and his close friends & family back home, all closely followed every communication as best they could. Although many prayed for him at the time, none of them ever lost hope for his safe return to land. Andrew is only the third man overboard in the race's 18 year history. The previous two being recovered in 9 & 20 minutes respectively.

This book sets the scene as to how Andrew initially came to be competing in the race, his team's eventful and truly amazing journey yacht racing over 45,000 miles around the world. It covers the epic story of his desperate fight for survival in the North Pacific, the search & rescue operation, Andrew's miraculous, surprising, and almost immediate return to ocean yacht racing, getting straight back onboard to complete the entire round the world race. And how the story touched &

moved so many people around the world during the days and weeks that followed.

Many of the events of that fateful day were captured, as they unfolded, by a TV cameraman traveling onboard for the race to San Francisco. This exclusive & amazing footage went on to form the basis of a 60 minute episode of the subsequent BBC TV series about the race. Global media followed the story for several days. Andrew has since been in much demand for interview, comment and public speaking. Both BBC and Channel5 in the UK have produced short documentary films about the event. NBC in the US have completed a 90 minute documentary with interviews from the race Skipper and several of the other crew involved in the search and rescue.

Andrew has also been working hard with the Clipper round the world yacht race team, and a handful of the key global marine safety equipment manufacturers since the event. To share his feedback from this unique learning experience in an attempt to improve ocean safety. This event is truly unique. The remotest ever man overboard recovery. The first time AIS safety systems have ever been used in this manner. And possibly the longest anyone has ever survived during an MOB in waters of such extreme temperatures. As a direct result of this work, some readily available marine safety equipment has been altered and improved. Training for future Clipper round the world yacht races has been amended and updated. New equipment has been designed, manufactured & purchased and is now standard kit aboard all of the 70' Clipper Racing Yachts.

These improvements & changes, along with a heightened awareness amongst the world of ocean racing yacht teams, as to the speed & ease at which a crew member can be lost at sea, will all contribute to future safety on board racing yachts. This publication is told in Andrew's very own words. It is his personal account of this epic, dramatic and life threatening adventure story.

179W One Seven Nine West

Contents

Acknowledgements

To Mum & Dad
Without whom, I would not be the person I am.

To Siobhan
*Monkey The pleasure watching you grow into a
beautiful & intelligent woman is beyond words.
I love you more than you will ever know x*

To Sean McCarter & the crew of Derry LondonderryDoire
*Thank you for sharing the adventure of a lifetime.
I owe you my life, an impossible debt to repay*

Foreword
Sir Robin Knox Johnston

The phone ringing alongside my bed was the first I knew of Andrew's adventure. I blinked awake, fumbled for the light and picked up. *"Robin, its Justin, I'm afraid we have a Man Overboard situation on Derry about an hour ago"*. My heart sank. The boats were in the North Pacific which is anything but pacific. It can be cold, very windy, and I knew there was a nasty storm running through the fleet. An hour meant that whoever it was had probably died of hypothermia by now. In nine races we had now lost three over the side, but have recovered the other two in less than 20 minutes. This was very different. Justin filled in the rest of the details. The casualty was Andrew Taylor, a steady round the world crew member, I knew a little and liked a lot. The yacht was conducting a search, OneDLL had diverted to help and taken over communications with us, but an hour in those waters was not good and all we could do was await further news.

I asked the obvious questions, had we clamped down on communications from the boats and had the PR team been alerted. The PR team were next on his list and communications were closed down. This was standard procedure to prevent any communications from the crew to family and friends until we knew the exact story and could ensure it did not get misrepresented, misunderstood and exaggerated. *"OK"* I said, *"I'll head to the office and suggest we all meet there as soon as we can"*.

I dressed quickly, got my car out of the garage and was just leaving when my phone rang again. It was Justin. *"They have recovered him and he is alive!"*. A wave of relief swept over me. It was little short of miraculous that they and found him in those conditions and that he was still alive after such a long time on the cold seas. I knew that the next few hours were now vital as hypothermia can still kill, but there was a qualified paramedic on the team on board so he was in good hands I returned home, put the kettle on, made a cup of tea and awaited further news. As I learned more I realised that we were going to be busy dealing with press enquiries once our press announcement had gone out to the boats and the media. It was important that we got this out as soon as possible so we could open communications from the yachts, but at least the facts were available then instead of rumours. I headed over to the office.

As more information came in we appreciated how lucky Andrew had been. He had been in the water an incredible 100 minutes, but was in his Henri Lloyd Dry suit which would have given him extra vital minutes of life. He also had a McMurdo AIS Beacon which is how the boat had eventually found him. We knew that Sean McCarter was an excellent skipper, calm and organised, a good leader and excellent seaman, and he had the search skills learned with the RNLI. Andrew owed his life to Sean's determination to recover him in appalling conditions, a commitment shared by his fellow crew members.

As more information came in I felt very proud of everyone involved. The accident was caused because Andrew thought he was clipped on but he wasn't. Then the training had cut in. I had had to do little apart from help with the questions afterwards. Sean and his crew had done everything right, Andrew had eventually got his AIS beacon going and kept himself alive, Ollie had diverted without waiting for instructions and the team at home had reacted immediately and implemented our emergency plan.

There are always lessons to be learned from these situations. I had a long and extremely useful chat with Andrew in San Francisco and I realised how lucky we had been. Suppose he had been knocked unconscious when he hit the rudder, he could not then have inflated his lifejacket nor set off his AIS Beacon. He would almost certainly have died, even if we could have found him. We needed to create something automatic for man overboard recovery.

Andrew has written a very honest and useful account of his circumnavigation. It should be compulsory reading for any sailor contemplating an ocean crossing. A circumnavigation is always an adventure, and a tough one at that. More than twice as many people have climbed Mount Everest as have circumnavigated our planet. But Andrew's adventure was more than he, or any of us had ever bargained for. He was lucky, but he made a lot of his own luck through his own determination. As a result of this determination, he has the rest of his life to look forward to and I wish him many years to enjoy it.

Sir Robin greeting Andrew as he arrives in San Francisco
and is whisked away to hospital

Photo Credit; Clipper Ventures PLC

Preface

I have always considered myself lucky, to be fit & healthy and able to travel the world experiencing adventure and pushing some of the boundaries of life. Climbing, skiing, scuba diving and mountaineering. I am under no illusion however, I am a very very lucky boy to have escaped this particular life adventure alive to tell the story.

Many of the fleeting moments upon that fateful day in March 2014 could have easily ended differently. As could the subsequent story's ending. If I still had nine lives at the moment I became the *'man overboard'*, I have definitely used more than one of them in escaping this.

Since the event, I have felt compelled to share the story. Many thousands of people around the world have shown such a genuine personal interest. I am often called upon to recount events and share some of the experience. On each occasion however, I can only share small anecdotes. Increasingly over time, it felt wrong not to do so in a more correct and complete manner. Whilst at the same time, giving something back to the two charities I support.

If we can also subsequently learn something from this experience, share the lessons and contribute something. Anything at all in fact, however small, towards improved marine & ocean safety in the future. Then the trauma, emotional stress & worry which was burdened upon so many, will all have been worthwhile.

I genuinely believe, as a result of some of the outcomes of this event, lives will now be saved in the future, and for both this and escaping with my own life, I am totally humbled and shall be eternally grateful to very many special people.

Bio

This is me, Andrew Taylor, father, son, mad uncle, brother, business partner, nephew, cousin, friend, confidant, associate, neighbour. I really am just me! I am not special in any way, just a regular bloke who happens to have a passionate penchant for the outdoors, living life and seeking adventure.

I was born and spent my youth in Newmarket, Suffolk. A quite beautiful place inhabited by some truly remarkable and hospitable people. I didn't realise this when I was a growing up there. But as I regularly return in later life my affection for the area grows significantly. Many of my family and close friends still live there. My parents in particular have always lived there. They have, and still do, contribute towards the town's success in very many ways, via chamber of trade bodies, local council, charity work and the various and many numerous sports clubs where they both hold office positions of club secretary, chairman, president or whatever. It is also where you are most likely to find them. They are rarely at home and even rarer sitting still, they spend their lives in and around sport. Which is almost certainly where my own love of sport came from, growing up in a sporting saturated and competitive environment.

My mother and father are two of the strongest people I know. They have been together since they were 14, still pat each other on the bum occasionally, smiling & laughing together all the time. My father is a supporter and a risk taker, always doing something for others. Mother is a rock, stable and secure with a positive, voice of reason view on life's reality. I like to think I have inherited a little of each of these qualities, mixed with some mad adventure and a high risk adventure desire. Which probably came from my Grandfather who gets lengthy mentions in dispatches, was extremely highly decorated throughout the Second World War, has public memorials dedicated to him, roads named after him, and as I remember fondly always had great stories to tell in his soft Northern Irish accent. He often told us with a wry smile of riding the wall of death on a racing bike as a way of raising cash to fund his early professional football career. A story we were captivated by and absolutely loved to hear again and again as small children sitting on his knee. Only to discover in later life that he actually did do this! It was part of Duffy's circus in Northern Ireland and I have since met some people whom actually remember seeing the spectacle and its sideshow attraction. My search continues however for any pictures or memorabilia of this.

After a standard and relatively poorly rewarded secondary education, I talked my way into college in Cambridge studying hospitality. Which led to an early and successful career as a chef, working for several 3star Michelin restaurants, including Le Soufflé at the Intercontinental London, with Peter Kromberg, and with Michel Roux at the Waterside Inn. Then later as executive chef for the prestigious Royal Scotsman Train amongst others. After winning some culinary Olympic medals and competing in National Chef of the Year several times, I moved out of the kitchen and into hospitality management whilst still quite young and established myself as a project director for big new build and complicated food & drink projects for distilleries, racecourses, motor circuits, concert venues, outdoor events and major new football stadia including both the new Wembley & Emirates stadiums. This culminated in me being approached to project direct all of the food and drink in the north Olympic Park for the London 2012 games. Together with an amazing team of people we delivered some 8.6 million meals in a little over 3 months, which totally consumed my life, working for over two and half years, virtually without a day off.

My daughter Siobhan, whom I only ever affectionately call 'Monkey', has an amazing sense of humour, a smile to melt a million hearts and has grown into a very beautiful, intelligent and incredibly special young lady. (Ok, so I do need to admit here, that might be a slightly biased father opinion!) I miss her intensely all of the time we are apart. As a result of this she designed for me a tattoo of a monkey, which I now have on my shoulder, keeping her with me every single moment of every single day whilst I am travelling or whilst we are apart. This has, until right now in this book, been a very closely kept secret only Siobhan and I have shared. However, it forms a part of this story, has had a profound and significant life effect upon me, keeps me motivated through all adversity and also keeps me grounded and safe.

I cannot sit still, rarely watch TV, have an insatiable appetite for media, technology, sport, food & drink and being anywhere outdoors. A normal day for me would start with an early morning run, fresh ground coffee and a list of things I want to do which never ever gets completed as it just keeps on growing. After a very serious accident a few years ago when I got knocked down by a hit and run driver whilst out running, my insatiable thirst for living life to the full had already grown significantly long before I took on the challenge of round the world yacht racing.

I am fiercely competitive with myself, always challenging and pushing to raise the bar. Run a regular route faster, swim further, climb higher or just fit more into work & play each day. My desire to take part in a circumnavigation as part of the Clipper round the world yacht race 13/14 is based upon this self-challenge.

Why
A question I never ask myself

Wednesday 6th July 2005, I am standing towards the rear of the temporary FA boardroom. Temporary whilst the new Wembley Stadium is being built. Along with many close friends & colleagues, all of us working together on the final designs and mobilisation plans for the opening of the new stadium. A hush settles over the room as we watch and listen intently to the live television broadcast from Singapore on the massive flat screen television on the wall, and several smaller ones around the room, all tuned to various global TV channels covering the live broadcast.

Jacques Rogge, the International Olympic Committee President steps forward, and with an absolute precise clarity of definition proclaims *"The International Olympic Committee has the honour of announcing that the games of the thirtieth Olympiad in twenty twelve are awarded to the city of-"*. There is a massive delay, an unfeasibly long pause, the exact timing of which is still etched on my mind precisely to this day, it seemed like a lifetime, everyone in the room is frozen to the spot, holding their breath.

Many of us over the last couple of years have worked on small parts of the original London 2012 Olympic bid submission. Ok, so in the grand scheme they were small contributions, but we had contributed none the less, and we were part of it. Part of this day is ours. London is on the up & up. The new Stadium is going to be magnificent. It is going to be late, but it is going to be magnificent. We all felt like we were on the very precipice of something great, this is our city, this is our London and the world is wishing us well and watching just as intently as we are

Jacques Rogge exhales at the end of his pause and says clearly and concisely the word *"London"*. A short sharp cheer goes up, followed by a pause and an intake of breath, after not breathing for so long during the pause. With huge wide eyes, there are hugs, smiles and even tears around the room. London is at the centre of the world's media for today, the 2012 Olympics are actually coming to town, and what a place to be to learn this first hand. Champagne corks popped and we spend the rest of the day celebrating and enjoying the moment, snacks and a small buffet arrive, along with more champagne and lots of beer and wine. The afternoon rolls on with the last few of us eventually deserting the office quite late that evening.

Less than 24 hours later, many of the same people are back in the same room watching the same TVs. The empty glasses, bottles and buffet remnants from the previous days celebrations are still all around us as we watch the incredible and totally unbelievable scenes of devastation created by the 7/7 central London bombings.

The terrible events unfold around us in the city center throughout the day. Once again London was back to the center of the world's media, albeit for very different and very wrong reasons.

We had a good number of stadium colleagues, team members, close friends and family out in the city that day. We spent the rest of the day tracking each of them down and ticking them off a list as contact with each was made. It wasn't until very late that evening, when we ticked the last name off the list. As we slowly double checked and the realisation clarified now that each and every one of them was safe, the same wide eyes, hugs, smiles and more tears once again filled the same room.

The events of those 48 hours changed very many lives all across the world, some fundamentally more than others. For me, they made me think more carefully than before about what life should hold in the future, how fragile life can be, and how lucky I was in my career and my health. Notwithstanding the birth of my daughter Siobhan, these were two of the very longest and most emotional days of my life so far, and even writing this now I sometimes have to stop to take a breath! Over the following few weeks I made two very big and life changing decisions, personal promises, which have now come to pass.

Firstly: I decided I was extremely lucky in being at a significant 'right place, right time' in my working life, and that I would concentrate on a full and total commitment to the next few years of my career. Firstly, completing the project I had already started as part of the team opening the new Wembley Stadium and then contributing in the best way I possibly could to the success of our home Olympics. Two greater opportunities would rarely present themselves, and I would be totally mad not to grasp the moment.

Secondly: I decided that in early 2013 I would stop, and go do something completely different for a while, after all, what ever could you possibly use to encore being part of these next seven amazing years in London.

So, alongside an all-consuming work life, balanced wherever I could with family time, I started discussing and planning a high altitude mountaineering expedition with my climbing friends for 2013, still some six years away. I had done this before in between projects. Always having a personal life goal to fulfil, something to motivate and inspire me on the down days and dark times you always find in large scale projects. A sort of self-bonus, these were often a closely guarded personal secret. I promised myself a special watch, a particular mountain to climb or purchasing my dream car. All of these came to pass and bought me much pleasure. I actually bought a coffee mug with the particular dream car's logo on it whilst mobilising Wembley Stadium and it really helped to keep me sane at times. It also made eventually driving and polishing it years later such a massive personal pleasure, reflecting on the effort and stress I went through to earn it.

I had climbed in some amazing places around the world. But, as time went on and the plans progressed for the 2013 expedition, I struggled to find that really tingly excited feeling inside. Then one morning at a railway station I saw a poster for Clipper round the world yacht race!

After several meetings, an interview, a selection day, much personal consideration discussed with my parents and some lengthy financial calculations too; I signed a contract with Clipper Race to join the race and circumnavigate the globe, 45,000 miles as part of the crew in the 2013-2014 race. Was I mad? I had never even sailed before at this point. But for me, that was exactly the point, the challenge of taking on something new, learning a new skill. It is exactly what I had promised myself I would do.

From that day onwards I smiled every time I thought about the race. I had once again found that really valuable personal goal, a self-bonus and a deeply cerebral personal motivation in life. Pausing only to reflect on my family, health, luck, privilege and opportunity to achieve this. Very few people knew about the race. With the exception of my parents and an extremely select number of close friends. I didn't wish anything to detract from the Olympics project and so for me it was a closely guarded secret until after the closing ceremony and the project had closed down.

Fast forward to the 10th October 2012, and for the first time in over seven months, I have slept through the night. No telephone calls, no interruptions. During our 24hour park operations I have been awake every night at some point, whether to satisfy my curiosity and check something, or to take a phone call and respond with assistance. During games time operations, our night work was critical to restock and re-supply the park for the next day. So much so, that I regularly spent the whole night in the park, grabbing a few hours' sleep whenever I could.

This full night's sleep signified clearly for me the beginning of the end of this project. Some seven years work in total. We had just served the best part of 8.6 million meals, in less than eight weeks!

This day was another massively significant day in this life journey. A few months of bump out from the park followed as we de-rigged the temporary buildings & operations, then a few more months of final operating reports and a mammoth financial close down. All was done & finished in early 2013. Around January time I stopped going to work every day, and by early March I had closed down the operations completely. Now I could really concentrate upon my race training and preparation, which had previously just been a dream to keep me motivated.

Training
Cold, wet, tired and ecstatically happy to be doing this.

I agreed to complete my early race training in October and February respectively. I wanted to experience cold and wet. I hoped for what regular social sailors might call 'bad weather'. There seemed to me little benefit sailing around in glorious sunshine with shorts and sun glasses on, in the Solent, as preparation for a round the world yacht race taking on the southern ocean, Bass straights and south China seas. I would not be disappointed in this regard. We did have some sunshine, but to boot we had a fair share of proper windy, wet and cold days. With some real tasty channel chop to test out our sea legs too.

I arrived in Gosport early one October evening, packed and ready for my first training week. Well, when I say ready, consider this; whilst I am pretty self-sufficient and well used to living out of a rucksack for weeks on end whilst away climbing, I am an amateur sailor. In this instance the word 'amateur' applies in the very true sense of the word. I have up to this point in my life, never ever been onboard a sailing boat! My head feels like it is going to explode with questions, thoughts, concerns and genuine interest & excitement. Simple stuff, which to me now seems inane. What is it like sailing at night? What is it like sleeping whilst still racing? What do we eat? How and where do we wash? I felt naive, I felt nervous, I felt well and truly outside of my own comfort zone, but most of all I felt excited. I was about to find out what this is all about, learn some new skills and hopefully come away from the end of the week knowing I had made the right decision.

Training with Clipper Race is intense, immensely enjoyable and pretty serious all at the same time. The training Skippers are mostly ex or current ocean yacht racing Skippers, a mixture of round the world racers and navy instructors. They all have a patience and practical training approach the like of which I have not experienced or seen ever before. Skills are built at a brisk, sometimes gruesome, pace. Once a skill or manoeuvre is grasped an almost immediate opportunity to take responsibility for this, plus our own team work & safety whilst practicing these skills over and over is afforded. In the very early stages of training crew take on much responsibility, and in what seems like no time at all we are out in the channel sailing through the night in a force 8. Cold & wet, leading our own watch teams on deck, practicing what we have learnt without a Skipper looking directly over our shoulder, albeit under the safe, close, watchful attentiveness of the trainers. The quickest way to learn, is to do something yourself. Perhaps even make a mistake, learn from it and never make that same mistake again! The trainer Skippers are never that far away; safety is absolutely paramount and regular de-brief, reflection & further learning is both frequent and in depth.

With teams of like-minded crew, mostly on board for similar reasons, we build and bond very quickly. It takes less than 36 hours aboard a racing yacht to be working as one. The 'form-storm-norm-perform' process which normally takes weeks on land in a working team environment passes at a most extreme rate. I think partly because of the environment and risks associated with being aboard a racing yacht. Probably more so the sense of purpose, common goal and aim of the team; all of whom have made the decision to deliver a personal positive & full commitment to this even before they even arrive at training. We all have a great deal invested, time, emotion and financial in this adventure. We have much to lose and even more to gain from contributing well. Grasping this thought and finding a way of achieving this approach within a land based working environment would be unbelievably powerful for productivity.

Repetition of safety procedures and emergency drills flows throughout the training, and with each drill we get progressively stronger at dealing with potential issues aboard. We received a total 'beasting' from the Navy survival instructors on our sea survival training. A totally exhausting session of life raft and life jacket drills in a controlled indoor environment. Which left us all in no doubt about the scale of the risks we face, how tough it is to get in and out of a life raft at sea, how uncomfortable it is once you're in, and how much none of us wishes to do any of this for real!

At sea we constantly review and repeat exercise for all manner of eventuality. Casualty on deck, loss of steering, fire, flood, torn sails, loss of mast, capsize and of course Man over Board (MOB). The latter of these is repeated tirelessly. MOB is by far the greatest risk to life, and it is most of the crew's worst nightmare. As our skills build & the team work progresses, one of the '10stone' life size recovery dummies regularly 'falls' off into the sea, assisted by a trainer of course. We all launch straight into our drill, crash stopping the boat, marking way points, rigging harnesses and dropping a rescue swimmer over the side. Recovery is manic, a loud but controlled process and in training takes anything around 8-25 minutes in the calm waters of the Solent or the relative calm of the English Channel. In a big cold ocean this could easily take longer, and the thought of being the one getting cold and wet amongst massive waves, or worse still at night, whilst awaiting the boat to come back is a very unpleasant feeling for all of us. We are however confident about MOB recovery during training. We all know how it works and have heard the stories about the two previous Clipper Race MOBs, who were recovered quickly in 9 and 20 minutes.

At this stage in training, I only have two real fears about the race. One is that the whole adventure will all be over too quickly and the other is falling overboard. This is a real live fear for me, and one I am managing within, learning how to move around safely, and using my safety line and the boat equipment to stay safe.

These drills are incredibly realistic, they really make you feel cold and your hair stand up, no-one is left in any doubt about how quickly and positively you need to work to complete this, just how difficult it is and how in the blink of an eye a casualty in the water is lost. We completely lost sight of a fluorescent yellow life size dummy with flashing lights attached to it, in less than a minute and in reasonable visibility during one of our less successful practice drills. Going into a search pattern, retracing our course to finally locate and recover it some 20 minutes later. If you take your eye off a casualty for a second, you lose them. If you are distracted in any way, you lose them. This particular lesson is a good one for us all, and for the rest of the week the spotter is in no doubt of the importance of their role.

Onboard completing level one training with me that same week, was Jason Middleton. A slight, but terrier strong and enthusiastic east Londoner. Who later on the race developed an enviable Lambeth cool fashion style all of his own. Becoming known as a jackdaw, for collecting up any leftover or lost kit, cutting it down to size, trimming away pieces and creating a stylish Bibendum style race kit all of his own. Jason is quiet and unassuming, but underneath extremely intelligent and articulate. We become good friends by the end of the first weeks training and subsequently request Clipper Race that we sail together on the same team in the race. Little did we know what adversity we would eventually experience so closely together months later. Whenever we drill man overboard, or require someone up the mast, Jason steps up, harnessed and ready, he gets straight in the water or climbs aloft without hesitation.

At the end of week one training, I leave Gosport with a childlike grin, the likes of which one finds quite rarely in life. Wow, what a week! All of my questions and concerns had been answered; my body ached all over, I was tired, hungry, sore, wet, cold, but most of all, more excited now than when I had arrived a week ago. This was truly amazing, I had absolutely made the right decision and could not wait to rejoin the next training session. I had made some fantastic acquaintances whom later became very good friends.

One of our offshore phases in later training was a 48 hour nonstop sail down to the Channel Islands, around the west and north coast of France then back across the channel. We split into two watches for this, and worked shifts of four hours on and four hours off in rotation, to replicate that used by some of the racing yachts during the race. The first period was calm but very cold and the sunset and stars of the first night at sea were quite astounding. One of the trainers who had previously completed the race suggested we would get bored of sunsets during 12 months at sea, surely not?

Early hours of the next morning the storm we were promised arrived dead on time, the temperature plummeted to around minus six and with the wind at force seven gusting force eight made the actual feeling with wind chill cutting and icy. Whilst this was something I had hoped for when agreeing to winter train, it was pretty lively at times and very good taste of what was to come further offshore. The Boat rhythmically crashed down off the big waves, heeled over with edges of the deck underwater at times, occasionally fire extinguishers would fall off the walls below deck, the galley got trashed a few times, and several people's meals made reappearances, which meant occasionally we were working on deck shorthanded. At times this was pretty hairy, but really quite exhilarating, and a great rehearsal for what was to face us later on the race.

On the second day at sea I was on the foredeck with the first mate making a sail change fast as the wind gusts had really increased, the deck was too rough to stand and so we were working on all fours strapped to the deck with fluorescent orange tight safety lines. After a while and some very deep strength and heaving we had the sail on deck and were about to secure it, when we both called 'WAVE' at the same time. 'Wave' is the shout of warning given at any time by anyone aboard for others to hold on. On this occasion we had both seen it coming. I took a deep breath, dropped my head down towards the approaching surf, just as the bow of the boat buried itself in the wave. We were immediately fully submerged, sufficient to lift us off the deck briefly and test our hand grips upon the safety jack stay lines. As the wave passed, after what seemed like quite enough time to be underwater, we were dumped unceremoniously back on the foredeck in a heap. We shook ourselves, looked each other square in the eye for some quick reassurance and then both called out 'yeeeehaaaa'! With big smiles. We secured everything and completed the sail manoeuvre before exiting the foredeck for breather, job well done and adrenaline really pumping. A few hours later, still very wet and now freezing cold, I decided upon purchasing a dry suit for the icy cold southern ocean and north pacific races, a decision I now in hindsight owe my life to.

In addition to the race training as part of the team for the Clipper race, I also took on some additional theory training and passed a good number of RYA qualifications. Clipper Race also offered me the opportunity to train as a Clipper Coxwain. There were to be at least two qualified Coxwain on each boat. In the highly unlikely event that anything should happen to incapacitate the Skipper in any way, then the Coxwain will assume leadership and responsibility to bring the boat home. On a previous race one of the Skippers had broken his leg, and a Skipper from another yacht transferred to take over, leaving his own yacht in the hands of a Coxwain.

On being offered this opportunity to train as such, I considered it very carefully. It would be such a massive responsibility and really not one to be taken lightly. I wondered if it would be a burden, a weight to carry which might in some way alter or change my race experience. I had no desire to carry extra burden around the world. With some very tough exams to qualify, I would also need to undertake much additional studying. However having been offered this on the strength of the feedback from my race training I was keen to take up the challenge. I also figured in my own mind, this should not be in anyway a position or qualification to be utilised, unless it was ever required, very few people even really need to know I have done this training really. Finally, if anything were to befall our

Skipper, I would like to be in a position to offer as much as I could to bring the team and boat home safely. After two months of proper hard study at home and two & half weeks of examination packed training, I am pleased to report I passed out and qualified as a Clipper Coxwain, including passing my Yachtmaster offshore theory certification.

Coxwain offshore training;

It was very early morning, Clipper training days always start early! There was a truly beautiful sunrise with a spring chill still in the air and frost coating the pontoons at Gosport Marina. The trainee Coxwains all proficiently carrying out their duties, engine checks, cleaning heads (that's marine speak for toilets) clearing breakfast remains away, stowing equipment safely and rigging the yacht ready for departure. James and I were nominated engineers for the week and were in the process of emptying the bilges which were half filled with a potent and slightly noxious mixture of sea water and diesel from the previous few days training in the Solent. We were all nervously awaiting our instructions for the offshore practical examination phase of our two and half week advanced training. Jim Dobie, head of training for Clipper Race, who was putting us through our paces for the training, called James & I to the Nav Station. I initially thought perhaps we had done something wrong with the bilge work, and like naughty school children we scurried along and waited patiently his thoughts. This was it however, this was our practical exam briefing. In inimitable Jim Dobie style went like this. *"OK guys, you're first up, take us to that way point there, out through the needles"* says Jim pointing at an unbelievably remote and tiny way point marked on the electronic Nav screen about 35 miles southwest offshore in the channel. I tentatively asked Jim *"anything else?"*. *"Nope"* he replied with a smile, *"OK"* says I, *"what time are we leaving?"* James enquires. Jim smiles one of his massive big broad ones, and replies the entire briefing once again! Word for word! Before walking away.

James and I had a quick discussion around what to do next, we were only half way through the bilge cleaning and this was important to be completed before we depart, but we would have a fair amount of passage prep work to do right now, tides, wind direction, shipping lanes traffic all needed close review before we could leave. The boat needs to be fully rigged, deck crew in place and jobs allocated to the team. The journey required could take us 6-8 hours to sail, guess we need to leave quite soon, was this all part of the test perhaps? We agreed it was, Jim likes to put the Coxwain candidates under pressure to see how they could cope in reality. We agreed James would complete the bilge and engine works and I would get us underway, which in a little under an hour or so, we were. Dodging the ferries and hovercrafts out of Portsmouth and heading for the Needles with a decent sail configuration making us around 9-10ktts over ground. As the wind changed around, we zig-zagged our course, around the headland and out into the Channel, heading for the major shipping lanes. Ship dodging all the way south west.

As we approached one the busiest areas of shipping, around an hour or so before reaching our destination, an unmarked but very specific waypoint at sea which we were now well on course to arrive at. I asked Jim what to do when we arrive at the way point? *"Oh no need to worry about that just yet"* he replied. Half an hour or so later I enquired the same question. *"It's all about to become clear to you"* he responded. A few minutes later, the next two Coxwain candidates arrived with their briefing which was equally short *"change of plan, we are going to Cherbourg"*. We handed over and the next Coxwain leadership teams work began in earnest, they would need to plot our change of course quickly, as in around 20 minutes time on this course we would cross directly into the main traffic separation scheme, the channel equivalent of stepping into the fast lane of the M25 and somewhere we are not allowed to sail on this week. *"Good luck boys"* we added as we stepped away and with a fresh brew we headed back up onto deck into the cold and gusty spray of a now quite lively English Channel.

We were exhausted; sailing a racing boat is one thing, taking full responsibility and leadership for it over the last 8 hours or so is completely another. Rewarding but very draining. And so that's how it was for the next three days. We never actually docked at Cherbourg, Poole, Dieppe, Swanage or any of the other mysterious way points we headed for throughout the day and night. As we rotated around responsibility, and maintained sail for the rest of the week.

There is no let up during any of the Clipper race training, every single moment is filled with something to do, learn, study or practice. Evenings over dinner are lecture and exam filled. Whilst at sea, the sailing and drills continue without rest. During meals we discuss race tactics and emergency procedures, debrief ourselves, tie knots against the clock and with our eyes closed. Whilst it is a great pleasure to learn new skills and we are generally all there through choice, it is not a holiday and as the week's progresses, mind, body & soul really feels the impact of this intenseness. I consider this to be a part of the learning experience, sometimes needing to dig right down deep into energy reserves just to do so, and this is only training the real race will be even harder still.

It is a rare opportunity to set yourself about learning a completely new theoretical and practical skill at this level. Especially in later life, and I relished every single minute of it. I cannot wait for the race to start, however the pressure of time is really looming. There are a little over eight weeks now to race start day, and I am away training and preparing with the boat team for five of them!

In the mean time at home the tension is equally building. Packing away my life as I know it. Finalising power of attorney, signing my last will and testament, and meeting up with as many friends and family for as much time as I can spare before we leave in between training is more than filling every single waking moment. It is all proving quite emotional too, which I hadn't expected to be dealing with this early before race start. Everywhere I go, everyone I see, is a harsh and seemingly final goodbye. I hadn't experienced anything like this before, the effect of me going away on the race was much deeper within my friends and family than any normal departure, and I would advise anyone on future races to consider this time very carefully and make best use of it. It all feels so strangely final.

Keeping fit and healthy consumes any spare time left. I complete several half marathons, 10k runs several times a week, a few triathlons and a daily upper body and core strength training routine. My boat kit bag is permanently packed as I travel back and forth from training offshore, and I still practice knot tying with my eyes closed with some spare ropes in the evenings.

Crew allocation & team building
The 22nd Crate.

Crew allocation has got to be one of the most eagerly awaited parts of the waiting game, prior to the race itself. Behind the scenes however this is a nightmare part of race planning for the Clipper race team.

The race recruitment team travel the world and recruit 500+ team members for the entire fleet. Then, in something resembling the world's biggest and most complicated table plan, the race office team split us into teams, allocate us to a Skipper and a boat. There are a few key priorities to this, for example if there are 12 crew with medical experience and 12 engineers then each boat gets one each. Beyond that it's about keeping the teams as fair and evenly matched as possible. With as near as possible equal numbers of round the world crew, crew doing single or multiple legs, plus as even as possible a division of age, gender and sailing ability.

Once this is completed, and a few months out from race start, crew allocation day takes place. For the 13-14 race this was held in the Portsmouth Guildhall, which given the numbers of crew and friends & family whom attended was barely big enough! It was a pretty amazing sight all the crew arriving in their bright red Henri Lloyd race crew branded jackets. Once we had squeezed into the Guildhall there were a couple of short presentations from Justin Taylor race director and Sir Robin Knox-Johnston himself with an update on the progress of the new fleet of racing yachts.

Then came the part we had all traveled the length and breadth of the country and in some cases the world for, crew allocation. The 12 Skippers were introduced one at a time on stage in blazers and chinos, all looking clean and sharp. One by one they stepped up to a lectern and read out their allocated crew names in alphabetical order. Each reading the first half of their full crew as the names appeared on a massive projection screen behind them. With 12 teams and 500+ crew this took a long time! The room however remained silent and pensive throughout, everyone looking for names they recognised and friends they knew to see who was where. Then came the second round of names, and with a surname beginning with T, I was going to be in this round. I had recognised a great deal of names from training and social events so far, as each of the crews were read out, gradually one by one there were complete teams I was not going to be part of. Then second from last Sean McCarter steps up and reads out my name towards the end of his crew list. I Skipped my eyes quickly through the names up on the screen and recognised only a couple of the 53 people we now had in our team. Jason was one of these, we had asked to sail together and this was the start of that becoming real.

The remainder of the day was spent in various break out rooms, with our respective teams to meet each other, start discussing how we would work together and what our objectives might be for the race. Sean had arranged bright yellow 'Team Sean' shirts with *'the beatings will continue until morale improves'* under a skull and crossbones emblazoned upon the back. It was a nice touch and really made us feel part of team, many other teams were really jealous of these at the party later. Some key roles within the round the world team were allocated out to willing volunteers, victualing to Richard Dawson, chief of staff to Michelle Porter, engineer to Charlie Crapper, medic to Susie Redhouse. Nick Blewer agreed to take on the task of arranging the team building weekend, and also stopover manager. Jason, as winch engineer. Conor, Bosun. Andy, sail repair. Kristi, media manager. And me, navigator & safety manager.

After a number of lengthy team discussions we left and did, as it would turn to be, exactly what Derry Londonderry Doire team do best when they are on land. We adjourned to the pub and partied hard the rest of the night away.

Some months later we all arrived at an outward bound center in Winchester for our team building weekend. Still known as Team Sean at this point. What a tremendous job Nick Blewer did arranging the weekend. Dormitory accommodation for boys and girls split, massive barbecue dinner and a bar called 'round the world'. Then a whole range of sailing, team and race themed games throughout the weekend, with points and prizes all round. Very much fun and a great team build weekend, with raft building and racing being the funniest event ever. Milk crate tower building and climbing being the most competitive, Sean himself managing to build and climb to the top of a massive stack 22 milk crates high, setting out the term '22nd crate' which followed us around the world, meaning to work harder and push higher. Nice touch!

On the Sunday we openly discussed team tactics, how competitive we wanted to be and what our team ethos and culture would look like. We all agreed, to sail safe, have fun and be competitive, always in that order. No silly or navigation penalties, look after the sails, be consistent, carry out regular 'night raids', always to go for the scoring gates and ocean sprint, but never at the cost of our overall race strategy. Then we set out and agreed our race targets; Top 6 finish in first race. Top 5 finish in race two. At least one race win. At least three podiums. Never finish below eighth. Each and every one of us absolutely bought into this and we left the weekend having signed up to and agreed with our team goals. More importantly we all totally agreed to have fun at all times and enjoy the experience. We went on to discuss and agree we would at all times be magnanimous & reserved in both glory and defeat. We would never slander or gossip around other teams and would always celebrate all other team successes, something we became well known for as the race progressed.

Sean had set himself out as a competitive and fun leader. He was already showing his 'quality over quantity' personality. A man of very few words, he has an inbuilt ability to captivate you as a leader and you find yourself listening intently to his short statements. Clearly very intelligent & articulate, with a wry smile and a slight shyness, he is an extremely likeable character and the team which still carried his name as theirs, were already growing to respect and love him for it.

As we packed and left Winchester, 'Team Sean' life felt really good. We had such a fantastic weekend, really very well organised & put together. The team totally now felt like it was coming together as one. There had been much laughter, some serious debate, and some random and silly conversations in the round the world bar. We had the makings of our team tactics and a culture we all agreed with & signed up to. About an hour into the journey home I picked up an email from Clipper race announcing our entry as a race fleet into the 2013 Rolex Sydney-Hobart race. Wow! Not only were we setting off on a circumnavigation and traversing the greatest oceans of the world, we were now entered into surely one of the most famous of all yacht races in the world. Even as an amateur sailor, this was something only dreams are made of. This was amazing news on top of an already epic weekend. I texted everyone on the team I had mobile numbers for and the news spread quickly with cheers and celebrations all round. I was absolutely buzzing, as soon as I got home I went for a massive run that evening and I didn't sleep for excitement.

Next morning, still full of energy and after another run and a long & late breakfast I logged on in my office at home, and bang! There in my inbox is a full colour picture of Sean & Sir Robin in Derry, with Martin Reilly the Mayor of Derry, announcing their sponsorship of our team and yacht. Sean had known this all weekend, he had left us in Winchester to go straight to Derry. How he had kept this a secret all weekend is a marvel, and a mark of his professionalism. I struggled to do any work for the rest of the day and ended up cycling to the pool and swimming lengths for an hour. This journey was really starting to come together. The sense of belonging to the team was palpable and growing all the time. We now had an identity, a strategy, a good deal of friends on board, a name, race targets and objectives. But most of all a sense of team. If I had won the lottery on this day, my life for the next couple of years would stay exactly as it was, I felt remarkable and ready for this adventure. Everything was coming together for me at the right time.

I could not wait to get together with the guys again, level three training was not far away and prep week close too. Race start was now just weeks away. Every moment of every day felt exciting, I had an enormous amount of motivation to pack my life away and leave my temporary home in Oxfordshire, I had used this as a post-Olympic bolt hole. I had really enjoyed living here, but it was time to leave and packing was easy. It felt good to be removing the trappings of life and packing up to leave. It felt absolutely right, and it just got better and better.

It wasn't however all totally fantastic. Siobhan was in the middle of her exams. She was having a really tough time. Working extremely hard and getting ever more stressed about her work load, she was finding life really tough. Her social circle was breaking up too as friends discovered boys, pubs, late nights and alcohol. Siobhan had little interest in this (apart from the boys bit which was kindling!) and had made her feelings outwardly known to some of her friends. As a consequence of which, she had discovered an ever decreasing social scene and some grief & bullying from some of the lesser cerebrally capable ones. It was turning into an incredibly tough time to be leaving her, and deep inside it started to hurt. It hurt a lot!

Prep week
Straight out of the box

Prep week for Clipper races normally consists of strategy planning, victualing and tasks to personalise your race boat, within the race rules. However, prep for the 13-14 race was to be fundamentally different. Clipper race were commissioning a brand new fleet of 12 super-fast racing yachts. Known affectionately as 'the 70's' by those close to them, on simple account of them being roughly 70 feet long.

The boats were being built as hull & deck in China, then fitted out and rigged in the UK. The overall project for delivery in time for racing was dogged with disaster. Several companies charged with their delivery went bankrupt and a number of senior people from third parties working on the project were allegedly involved in murder & espionage, resulting in the schedule becoming ever more fraught and tight as the final race start fast approached. Throughout this time, the Clipper race team worked tirelessly and efficiently, whilst always maintaining outwardly that the boats would be ready in time. They all stayed incredibly positive at all times in both their internal and external communications, which is a credit to them all under pressure.

The early boats including CV21, already named and branded as OneDLL, were on the water in the late spring for sea trials and were proving really successful whilst being used for race training. We were allocated YachtCV30, and we waited patiently for her to arrive.

A few short weeks before we were due to move the fleet to London for race start, she arrived looking grubby around the edges. Her rigging was incomplete, she had no boom or sails and below decks was a workshop, full of tools and dirt from the build. No bunks, galley unfinished, no navionics and most below deck equipment was incomplete. She was plain white, although with her transport from China, dust & dirt all over her, this looked more like an off white or dull cream colour.

Initially this was a shock to us all, but with some time and discussion, we turned this around into a positive team opportunity. We would now have the chance to complete these tasks and be an integral part of the build. This would give us a massive upper hand over some of the other yachts in the fleet, we would get to know our yacht inside out, we would have the opportunity to complete the build & fit out of a brand new racing yacht, and when in life would any of us ever get the chance to do this again. For those of us that had the time and inclination to get involved, it became part of the overall race experience.

Over the course of the following two weeks team members came and went whenever they could spare time. Between us CV30 began to take shape and feel like a racing yacht. There were some frustrations throughout this time, waiting for parts and specialist engineers to help us get her operational. Tools and some spares we needed desperately were in short supply, and with all 12 yachts now on the water, all needing attention at the same time, it was a stressful time for us. We inspected the systems inside and out, took all the floors out, traced & mapped all the pipework and electrics so we understood it all. Checked over, cleaned and serviced all the winches. Tested & configured the navionics as they were installed. Our full set of new racing sails arrived and we set about unpacking and checking them over, we added some luminous arrows onto our spinnaker and yankee to make them easier to trim. Once our boom and vang arrived, on board CV31 Jamaica Get All Right, we man handled and fitted these, then loaded our sails aboard. She was so close to being ready to go out and sail for the first time now and we eagerly awaited an official sign off to do so.

There were a good number of practical jokes around the fleet during the week and the atmosphere was one of great fun. 'Cut here' with a dotted line and some scissors was added to our mast base in permanent marker. Cabbages appeared balanced upon booms. DLL Smurfs started making an appearance hidden around the fleet. One morning we found a pink logo added to our transom, which read *'powered by fairy dust'*. It was meant as a joke, but we absolutely loved it and it became a tag line for us right the way throughout the whole race. We even had some of the letters replaced later when they rubbed off.

CV30 the first time out:

She was at last ready for her sea trial. We waited with tense anticipation to get sign off to take her out. By the time this came, it was too late and we slept on it. Rising for an early breakfast next morning the excitement was growing and we set about rigging sails and prepping her ready to slip. After a Skipper briefing and some last minute safety and rigging checks we slipped our mooring lines and quietly slid out of Gosport.

We have done this so many times before on Clipper race training weeks, but this was different. No, really, this was very different! We were aboard CV30, the very latest arrival of the brand new fleet of 12 round the world 70' ocean racing yachts. She is pure white, brand new, straight out of the box, spotlessly clean and meticulously well prepared by us, our own race team, now ready for a proper sea trial. Skipper Sean McCarter, myself and 12 other team Seam crew were given the honour to do so.

We were locked and loaded ready for a full week at sea, with 5 other Clipper racing yachts going out with us, and weather permitting we were planning three 'friendly' ocean races of 60, 120, and 230 miles during the following week or so. OK they might be friendly races, but we are team Derry and this was important pre-race psychology to set some markers down.

Ever since I signed my crew contract to circumnavigate aboard the 13-14 round the world race, I have thought a lot about this moment, and after the rope slip and some sweet manoeuvring out of the marina by Sean, I stopped and paused on deck to take in the moment. Wow! This was it, at last the first trials on the new boat, it felt awesome, a lump of expectation and anticipation in the throat, with a schoolboy tingle of excitement, the likes of which I really cannot remember feeling for some time. My thoughts shifted briefly to race start day on the Thames in a few weeks time, all 12 boats leaving to circumnavigate for 12 months, parading and departing under Tower Bridge. Blimey, whatever is that going to feel like if this felt this big just for a race training week?

Our first two days were 30degrees plus and absolute flat calm, great preparation for the Doldrums, but not really what we needed to try out CV30. We made use of the time really getting to know her, which basically involved taking as many things apart as we could, cleaning, checking and putting them back together again. This is invaluable practice as any one of these tasks might need to be performed under massive pressure in heavy seas or perhaps in the dark, so once completed, we did some of these again and again. As the week progressed, winds picked up and we got our chance, 10-15-18+Ktts of wind, well heeled, and requiring some tight manoeuvres, CV30 performed amazingly well, continually coming back for more, she is quite beautifully balanced and feels really smooth under power. We pushed her over as far as we dare, and got some incredible pictures of one of her twin rudders fully clear of the water with the sunset glistening off it.

Below decks she is quite basic, everything is white, very hard and slippery! We hot bunked for the week and crammed ourselves into as smaller space as possible to replicate big ocean racing and everything worked really well. We made some notes throughout the week on the future retro fits we might make, to pass on to our shore team, via the race office for approval within the race rules.

We out ran several other boats and on one race we chased in close quarters with OneDLL for over 15 hours, gaining a bit, losing a bit but gradually reeling her in. Great practice for the race and a really nice opportunity to work as a team together aboard our brand new 70' racing yacht.

St Katharine dock & race start day
Irish stew

The final days building up to race start were increasingly hectic, boat preparation continued right up until early evening of 31st August. Lists had been progressively prioritised several days before, and with a crew task list now in place for the stopovers in Brest and Rio, we finalised our London tasks and were ready to race.

Throughout the week in St Katharine Dock, very many crew friends & family visited the boats. All of our leg one crew disbanded ashore spending final moments of time with their loved ones wherever they could, in-between a great deal of work still required to be completed. My parents arrived on Thursday and after meeting them at their hotel and finishing some last minute business tasks & paper work with my father, I walked them the short 5 minutes down to the dock to see the fleet for the first time. Mother was quiet & pensive, this was the first time she was to be exposed to the fleet in all its glory, and somewhere inside, I knew only too well she had a trepidation and growing motherly concern of my impending departure around the world. Which I had become acutely aware of quite a while ago. I had long since stopped telling her the stories of the 'drama on the high seas' from previous races which excite most people I talked to about the race, and I had very specifically not at any point told her about the cuts, bruises, broken bones and dislocations our team had suffered already during training. Figuring, or assuming at least perhaps, this would protect her from some of the pain. Father was quite excited, questioning me all the time as only he can. Mostly around how the week had been for us, and what we had been up to. But always with a calculated slant to capture the essence of how I was feeling. He has a certain quality of asking clever questions which establish greater depth of answer, probably developed through his early police force training many years ago, and possibly reinforced by his desire for greater knowledge and understanding of what's going on with the family, in a patriarchal consciously responsible way.

My parents support has never been short. They are the only people I know whom have always truly and unconditionally offered me their full support, listened and guided me through life. I truly admire the fact they have been together since they were fourteen, celebrating their Golden Wedding anniversary and their seventieth birthdays during the time I am away. I tell this to many people I meet, reinforcing to myself just how significant this fact is to my life. Absolute consistency and reliability is such a gift, and without this I could not have ever done any of the things I have achieved and without this I could not even contemplate taking part in this particular adventure.

We arrived at St Katharine dockside, the fleet was posing magnificently in the sunshine and the atmosphere around us was once again fantastic. I showed them around the village and introduced them to as many other crew & Clipper race team as we met along the way. I was able to get them onto the pontoon by the boat, but the 4' climb aboard over mooring lines and fenders was sufficient to prevent any closer inspections for them until 'showboating' the following day. We had dinner in their hotel, without alcohol as I was now pre-race 'dry' after a long week with some late nights and much red wine in between working hard on the boats. We talked around the race and the plan for the next few days so they were clear. I was consciously managing their expectations all of the time. They gave me a great 'bon voyage' card with some really nice words written inside by mother. It said "the world is truly round, and it seems to start and end with the ones we love" (Nelson Mandella) Both Mum & I cried. After some hugs I dismissed myself and walked back to the boat, pausing on Tower Bridge to take in the night scene. It was a most amazing night, clear skies and lots of stars. I tried hard imaging and self-imaging some clarity to myself of what it would be like in a few days time to be down on the river, crossing under a raised tower bridge and looking up, from below where I now looked down.

Any thoughts I had at this time and any images I captured to myself turned out to be pretty woeful in comparison to how massive the day actually was, nothing had really prepared me for the scale of the day, the size of the crowds and the emotional atmosphere.

On one of our final prep days Father John from the Church of the Martyrs, Tower Bridge came and joined us on the boat. Holding a short service in the cockpit. With around half the crew in attendance. He told some stories of great ocean voyages and historic references of much interest. He told us of support and sanctuary, explained how we might find greater faith and support in this and blessed our boat, and some of us in the process as he tossed his holy water all around with some gusto!. Then he smiled and exclaimed that we might now go on to be extremely successful and he could then claim all the glory for this. He stayed around for a while and I had a really good heartfelt private chat one to one before he left. I have never been overly religious, frequenting church only at Christmas, Easter and family occasions. But I do have my own beliefs and a personal strength of soul sufficient to want to chat one to one with him before he left. Sharing some private thoughts which I shall now keep with me around the world. I am most grateful for his visit to our boat and the time he gave to us.

A good many close friends and family visited the marina during the week in St Katharines, and as much as I could I took the time out to share the race experience with them and show them the boat. I have said many times how lucky I am to be able to do this, and it would be totally selfish of me not to share it where I can, with those who wish to.

Our boat naming day arrived, she was sparkling clean, now fully branded and with lots of additional team colours. Flags & bunting flying, she was moved onto the show pontoon for pride of place. We met with the Mayor of Derry LondonDerry and a few of the council officials responsible for the Clipper race sponsorship. They presented to us what the sponsorship meant to the city and how successful it had been previously. There were options for us to expand on the plans for our 'homecoming' port visit next year and a team of land based crew support to assist with this was established. As part of the presentation they showed a short video of Derry LondonDerry, its history, culture and the Freedom Bridge, with soft focus and romantic Irish music & lyrics. Another sunglasses moment for many of us (hiding the tears behind dark glasses); really quite moving. We moved onto the show pontoon, posing for photos and cheers from the crowds. Collecting my parents along the way we moved down onto the show pontoon, where there was music playing and a drinks reception was in full swing.

I managed to get a really nice photo of my parents with Sir Robin Knox-Johnston, Skipper Sean McCarter and Martin Reilly the Mayor of Derry LondonDerry. I was actually in the original of this picture too, but I cropped me out before posting and publishing it, this was for them not me.

After some more photos, an official speech and some champagne spraying from Martin & Sir Robin, then some more photos and some more champagne, we arranged boat tours for our friends & family, and now finally I had an opportunity to show my parents the boat. They both thought it was bigger than they had imagined, at least until they stepped below, both banging their heads at some point whilst touring. Again Dad asked and inquired about lots of things and showed much interest in the technical stuff. Mum was quieter but was clearly enjoying the tour and appearing to enjoy the privileged position of being aboard our yacht.

It was also interesting that at this point she seemed to show more interest and asked many questions about life rafts, safety lines and life jackets, which really made me smile, but also really pleased me, as hopefully this went further toward softening her concerns at this time. I spent some time explaining and clarifying just how much training we had done with this, how effective the equipment was and how safe in reality we actually are on board these boats out in the ocean.

The remainder of Friday & Saturday proved totally manic. Friday was pretty much dominated by the naming ceremony and it was extremely difficult to get anything else done. Saturday, our last day before departure saw friends and family on and around the boat pretty much all day, which was fantastic to be able to share with so many, and whilst frustrating where we still had work to do, it was important for family to get this access and time with us all and I invested time and effort into talking to everyone and making them feel welcome. During the afternoon we made our way to the Grange hotel for our final pre-race briefing.

Dressed in team colours, we walked the 15 minutes or so to the hotel together as a team and took up the first three rows of the second tier of seating. Justin Taylor, race director started the proceedings and called for a cheer from Henri Lloyd, like a kind of 'hello London' moment. A single cheer went up from the back of the room to some cheerful laughter from the rest of the teams. He tried again and not much more. He moved on to team after team, each of whom tried to outdo each other with cheers and screams. As he moved though the teams, Conor suggested a novel response and passed word around to team Derry. So each team gets louder and louder with cheers and whistles. Then Justin says *"welcome Derry LondonDerry?"* as a big question awaiting a loud response. We all waived a silent cheery wave, no noise, and absolute silence. Genius! Absolutely fits with our strategy of being a no fuss team to have fun. The whole room laughed and Justin did too. A terrific moment for the team and we all laughed about this for several days afterwards. We agreed this would stick and should stay with us as our intro. Absolute genius Conor, great and quick thinking.

Once the evening approached and things quietened down we were able to compete our pre-race checks and stow the last of our equipment ready for departure. A final jet wash, a wipe around below with damp sponges and she was ready and looking absolutely fabulous.

As the daylight faded on Saturday, I found myself alone on the boat and sat out on deck for a while, contemplating how far we had come in the last few weeks. CV30 LegenDerry was but a shell hull when we first got our hands on her and was being used as a tool shed on the dock by the Clipper race maintenance teams. One small advantage of this was that we never had to go looking for the maintenance specialists as they regularly returned to our boat for supplies. This also gave us the opportunity to feed them with doughnuts and tea (plus the occasional evening beer) on board, which paid many dividends to us later in the race having made good friends with them all. We were ready to leave, we were all tired after much hard work, but the adrenalin was flowing and this would get us through the next few days with ease.

I decided to walk over Tower Bridge and survey for one last time from above where we would depart from the next day. On the way down to the bridge I passed an office block with the blinds open and the lights still on. Desks inside strewn with the previous weeks corporate debris, charts and white boards around the walls, some badly photocopied 'staff notices' stuck to the wall at an angle with parcel tape, half empty coffee cups, some shoes & jackets. One desk had an open sandwich, half eaten on a plate on the side. This was a world I was keen to escape right now.

Sunday morning arrived and I woke at around 04:00, having not really slept much aboard in anticipation of the day ahead. I went for a shower in the marina facilities and watched the most amazing early morning sunrise over the marina basin where the race boats were moored. The scene was quite magical; absolute still, calm and peace. One lonely yellow jacketed security guard walking slowly & quietly around the pontoons and a few ducks sheltering under the bow of the GREAT Britain boat.

I got back to the boat where a few others were still sleeping, quietly I began to make bacon sarnies and coffee for all the crew as they stirred and rose with the smell, or arrived with their kit from nearby hotels. Gradually more and more team arrived and with smiles all around the mood was buoyant and became excited as the morning progressed. There was little left to do except stow our kit and make the final boat checks, and by shortly after 08:30 we were ready for our final Skipper briefings and got into our full team colours ready for the departure presentations ahead.

A few close friends arrived to wave us off and I made a quick visit to the public viewing areas each time for a hug, high five or departure kiss. Then my parents arrived and I spotted them on the gallery above us, I jumped down off the boat and headed up the ramp. In many ways I had dreaded this moment, and a great lump in my throat appeared. I took a deep breath and met them with a hug and a cheery smile, exclaiming what an amazing day it was turning into already. We spent a few minutes together exchanged a few last personal thoughts, a hug and a kiss. Then, as calm as I could, I said farewell as I might do when popping out for a bit and promised to call from France. Toughest moment so far and I could see both of them filling up a little. I got back to the boat and Michelle, another of our round the world crew, who had been watching where I was came and gave me a hug, we both had a little cry together.

All 12 teams were now assembled onto the foredeck of their respective boats in team colours, a great spectacle and excellent photo opportunity for the crowds. Clipper race had arranged a fleet blessing for race start day. We were then quickly ushered around in teams to assemble behind the stage area ready for race start presentation.

Clipper race time was now well in control and our next few hours were timed to the second, with no prisoners. We assembled beyond the marina office in a kind of 'backstage' open air green room, behind GREAT Britain, Qingdao and OneDLL, the order in which we would leave the dock shortly. After a few moments I realised we were behind the crowd viewing area above the stage where my parents were likely to be. I slipped ranks and made a squeeze through the crowds to where they were. We all had a big hug and, to be fair, I don't remember us saying anything to each other, it was just a final fleeting moment together.

Qingdao were on stage as I rejoined the team and we were shuffling ever closer to the security gate at the top of the ramp leading to the stage. I suddenly realised the significance of this gate, we would pass through here and not come back. We had spent the last week or so freely moving around, on and off the pontoons back and forth, with full freedom. This time there was no going back, we would pass through here, be processed through the Clipper media system of presentations & scripted manoeuvres along the pontoons and straight to our boat, which was fully rigged ready to slip already, and would do so almost immediately upon our boarding. I really hoped when we return to St Katts after a year away we can exit via this gate completing the exact circumnavigational loop back to from whence we came. I took a moment and captured this image clearly in my mind, I carried the image of this gate with me around the world, as clear as if it were there with me now, to return through it safe and well.

We were called down to the stage, with our battle song, The Script, Hall of Fame, playing loud and proud all around the marina basin. The crowds were amazing all around us cheering and waving flags, I was able to spot so many faces too, friends, family & Derry crew too all supporting us. We were introduced and the MC for the day linked some news about Derry LondonDerry and welcomed Martin, the mayor, to the stage who said a few words and wished us well, then a few questions to Sean about the race and to a couple of our crew about their feelings on departure and 'why they are doing the race'. We were wished well and left to walk the short walk around the lower pontoons to the boat.

It was like a gladiatorial amphitheatre with crowds all around above us cheering and waving, quite fantastic with many familiar faces and some great moments of shared glances, blown kisses and waves. Eye contact is such a strong and personal medium, you can hold someone's glance, a short stare with a smile, there is no need to wave and scream to each other. Nothing need be said to those closest, you know what this contact means, and some of these really hurt.

Back on board and we slipped lines, rotated around 360 on the spot, into the lock and held station with the three other boats which were exiting together. A slick piece of manoeuvring under much pressure from around him by Sean. It takes around 45 minutes to get each group of four boats through the lock and out onto the river, and boy is it a tight squeeze, with no more than a fenders breadth all around us, we needed to concentrate hard on this manoeuvre. This would not be a good time to bring two boats together or touch a dockside. Chance for some more crowd face spotting and waving, in between managing roving fenders and spotting distances.

The dock gates were lowered and, one at a time, we exited out into the river, at the last minute pulling fenders inboard and forming a team line up on the port side forward deck for the first river 'money shot', photographers lined up on the north bank to get us in formation with Tower Bridge directly behind, a great shot resulted, well planned and well executed.

We started a slow 3 mile loop, down the river and back, about two boat lengths apart at spot on 5ktts, the loop takes us exactly 22 minutes, so second time around we collect the next four yachts as they exit the lock and continue around. Once all twelve are out on the river we have to be more precise with timings and vhf radio talk between the formation counts seconds and marks points along the way.

At exactly one o'clock, Tower Bridge begins to open and GREAT Britain, Qingdao, OneDLL and Derry LondonDerry Doire pass through under the raised bridge. Wow! What an amazing sight and experience, as we pass under my phone rings, it's a great friend, Barny, who's up on the bridge looking down, we exchange some fond words and share a close moment together, then end the call to continue to take in scene around us.

The four yachts hold station next to the Mayor's office by the south bank, and the crowds close by get a good look at us and some more great photo opportunities. More faces in the crowd and another call from a good friend, Sam, who explains her accurate position and I can spot her and wave directly, another great moment shared. We share some thoughts on the day and our respective excitement, then wish farewell and good luck. So many goodbyes are increasingly difficult throughout the day. Emotions are running very high now.

Again the radios are calling marks and seconds counting down, we realign our formations and start to rotate around to exactly one thirty when the bridge reopens and we pass back through to meet the returning eight boats completing their final loop on the other side, we fall in line astern, one boat length apart and at 5ktts we head out down river.

The spectator and support boats fall in behind us as we make our way down to the Thames barrier, one by one they slowly overtake the formation to get a better look at us. Some of the RiB's and yachts following us cause a stir as they occasionally get too close. The media boats are buzzing all around and the helicopters occasionally pass over head.

We raise the pace slightly and head out of the estuary, the spectator boats start to hang back and turn around and soon we are alone in our formation. Once out further we drop the ceremonial flags, colours and banners and stow them safely below. We rig our mooring set for the evening and a couple of crew go below to fire up a hot meal for dinner. Once anchored, we stow our gear and meet back in the cockpit to debrief the day and discuss again plans for the next morning's offshore race start. Reflecting upon the day with the crew together is a pleasure, emotions are still high, but we are focusing on racing now and settling down for some sleep after a manically hectic 36 hours.

We are then presented with two luxury gifts to round off quite the most awesome day:

Possibly the best sunset I have seen in a very long time, it silhouettes the industrial landscape of Gravesend and graduates the whole sky with a soft glowing and moving colour-scape. I spend some time taking this in, and reflect on the dramatic colours bathed across the water, sky and the industry we are leaving behind us as we depart tomorrow.

A great big, hot & steaming bowl of Irish stew. Courtesy of Dee, a crew member from Derry.

Leaving London, 1st September 2013
Photo Credit; Clipper Ventures PLC

Rounding the windward mark, race 2 start, Brest
Photo Credit; Clipper Ventures PLC

London to Brest
South into the fog.

After the parade of sail down the Thames and out to Southend we spent the night at anchor just off Gravesend, with a two hour rotating anchor watch, allowing leg one race crew some much needed sleep before the actual race start next day. We spent the evening reviewing our race tactics and specialist roles for the start line, so we were all clear on what we were doing. Skipper allocated watch duties and I was nominated as assistant Watch Leader. Wow, what an honour, I felt really quite touched and quite proud too, to have been given this opportunity for the first leg to Brest and all the way on down to Rio. I had been assistant Watch Leader on the 300 mile offshore delivery race to London from Gosport, and in the second half of that week, after dropping off our Watch Leader in Brighton, I was promoted to Watch Leader for the second half of the delivery. However for all of leg one, all the way to Rio, on my first ocean race crossing, I was proper stoked to have been given this, and thanked Sean afterwards, promising to work hard and do my best for the team. It was a consciously high level of responsibility at an early stage in the race for me. When the Skipper sleeps, the Watch Leaders basically have ultimate responsibility for the team and the boat safety. I have never been afraid of taking responsibility in life, but this is a big step for me, two years ago I had never sailed before, now, as we rotate over the next few weeks there will be many times when I am totally responsible for the whole boat and the crew.

Our agreed watch system works with two watches of around 8 people in each. You share a bunk with your opposite number in the other watch, as you are never both sleeping at the same time. Within each watch there is a nominated media person, Bowman, Medic and Engineer. A Watch Leader runs the deck work, all sailing manoeuvres and trim. Then the assistant watch leader manages the team, tactics, navigation, radar and all below deck works such as hourly log, bilge and safety checks etc. On our watch, I was assistant to Conor O'Byrne our Watch Leader. A 6' 2", prop forward built, softly spoken Irish Garda, with a dry and infectious sense of humour. Conor & I had only ever worked on opposite watches previously, but we were already pretty close friends from training and pre-race prep work, we understood each other well and were both really happy to be working together, giving each other a big hug when we knew this. We went on to discuss how our watch would work in principal and what we each needed to work together, though neither of saw this as a particular challenge.

A super early start saw us off our mooring and away into the estuary at dawn to do some last minute compass and instrumentation configuration. The fleet grouped up just off Southend pier, tacked & gybed together with shouts of *'no water'* and *'back off'* between the Skippers at the helm. In the cockpit we were in fixed specialist positions practiced over the last few weeks, everyone sharp and working hard. Only the Skipper's instruction and some occasional repeats of confirmation were heard on deck. As the minutes ticked by we positioned ourselves well and crossed the start line in third place. For the first few miles out to sea, the yachts were all within close sight of each other and made for some great photos, especially when our new branded spinnakers were flown. The media guys absolutely loved this and we were constantly buzzed by helicopters and RIBs filming and photographing us, the results of these were amazing and a great start to the race media campaign.

Over the next few days we pulled out a close fought lead together with Henri Lloyd, never more than a few short miles between us, and most of the time within sight of each other. We continued some great close sail racing and gave CV30 Derry a really nice testing shake down, she creaked and groaned with distaste, almost under protest as we pushed her increasingly harder. On one afternoon during a powered up manoeuvre she started to crack loudly and with the enclosed sound-box effect of down below, alarmed a few of the crew sufficient for Skipper to call the helm to back off a little. After some inspection, whilst concerned faces of crew looked on we discovered the cracking to be around the base of the mast, alarming at first, but upon further inspection we were pretty sure this was only cosmetic and not in any way structural. We gradually loaded her back up again and progressively forced another crack in the same place which confirmed our suspicions. Some conversations with our maintenance team across the Sat-Phone and we soon had a team of specialists on standby in France to meet us and undertake the repairs.

The winds backed right off to virtually nothing and for a day or so we were fighting to make any headway at all. Eventually we stopped and, drifting backwards, we actually anchored, with possibly the longest anchor warp I have seen, well over 300m of line, which later took almost an hour and much sweat & muscle grind to retrieve. Perfectly legal in the race rules, this saved us almost 8 miles of drifting on tides in the wrong direction, one of the boats lost almost 10 miles just tidal drifting.

Then a final cruel twist; Fog! Lots of it! So thick we were down to maybe only 10-15m of visibility at times. On one occasion we knew we were close to Henri Lloyd, we could actually hear them calling their gybe on deck then drifting away from us in the other direction, but could not see them at any point.

Race office called the race distance early, giving us a new finish line and a two hours to a *'closest to the finish line'* result notification. Disaster for us; we had stuck to our tactics thus far, remaining as west of the pack as we could in the conditions to give us a better final finish line run into Brest, this was in the main part working well for us and we had shared the lead for some time with Henri Lloyd. But with the new finish line so far south, little or no wind, and only two hours now to the newly allotted finish time. We had absolutely no chance and ended the race equal eighth. A bitter blow for the crew who felt cheated and down about the race office decision. We had a good old rant on the boat and then agreed that that was it; no more after we arrive in port. We had agreed with our behavioural strategy and this would now test it. We would congratulate the winners and be magnanimous in defeat. This is a round the world race and there is much still to play for. We kicked the donkey (started the engine) and motored the remainder 100 or so miles into Brest.

Our first port stopover arrival was a really tough one. We were down about the race loss and tired from the race start adrenalin now easing off. Deep clean and prize giving that evening were awful, turning out to be one of the most stressful events of the whole race. We did well to escape this as a team, still together and friends.

In consolation for the above for me, as we entered the harbour at Brest, on the end of the wall were two of my very best friends whom had come out to meet us into France, Dave & Magda. What an awesome surprise, so great to see them and have a special welcome. I managed a distant handshake and kiss from the dock as we entered port, and then spent most of the next day with them enjoying a very long Brest lunch after showing them around our boat, good times, good memories, and great people, true and proper good friends.

Next day we were back to work, still a great deal to do as there always has been on our race campaign so far. Much time & effort went into protecting lines and blocks from chafe, whipping new strops and block harnesses ready for all kinds of use on the race. It was so good to be working down to this level of detail, and it lifted the team. We watched some of the other boats rigging stanchions and at least one we knew still didn't have a working water maker. We were conversely in great shape, through much hard work from the team. A self-perpetuating prophesy of team motivation.

We left the boat early one afternoon to visit some local farms and growers, whom we contacted via some friends of Michelle Porter, round the world crew member and our teams Chief of Staff. Michelle, 6'3" with gorgeous long flowing hair and a truly charming and potentially heartbreaking smile.

What a fantastic experience selecting French home grown garlic, tomatoes and onions. Absolutely fabulous, top quality local produce and a very welcome addition to our dried and carb loading food on board. The onions were stowed deep in the lazerette and decanted as required, the garlic was peeled, stowed in oil packed into zip lock bags. Both of these proved to really liven up our meals over the next few weeks, and with the addition of some fresh courgette and tomatoes, the first few days at sea were really most welcome.

The same friends, Didier and Nicole, who took us to the farms, invited a few of us for dinner to their converted barn about half an hour or so from Brest, and drove us there in the evening. A glass or two of local wine on their terrace at sunset, overlooked by a noisy donkey, was a real treat. But nothing compared to the next few hours of local Brittany foods, pancakes, cheese, eggs, fruit and cake. A magical buffet for many hours, accompanied by local wine, cider and truly very genuine and beautiful hospitality from Didier and Nicole. We stayed overnight at their farmhouse, which was a real treat and the first time I had been off the boat for almost a month now. We shared the two bedrooms, three boys in one and three girls in the other. I shared with Conor & Jason. We had a small double bed, a single mattress and an inflatable double air bed. I suggested we *paper scissors stone'* for bed allocation, much to Nicole's amusement. We staged a best of three and I got the bed, yay! It turned out however to be a little on the small side and I was only able to sleep diagonally across it, which caused much laughter and piss take with Jason & Conor. However, it was really and truly great to sleep in a real bed and have a proper shower before an epic breakfast of French rustic breads and fresh coffee for several hours with our new friends. What a great start to the day, then back to the boat for a final days race prep before departure to Rio.

Nicole's car had a puncture, and so for the journey back to the port of Brest, all six of us crammed into the back of Didier's small white van, along with our onions and garlic! We sang some songs and laughed all of the half an hour or so it took to travel back. Not the best way to travel with a hangover, but some really good times and some great memories with really great new found friends.

Race start day morning, we met as a full team away from the boat for some privacy in a local coffee shop for our final race brief strategy meeting. As well as a review of our race strategy, we did a final run through the ceremonial stuff for the dock departures and the route for parade of sail, always the tricky part of race start days. Clipper race plan and time these days almost to the second, and with 12 x 70' race boats in close formation under the gaze of the world's media from chase boats and helicopters; there really is no margin for error. Dress code, where to stand for photos, who to wave to, when and how, yes we even agree how to wave sometimes, just to make this amazing spectacle look even slicker on the water.

Once we were back at the boat, changed and ready, we made our way out onto the pontoon and along the route to the stage for team presentations in front of the DLL spectator boats and crowds gathering to see us off. We walked along past the other Clipper race boats, to applause from the other teams, up onto the dock and along to the ramp to the stage. As we walked along we were met out of nowhere from the crowd by Didier & Nicole whom had come down specially to wave us off, with big smiles and hugs. I broke ranks and paused for a moment shared with them both. We exchanged a few words and parted with a hug. As I walked onwards to rejoin the team, I put my sunglasses back on to hide a tear behind once again, I had only met these people for the first time yesterday; they had made me feel so very welcome in their home and shared some of their time with us. Truly good people and I really hope I shall see them again sometime after the race. A brief presentation on stage with a few questions for Skipper from the Race Director, playing to the crowds, then back to our boat past the other teams. I paused along the way and exchanged some hugs and high fives with many people from the other teams, I have made very many good friends along the way training together thus far and very many of these people like me have not sailed across an ocean before. Whilst we might all have different motivations for doing this, we all shared today a similar depth of thought and apprehension about what we are about to undertake and I can see this in their eyes as we meet and depart at the same time. The next time I see these people we'll be in Rio after 4,800 miles of ocean racing.

Brest to Rio
broken ribs

Race two started just off the coast of north western France. We absolutely nailed the start and led from the outset, totally fired up after our race one defeat. We led the pack and crept out a lead of nearly 200 miles within the first few days.

We settled into our alternating watch routines fairly quickly, consisting of two six hour day shifts followed by three night shifts of 4 hours. At our mid-day watch changeover, both watches give up half an hour each to a happy hour, where all crew meet together, exchange update information and strategy, catch up on news and listen to music. This is strangely sometimes the only time one might see people on the other watch so it's a great addition to our routine. On many days however, we also end up using our happy hour to carry out tasks requiring many hands, we are a racing yacht after all.

Every six hours, on UTC time, with a regularity of precision the 'scheds' arrive. These are auto generated position reports for the rest of the boats in the fleet, showing us their distance to finish, latitude & longitude. As we adjust our boat time to our own version of local time, this six hour rotation shifts out of line with our clock on board and the watch system. This breaks the monotony of the day, which helps one focus on remembering what time it actually is.

UTC, or Universal Time Coordinated, replaced GMT, Greenwich Mean Time, for aviation and maritime use in the early 1960s. As a compromise and more accurate method of calculating time offset for time zones around the world. Often referred to as Zulu Time. In reference to Zero hour, designated by the letter Z, which in phonetic speak becomes Zulu. I know it sounds complicated but it does avoid any confusion as Zulu time is always the same base line and does not change the world over. Our boat time however is just whatever works best for us onboard, we adjust this to make best use of daylight hours and it bears little or no reference to actual time zones whatsoever.

The 'scheds' provide our update to the race and as soon as they arrive, there is a clamber of anticipation across the boat for the updated info. We plot the positions into our navigation software, add the mileages into an ever growing spreadsheet and review what the data means for us in lost or gained mileage. As soon as we have the news it spreads around the boat like a breeze, often some crew are woken by request for the updates or occasionally set alarms to get up and review it before returning to bunk. Our race strategy is clear and our daily planning precise, but on occasion when the sheds arrive we question why some boats are gaining or dropping back on us, then review what we are doing and how we can change our plans, turning up the heat as and when required. I have heard of previous races where some boats didn't feel like they were racing. Our team approach has always been really clear. Have fun, stay safe, and be competitive. In that order. I felt at all times we were working to this, and we were always competitive, for most of us it felt like part of the fun, which just made it easier anyway.

As we made our way out across the Bay of Biscay and further into the North Atlantic out to the north west of the Canary Islands. We picked up some bigger Atlantic swells and a good strong and reliable force 4/5 north westerly, our first chance to really start to wind up CV30 properly offshore. We lined her up, trimmed the sail pattern to match perfectly the conditions then set about balancing her on the swell. With each progressively larger wave and a steady breeze we surfed her along 15-16-17 ktts, she felt amazing; so perfectly balanced and true, starting to hum and vibrate gently above 15 knots. We moved some weight around both above and below decks, shifting our emergency water supplies and all other heavy stores into central locations primarily around the keel and mast base to help with the balance, all crew not involved in sail trim and helming sat up on the high side rail.

Then we set her up again to surf some more, balancing her along the wave roll, she sat atop the first big one and slewed forward gently cutting through the water ahead of her with a loud fizzing swish. The acceleration was beautiful, a wind rush and it was like someone had changed gear as she increased right up to 19.2 ktts. Big smiles and cheers all around the deck. Again and again she lifted up and sloped herself forward racing down the surf 19.4 then19.6. The crew willing her onwards. Then the big one, with Jackie on the helm and Skipper Sean assisting her, a beautiful long surf holding herself just right on the downside 20.4 knots, a big oooooorah cheer went out! And Jackie gets the prize and kudos for today. The first helm over 20 ktts. I have no doubt we will beat this later this afternoon and in the southern ocean swells too which should take us to 30+ knots easily, but there is, and will only ever be, one first time over 20 and it belongs to Jackie Ford; well-done Jac.

Consider that CV30 is 23m long, 5.5m wide at her widest point, with a mast of over 28m high, supporting a main sail bigger than a tennis court and a set of down wind surfing foresails almost the size of a football field. She weighs in at 36tonnes, and we occasionally refer to her as 'the bus' on account of her size and weight, but right now, she is tight, responsive racing onwards at high speeds, and on these big waves, you could very easily water ski behind her, as she kicks up a small rooster tail at the transom with her bow slicing through all but the really big waves ahead as they crash over her and rinse us thoroughly on their way across the deck.

On our regular rounds of bilge checks we find the crash bulkhead, the smallest water tight compartment right at the front of the boat, is taking on water, and lots of it! 8-10 buckets are pumped and scooped out from here 6 times a day, which becomes a real chore, and quite hard & dangerous at times in heavier seas. It is important we keep this empty as it effects the balance of the boat having all that extra weight right on our nose. No chance of a fix now till Rio either. We email the shore team and arrange parts to be waiting for our arrival to rectify this.

And so we continued in this manner for the next day and a half, rotating the helm every hour or so. In these conditions an hour is about as much as you can do. Helming a Clipper 70' in big seas is a mixture of delicate art, sensitive touch and balance, coupled with the enormously hard physical work of just holding or turning the wheel, whilst balancing yourself on the ever changing floor angle. It taxes your concentration levels and physical strengths all at the same time.

I took my turn at helming for just over an hour, thoroughly enjoying every single minute of it. Certainly feeling like I had experienced a full body muscle and cerebral work out afterwards. I handed over to John Gray and stayed with him whilst he settled and picked up the rhythm, then moved across to the other helming position to continue to watch the instruments and monitor our progress. A short while later we were picking up some side waves occasionally which was making John's task ever harder. As a side wave picks you up and twists the boat across the wind, you can lose the wind angle really quickly and need to try and anticipate this and prevent crash jibing if you can. Just one such wave caught us, catching John off guard, twisting us sideways to wind and heeling the boat quickly and progressively further and further over. I watched forward as the bow started to bury into the waves on the port side, finding myself now ever closer to the water, which was fast becoming my ground horizon. She twisted through a full 90 degrees, and I started to grip tighter still to the guard rails around the helm positions whilst my feet, then ankles, then knees went underwater. The full force of the wind then caught the sails exactly how we had discussed it might. The wind slapped us right over into the water, the deck now standing upright at nearly vertical angle, the boom and mainsail touched the water. Everything seemed to happen in slow motion now,

John lost his grip on the wheel and fell down towards me, his safety line catching him, breaking his fall towards the water and giving him just sufficient traction to start to think about getting back up as he reacted quickly. Around him, I could see Suzie and Richard hanging on too.

As John lost his grip and the wave passed us, simultaneously the wind picked us back up, getting underneath the sails, slamming us right over 180 degrees from where we were, boom now back in the water but on the other side. The retainer we had fitted earlier (a safety line to stop the booms lateral movement) really couldn't stop the full weight of the boom shifting from one side to the other, but it did an excellent elastic job in slowing down the swing across at least. The weight of a lateral boom slap and crash jibe in these conditions could easily bring down the full rig and mast. I had just about managed to cling onto the helm stanchions throughout, and I was now in a reasonable position to assist, taking the wheel we started to bring her back up to wind and managed briefly to get her level, with the boom aloft and heading back into the wind for some stability. The others got back to their feet and we did a quick check *"everyone OK?"* All was well, some pretty star eyed looks back, but all was well. But what to do now? I hesitated and was really unsure, the boom was back the middle but was not pinned or powered either way, an extremely fragile and unstable position to be in. I thought to myself, do I stay with the jibe position, or risk crashing the boom back the other way to reset where we started from? Just then, and at exactly the right moment for me, Skipper appeared at the companion way in just his shorts, with a life jacket in hand. *"All safe, but crash jibed Skip"* I called across to him *"which way?"*, *"hard a starboard"* came his reply, I quickly obliged and as gently as I could I settled the boom back to its original place far out wide on the port side. By the time I had done so, Skipper was next to me, life jacket securely fastened, just how he moves, Skips and jumps around the boat quite so quickly in these conditions in his bare feet is a mystery to me, but a real joy to watch, when you can catch it. We recapped what had happened and did a quick and thorough full rig check before powering her back up and continuing on our way, shaken but not stirred, this is a race after all! So straight back up to 20+ knots, learning from the experience and continuing on our way south west.

Next day, I was back on deck organising a new pump arrangement for the emptying of the crash bulkhead. There was no sign of us achieving a repair until we got to Rio, so if we could make this easier with some kind of pumping system then this would benefit us all. I had the pumping kit I was going to base my build on and was making my way forward, to go back down below. I passed the kit forward via Richard and Andy who were sitting on the high side and stepped forward over the traveler and into the cockpit. The boat slewed upwards and over to port, Richard in front of me lost his footing and was heading forwards towards the water. Grabbing hold of him, we went forward together over the coffee grinder, I ended up over the handle with Richard in a kind of piggy back, and as the boat raised up into the opposite direction, I started taking way too much weight on my ribs directly upon the handle, I waited and expected to break something, apparently groaning a little as we came back over, though I don't remember doing this. We got back over to the top side and the relief of getting off the handle and getting Richards weight off me too was immense. I sat onto the deck and briefly thought I had got away with it. I took a deep breath, and couldn't breathe. Pausing for a moment I realised now I had hurt myself and lay down for a second. Some of the crew who saw this had already realised I was hurt and by the time I sat back up, Suzie our boat medic was already donning her life jacket and exiting the companion way stairs. Susie, is one of the most unassuming and modest people I have ever met. Clearly intelligent and expert within her medical field, she stays away from praise and is truly humble. She also has one of the very best senses of humour on board, and an instinctive capability to bring a team together with wit and banter. We would come to call upon Susie's medical skills a lot around the world, and truly test these skills.

I got up, insisting I was fine and made my own way carefully down below, stubborn as I am. By the time I got to the saloon, I knew I was potentially in trouble and hurt.

I striped down to the waist and Suzie examined my ribs and back. Wow, shooting and proper sharp pain to the touch in several places, conclusion probably broken something, not exactly sure what, so lots of pain killers, full med check all over and confined to my bunk until further notice. To be honest it was uncomfortable just lying in my bunk so I knew something was not good. Suzie warned me of possible shortage of breath and we discussed pain levels and possible treatments. She gave me the strongest pain relief she could without stepping over the morphine line, which we agreed would be the first step towards medivac, and I really did not wish to do this. I slept for the rest of the day and through the night with Suzie checking in on me periodically. So a pretty eventful 24 hours to reflect upon, and not until I started to get back into routine, did I realise what this had done to my overall confidence on deck.

Next day was a complete loss for me, I felt like I had been run over by a bus, ached all over, finding it increasingly hard to breath, cough or move too far. Further examination concluded, almost certainly broken something, likely to be one or maybe even three lower ribs, and maybe a rear floater rib broken or dislodged as I had much middle back pain now too.

And so 2-3 days of recovery followed, increasingly frustrating stepping out of the watch systems and not being able to move around too far below deck. I made myself busy with navigation and position reporting. After 3-4 days I made back onto deck, after another day or so I was back into watch system fully, just not winching or grinding anything, and occasionally sitting out deck work when it got tasty and bumpy, just to be safe. The pain continued all the way to Rio and breathing was hard, sneezing or coughing were excruciatingly painful. On one day I had hiccups, talk about kick a man when he is down, I hung a towel across my bunk for some privacy and cried for an hour as each hiccup hurt more and more.

I decided not to tell anyone back home. I know some of my close friends & family, particularly Siobhan & my Mum do worry about the dangers of the trip, so a story of broken ribs this early into the race might not help the rest of the year away.

We raced hard onwards to the first scoring gate, frantically checking and rechecking positions and plotting navigation against wind & weather for best course. It felt tense for the whole crew, and in a last minute play out with Henri Lloyd we pipped them for three points and passed the gate to the west of them, celebrated a day or so later when the news was confirmed by the race office.

Still holding the lead we landed into the doldrums and lay becalmed on and off for eight days. The Doldrums, or Inter-Tropical Convergence Zone (ITCZ) to give it its full name. Is a low pressure area around the equator where the centrifugal force of the earth makes air rise and travel north or south, becalming sailing vessels for days, sometimes weeks on end. Occasionally this air returns in the form of violent squalls and hurricanes so whilst nothing is occurring, you can never ever let your guard down.

Totally frustrating and hard work staying alert to every single breath of wind 24 hours a day and constantly changing our sail set to maximise whatever we could. Amazing to go from flat calm with no breeze to 20 knot wind and heeled over doing 15 knots plus, then back to nothing again as the conditions continue to circulate around us. The frustrations of this, coupled with the unbearable heat, 40 degrees+ below deck, made it virtually impossible to sleep whilst dripping with sweat, sapping energy levels. One or two of the crew succumbed to dehydration and exhaustion, taking time out to recover below deck, trying hard to find some respite from the heat in the shade.

We tried hard to keep ourselves busy, erecting tarpaulin & spinnaker sun shades over parts of the deck, whilst we serviced winches, repaired halyards and generally did as much as we could in the circumstances, without jeopardising racing. This in itself is hard. You just know as soon as you erect a 'Bimini' (deck sun shade) then the wind will pick up and we take it down and go sailing again. Then, as soon as anyone goes to sleep its 'all hands' as a squall comes in and we maximise the passing winds for as much mileage as we can squeeze out of it as it passes. Seven days passed and we made only 250 miles south, we had previously been making this distance in a day! When the big squalls came, many of us readied buckets and collected water for washing clothes, as fresh water on the boat is reserved for drinking only. We also showered, using the rain water as it poured down off the main sail and through the boom as a shower, boy this was refreshing, the girls relished the opportunity to wash hair too. On one such occurrence we were caught with too much sail up as the storm intensified, the wind increased and a team of us moved quickly, changing sails still with shampoo lather all over us, too much hilarity and laughter for days to come.

Then, on one morning we gained a slight breeze from the south east, it held for an hour or two which was bliss. Then building slowly into a steady push giving us 4-5 ktts, which at the time felt fast, having not moved for so long. We were anxious not to celebrate this too early, but as the hours rolled on it seemed we were free. Miraculous; where did this breeze just suddenly appear from? It was like passing through a window; even the skies started to look different with more 'normal' cloud formations and less of those high altitude rollers we had been used to for the last week.

On the 23rd September it was my father's 70th birthday, it was a contemplative day for me, as I had been unable to call him as I had hoped to do so. A surprise phone call from me, mid

Atlantic, I know would have made his day. Our sat-comms were out of service for a week or so, and I really missed this opportunity which I had planned out for some time. I commandeered the daily crew diary and wrote a piece about life on board, thinking of people at home, wishing him happy returns, then accompanied this with a photo from the boat of the whole crew holding a sign and wishing him happy birthday. I managed to get an email out to him, and got a short reply, so at least I knew he had received it. Then later that day, Skipper posted in his diary a personal happy birthday to Dad too. Dad was proper stoked with this and told 'everyone' and I mean everyone about it. Even printing a copy and taking it out with him to bowls events.

All of the boats were suffering minor damage as the crews got used to racing them. Some had lost halyards, some had blocks & shackles which had failed. We seemed to be doing OK by comparison, but to be sure we initiated daily rig checks. Chafe was our biggest worry and for us and we started a chafe watch every hour on the key points. Our main halyard in particular was bad and we removed this before leaving the doldrums to protect what was left for repair in Rio. We tore our code 2 spinnaker on a spreader, which required a 5 hour repair job below decks. Still pretty lucky by comparison, at least one other boat already had spinnaker out of action through damage.

A few days later we crossed the equator, at 06:00 local time on the 29th September, to a beautiful sunrise. All 20 crew held the helm together as one as we crossed over from Northern hemisphere to Southern hemisphere finally becoming a 'shellback' no longer a 'polywog'. These are the mythical names given to those whom have, and have not, sailed across the equator. Later that afternoon we were visited by 'king Neptune' himself and his assistant 'Davy Jones' for a ceremonial completion of our crossing. We offered up a toast to Neptune, apparently made up of anything red and spicy onboard, Tabasco, chilli, tomato sauce and marmite were apparently the key ingredients! Then followed with king Neptune's pancakes, a raw egg mixture poured over us, then dusted with flour. Finally a lock of hair from each of us as an offering, cut deep with Clippers by Neptune, leaving a bald exposed white patch on each crew members head. Those that know me will know there is not much hair left to cut deep into. I did however receive a deep cut bald patch on my chest to show for this with honour, which itched for several days afterwards.

We saw a number of small pods of dolphin along the way and a few different birds. The most spectacular wildlife sight however was the bioluminescence in the waters at night. Sometimes this was just small flecks barely visible. Once or twice it was a mass of hundreds of large balloon shapes, a smack of jelly fish, cascading away behind the boat like balloons being released to the wind but lighting up the darkness with a soft green/blue hue. Then the very best show, which is thousands upon thousands of small flecks within the bow waves of the boat on both sides, like a welders sparks flying away from the wake as we crashed forwards, the light this omitted was occasionally sufficient to light the darkest of nights and illuminate the whole deck. We referred to this as our fairy dust, relating back to the sign from prep week. I would have so loved to have filmed or photographed this spectacle but all attempts failed with my limited camera equipment, and it shall now be confined to memory, but oh what a memory.

Around 6-7 days out from Rio we were now placed in mid table. We had already bagged the 3 points from the scoring gate, which if we were to end in 5th place, would give us the equivalent of second place points. Not the same as a podium finish, but some consolation at this point. One of the most pleasing factors at this point in the race was that we had stuck to our game plan. Stay safe, have fun, be competitive. At all times since leaving London we had been competitive, the team spirit and desire to do well in the race on board was excellent.

Very shortly after our exit from the ocean sprint, we cracked our Code2 spinnaker into the wind, and turned downhill towards a sharper course to Rio. Sailing with the Code2 was beautiful, and a welcome respite from the beating south course we had tried to maintain previously for the ocean sprint. We would sail this pattern for several days now and we set about recovering from the toll the ocean sprint days previously had taken on the team, getting some good food on the go and some extra rest in rotation.

I could still feel the constant pain in my ribs and it was enough to keep me in check and sometimes stop me doing too much. I concentrated on making it to Rio in one piece, ready to recover fully and get stronger again.

We experienced some of the clearest nights ever; star filled skies with more stars than one could possibly ever imagine. We also see in excess of a dozen or more shooting stars every night. We spent some time identifying constellations and galaxies; some of which I had not even heard of before.

Once we were in sight of Rio, we changed back to white sails and started to tack a course back & forth inside the way points at Cabo Frio. The lead three boats were now in easy sight of the finish and out of our reach, Jamaica Get All Right & PSP Logistics eventually crossing the finish line with only 19 seconds between them, the closest Clipper race finish ever. We could see both DLL and our nemesis Henri Lloyd a few miles ahead and we set about a sprint finish, heads down, full on racing once again. We pulled in slowly but surely gaining on Henri, and when we switched down early from Yankee 2 to Yankee 3, their late call proved too much and they were seriously overpowered allowing us to slip through as they battled with the increasing wind. We continued to pull out a lead and tacked their identical course to ensure no advantages were taken. OneDLL were still in our sights and, as we maintained our charge, we drew up to within 5 miles or so of them as we turned into the bay for the final run into the finish line. At the entrance to the Rio natural harbour lay two small islands, we had studied these a few times and were still unsure of the best route through. It appeared OneDLL were going for the gap and I took up position in the Nav Station to monitor them closely. We held our line maintaining the option to go around if OneDLL fell into a wind hole behind the islands. With Sean on the helm I relayed their stats continuously up to him. We held and held, they slowed right down 10-9-8-7 ktts, appearing to stall in the wind hole as we had expected. This could be our chance. 6-5, 4 ktts now. I measured quickly the alternative route and calculated we could pass them if we maintained the current 12 knots we had, but could it be done. Sean & I exchanged information at an ever increasing rate and the moments became increasingly fraught. Last chance approaching now. *"Inside or out?"* he called last chance. Hang on, hang on, hang on.......one last check on OneDLL......6knotts and increasing, no wind hole, *"go inside".* I shout back. We sharpened up our course, headed for the island gap, and prepared a spinnaker for one last dash. As we exited the island shadow we cracked open our spinnaker, dropped the head sails and accelerated towards OneDLL. It wasn't quite enough and they crossed the line only two miles ahead of us, after over 5,000 miles racing. Henri passed the line about 25 minutes later and although a redress time bonus for assisting another boat earlier in the race would see them finish above us on the table, we had our morale victory over them which counted for more to us on this occasion.

We made our way over to OneDLL and congratulated them, exchanging some laughs and brief stories as we prepared our boats for entering the harbour. The nighttime views of Rio were pretty amazing, Christ the Redeemer statue glowing on the mountain top and the city lights buzzing with life. The airport was located just past the harbour entrance and we were buzzed by a couple of big planes as they took off and we joked about having our navigation lights on!

The Clipper race RIB was out to escort us into our berthing, giving us clear instructions and a *'follow me'* process which takes much of the strain out of this part of the journey after an ocean crossing. As we turned and entered the harbour, there were cheers, whoops and whistles from the dock side. We could see a small crowd of around a 100 or so people cheering for us. As we drew closer we could see some familiar faces of friends, family and crew joining for the next race. A short briefing from the Clipper race team, accompanied by a cooler of beer and soft drinks, then we were allowed off the yacht, but not out of the marina. A small bar and food area was open on the dockside, and we were instructed it would stay open until the last person left, pretty dangerous tactics as it turned out, and they eventually served us breakfast next morning, staying open throughout! A great evening and celebration of our first major ocean crossing.

Next day we set about our deep clean and remarkably finished it in relatively quick time, much better planned and organised than the previous stopover. I was taking part fully in the work, just avoiding lifting anything heavy, so I got down low and cleaned the bilges, a pretty mucky job, but one I could physically do without too much trouble. I had arranged a rental house through a local contact. Seven of us were staying there and a mini bus & driver arrived to collect us early afternoon and we set off together to the house. I had my medical appointment for later that afternoon, and decided to get dropped off on the way and meet the team back at the prize giving that evening as this would make better use of time. Julia Debasse, our local agent was escorting us to the house, her mother was visiting and she asked if we could give her a lift home. When we arrived at the hospital Julia's mother offered to stay with me and translate if I needed it in reception. As it turned out, no one spoke English at the hospital and she stayed with me all afternoon, above and beyond normality and worthy of the flowers I later sent her from Cape Town. I spent around 5 hours at the private hospital and after an X-ray confirmed two very badly broken ribs, followed by an MRI scan to confirm no other damage or dangerous loose fragments, they gave me a prescription for ibuprofen and a medical note sent to Clipper race team and the insurance company confirming the above with 6 weeks to fully heal, all in order, good news.

I breathed a sigh of relief, as this meant exactly what we had thought and was an easily manageable full recovery. I jumped in a taxi and headed back to the marina for the prize giving ceremony.

We congratulated the victors magnanimously as always and stayed for a social evening and Brazilian barbecue. Throughout the entire evening it rained and rained and rained, some sheltered, most just put hoods up on their wet weather gear and enjoyed the evening; Clipper race crew are a tough bunch. We headed back to the house, arriving there in the early hours with some red wine and cheese awaiting us. JC and Ana, two new arrival crew had already arrived at the house from the airport and we stayed up relaxing for a couple of hours, really very nice treat just sitting on the sofa and chilling out in comfort after a month at sea.

Next morning we headed back to the boat, and back to work again on some repairs and maintenance. I received a note saying there was a message for me at the race office, so I popped in around lunchtime to check in. I met Gillian our crew manager and she stepped outside to talk. She said the insurance company have my medical report, which says 6 weeks to heal, so they are arranging flights for me from Rio to London and then back out to Cape Town, I would now miss leg two.

I paused in the surreal of the moment, 'what?' 'really?' 'why?' My head was spinning; this wasn't the outcome, the X-ray says healing well, the MRI says no other danger! I knew of at least six other people on the race who had broken their ribs on leg one and not been for a medical checkup, the race office knew of these people too. I needed some time to take this in and reflect, I wanted to argue and persuade right now. This was not the time to do this; experience has taught me in any situation like this, go think it through. I grabbed copies of the reports and went for coffee on my own out by the marina.

Sitting out in the sun, I struggled with this and wrestled with my options. For me this is a *'round the world race'*, not a *'get off and come back later'* race! Michelle came over and sat with me, she had heard the news from Gillian, but didn't let on at first; allowing me to tell her. I struggled as I told her. We chatted through the options and Susie (medic) joined us too, we looked through the forms and checked the information looking for options.

On the Clipper race medical form, it says signature of a medical practitioner declaring fit to race required. I had tried to get the hospital to sign this yesterday, but there was no one either prepared or qualified to do so. Susie made the obvious link, I have not been seen by a medical practitioner yet! I went back to the race office later and talked it through with them, then contacted the insurance company directly and reopened the case.

For the next 36 hours they called and emailed to and fro constantly, whilst trying to arrange an appropriate appointment for me. This time was stressful to the extreme; I tried to help working on the boat, but was pre occupied with constant calls to phones and email. I took a morning off & stayed at the house to try and force the issue; this was a last chance now with only 48 hours left before we sailed again. I badgered and badgered the insurers whilst using contacts in Rio to get local information and medical contacts for them. I also discussed with them the possibility of Susie submitting a report declaring me fit. Susie was a medical practitioner and had treated me from the outset and would continue to do so on route to Cape Town. Surely she was the most qualified to comment? To my surprise, they agreed to this. I had no way to contact Susie as she was out on a corporate sail and had no phone, so whilst waiting for the final call back for my appointment, I made my way back to the marina to meet the boat back in.

Thirty minutes from the marina in a cab I got a call; my appointment was now at 14:00 today, they would give me the address and it was about 15km from the marina. I looked at my watch, it was already 13:30. There wasn't a chance to get to the marina and back out to the clinic, or even directly there from where we were in just half an hour. I explained this and they said *'but its only 15km away'* obviously no concept of Rio traffic from their call centre. I asked them to try and make it for 14:30, which they did and we continued down to the marina. The traffic was horrendous and it seemed to take an age to get to the boat. I was worried now that I would miss Susie and I tried to call everyone else I knew at the marina to ask her to wait for me, with no joy. I was getting ever more stressed; this felt like my last chance to get back on board and it was slipping away in traffic and time. I got to the boat and met Susie, then headed back to the car and made our way across the city to the clinic. We checked in upstairs and discovered their osteopath clinic was actually 10km away and we needed to take another taxi. One of the doctors, who spoke good English, assisted us and we were off again across the city, getting dropped off at the new address. We went inside and it was a shopping precinct! After some exploration we found the clinic was upstairs, after abandoning the biggest lift queue I have ever seen anywhere we went up the fire escape to eventually find it and check in. They didn't have my appointment, made some calls to check and after some discussion it was agreed I would see their osteopath shortly. Then his PA came out and explained he only treated hands, not ribs. Really! You couldn't write this stuff! Lots more calls, loads more waiting, testing my Spanish and Portuguese language skills to the limits, they agreed I could see a private practitioner in the same clinic. We waited some more and tried to make light of the day. Once we met with the osteopath, he seemed quite satisfied with what he had seen on the MRI and X-ray and just wanted a full check to satisfy himself I was Ok.

I stripped down and he gave me some exercises to do, every single one of them hurt like hell, but I did each and every one with a smile, saying I was fine. Then he stood behind me and started pressing on points around my ribs, working his way gradually down my chest and back. He was digging his thumbs in deep and I knew at some point he would get to the damage which was going to hurt big time. I was facing Susie, she smiled and frowned at the same time, I guessed she was hoping this would go well, but she knew what I was about to do. She recounted afterwards all she had in her head was *'don't flinch, don't flinch, don't flinch!'*. He pressed and pressed some more, stopping to press the broken ones one extra time. I held my nerve, though I really don't know how I didn't pass out with the stinging and burning pain.

He said I could get dressed, and I tried to do this like I was OK, but I was again in a lot of pain. He said all was fine and he would write a report saying I could carry on as normal, rejoin the race and just no heavy work.

Then, when all the reports were written, he explained he could not stamp and sign the report I needed, as the insurance company relationship was with the first clinic we went to. So back across the city again to the first clinic, it was now around 16:30 on a Friday, and all I could think of was they would close before we got there. We were so close to having what we needed, again the traffic was awful and it took us an age to get there. When we arrived all was well, but they said they could not sign the form as they were not the examining doctor and the previous guy had made a mistake, oh boy! What a day this was turning into!

After more discussions & explanations in a mixture of Spanish, Portuguese & English, plus some outrageous flirting with the receptionist! They compromised, copied over the previous doctor's report and stamped the form. This could be it? I might actually be there now? But no celebration until it's confirmed. I had them email the form directly to the insurers who called and said they would pass it to their medical team and Underwriters first and get back to me tomorrow, this was going to be tight now. There was nothing else we could do with this. We exited the clinic and after realising I had deprived Susie of a corporate lunch, agreed to treat her. We had absolutely no idea where we were in Rio, so we walked a little then spotting the sea, headed down a side road and found ourselves on Copa Cabbana beach, about 150m from the palace. *"Pick a beach cafe Susie, any one you want, my treat"* I said. We found a great spot, right on the beach and had the most amazing lunch together.

The insurance company called like clockwork every two hours for the next 12hours to keep me up to speed with progress and copied in the Clipper Race office at every stage. The girls in the call centre, Natalie & Simone, were excellent, they showed an interest in solving this and working together, they were pleasant and courteous and it felt at every stage like a personal service.

The following morning, around mid-morning I went to the race office to check on the latest status, all fine they said, we had the report in yesterday evening and it confirmed you are all fine and fit to race, welcome back to the team. I was back on the team, I grabbed a coffee and sat outside to take it in, still stressed and boiling inside, I tried to settle myself. Andrew Richardson passes by and I stop to chat with him. Andy was a round the world crew member with us on team Derry; a retired Yorkshireman who has travelled the world and been extremely successful in his own business. A more delightfully pleasant and gentle man you could not wish to meet, who spent very many hours just tinkering away fixing and improving our environment aboard, sorting and tidying the tool shed, inventing things and stitching the sails, with never a bad comment or fuss ever made.

Andy's equally delightful wife, Wendy, had flown out to Rio to meet him, carrying with her the news that his father had died about two weeks ago! I spent a good deal of time chatting with Andy, or rather listening and sympathising along with him. I cannot begin to understand how he felt, but I can only admire how he managed himself and dealt with this during our stopover in Rio. He stayed with us continuing with the race and once or twice we touched lightly upon this again, as and when he wanted to. In the grand scheme therefore my problems with getting back on the race were actually insignificant and I should simply be grateful for my luck, life, friends and family, who are all fit and well.

We had our race briefing, hosted this time in a disused 'shed' at the back of the marina, next to the airport. It's not all glamour for race briefings. There was some useful as ever information about scoring gates and sprints, plus some great weather briefings. Sean followed this with our own team briefing and shared the final race strategy with us. New watch teams announced, a shuffle of the teams and chance for others to take the lead. He announced a new role within the team as head navigator, me, assisted by John Curtis from the opposite watch. This gave me some real team responsibility and a chance to still contribute whilst recovering to full fitness. And so ended the most hectic and stressful few days in Rio.

On race start day morning, we took a last shore breakfast on the Marina side in the sun and made our final preparations for departure. Our local contact from the Irish embassy arrived about an hour before departure with an Irish band, who played live Irish jig music for us on the dock and we all danced and sang the last few minutes away on land, much to the pleasure and amusement of the other teams and spectators. It was a welcome moment of pleasure at a perfect time, raising morale and team spirit right before the off. We slipped the dock at just after 11:30 and headed out for a parade of sail. Flags and banners flying in a blaze of colour and spectacle.

Rio to Cape Town
Southern ocean sailing

After an increasingly fraught choreographicall commentary on VHF from the media team on their chase boats and helicopters for the money shot under Sugarloaf Mountain, we dropped the brightly coloured flags & sponsor banners on board and set about getting ready for the business of race 3 to Cape Town.

We set up on the start line, did some trial circuits and then rounded back away to run up to the line with the fleet. Jostling for position, whilst counting down the timings out loud from several synchronised stopwatches on deck, we approached the start line. Tight for space, we jostled for position and set up at the last minute along the end of the line, fast approaching the windward mark, we turned and crossed the line at exactly the moment, with barely a few yards to go. *'Ooops that was a close one!'* Says Sean on the helm with a wry smile. We have made the start with perfection again and lead the fleet across the bay. We squeeze as much as we can up towards the wind with, who else? But, Henri Lloyd underneath us. They push us almost onto the beach on the other side of the bay, before tacking right at the last minute; leaving us little or no space to complete ours with only a few metres to spare. All advantage lost and now back in fourth, possibly even fifth position as we head out of the bay. I take up position on the Nav station down below as agreed and call the distances and max closing depths to the two islands at the entrance to the bay, adding the best course to mark as we pass by and I also call the safe turn point distances out loud. We head out across the bay towards the mark at Copacabana beach, rounding it in third place. All the time, Sean and I are in constant communications on distances, depths and our best course to the next mark just off Ipenema beach. We round the headland, pass the next mark and turn to head out to sea. There is one more obstacle of the last landfall of Brazil; some remote rocks and islands around 3 miles out which we pass by safely. I come back up to deck for some air as it's been a pretty stuffy two hours down below. There are stories around the crew of how great Copacabana beach looked and what a spectacle it was racing around the cans so close. Shame I missed this, but playing my part for the team down below and a pretty great lunch at the Copa only a few days before is more than consolation for this. I am in truth just happy to be onboard, I so nearly missed this one.

The next few days are really hard; we beat hard directly into the wind due south and the boat and team take a real beasting. The environment below deck decays as we work hard just to survive as a team and maintain our life aboard. It is traumatically hard work as the boat bounces and writhes around on the head of the waves. Working on deck is hard work with little or no footholds and a constant shift of the deck. Below decks, even standing in one place is almost impossible at times. We reduce down to emergency food rations, eliminating the requirement for cooking, and also allowing those not feeling so well to eat on deck. Watch teams are shorthanded and those of us that can make the extra effort to rotate in support of each other, reducing sleep even further. I am fit enough to join the watches but still pretty limited in what I can do on deck. I get caught out in position a few times and join in winching lines, it hurts like hell and once or twice I retreat to bunk, after my watch duties, in agony. However, once in my bunk, and attempting to sleep the experience isn't that great in these conditions anyway, and so deck work becomes the best place to be at times.

After five days or so beating south, we break off to the south west and raise a code two spinnaker. Levelling out, the boat and increasing our speed at the same time, this brings a welcome respite to the team, who bring themselves out of hiding and back into play. To add pleasure to this, the sun is shining and we take lunch on deck, full team together and have a general catch up on where we are, and our strategy so far. The scheds continue to arrive at a familiar regularity every six hours. We are placed fourth to PSP Logistics, GREAT Britain & Team Garmin. The position measured is a straight line distance to the finish which takes no account of rhum lines or best course, so we believe we are probably placed first or second in reality. We are flat sailing and surfing, covering 60-70 miles every six hours and we creep back into first place, which, whilst 'not' part of our strategy at this point, is nice to do and reminds the fleet we are still here to contend with. We sharpen up our course and head due east, changing our clocks by an hour each day over two days to make better use of the daylight hours. This provides an added bonus of a sunrise directly on our bow, which looks amazing and greets the next few days early dawn shifts with some beautiful skies. I continue to use this leg to get back my confidence and we are around 7-8 days in before I get a sense of moving freely around the boat both below and up on deck. Still struggling with some big twinges of pain, but feeling much stronger now. I know it's a long race ahead and I need to work hard to resist doing too much, but nonetheless I push myself each day further and further.

Our crash bulkhead appears to be better than before after the remedial works in Rio, it still leaks, but now it's only a few buckets a day. However, to add insult to our injury, we now we have a massive leak around the rudder and steering seals in the lazzerette.

It's a beautiful sunny afternoon, we are tripping along nicely with the Code 1 spinnaker out front making around 10-12 ktts. The crew were going about their business it was a quiet afternoon watch and we were all relaxed. I was down below, had just finished plotting positions and was drinking hot chocolate whilst updating our crew notice board with the latest scheds, when a spinnaker slap occurred. This is when the spinnaker loses wind, deflates and then re-inflates, slamming enormous pressures directly upon the rig, invariably crashing as it fully tensions the lines and blocks which crash and bang off decks and blocks as it happens. It is inevitable this will happen when flying spinnakers but the risks to the rig and sail are great & many. We do everything we can to avoid it and recover as quickly as possible. This one slapped again and again, then powered up horribly quickly as the boat rolled, quickly healed over and then came back up again. I sensed all was not well with this one as the power increased and increased, so grabbed my life jacket off the side rail where it was hanging and slipped up onto deck quickly fastening the catches as I did. The spinnaker was in the water already, the boat heeled right over and Sean was exiting the rear hatch and about to take the helm. *'ease the sheet'* he calls, Jacky eases as he continues *'more, more, more'* the boat continues to heel over now almost vertical, *'release the vang'* calls Sean, I am next to this by now so jump to it quick time, leaving just enough tension in it to reset when we settle. I load it back onto a winch, plant a winch handle in it and clip on; all of us are now clipped on and scrambling for hand holds as the boat makes almost fully vertical heel over. The boom digs into the water and the main sail dragging pulls the boat around, slowing it and steering us like a sea anchor braking one side and twisting us around. As it slows and we turn, we pop back up and sway over, boom comes across the deck to shouts of *'heads up, boom over!'* It briefly touches the water on the other side then swings back to centre. Oleg snaps to the main sheet and settles the tension back into it; we now had the boom under control. The spinnaker, almost under control, gets pulled in on the sheets at a most impressive rate by Jacky, whom a few moments ago was dangling legs out and hanging on with both hands, but is now standing solidly by the winch pulling in armfuls of sheet, whilst Andy grasps the grinder and tensions it up nicely ready to re-fly. Vang back on, main tensioned, sheets ready, the boat settles back into full sail and we continue along our way. *'Nice recovery team'* says Sean as he slides back down the hatch. Everyone checks all are ok then we settle back into afternoon watch routine. I slip back down below, recover my hot chocolate, which amazingly has survived the event in its thermal mug with the lid tightly secured, and continue where I left off. Just another quiet afternoon on watch in the sunshine, and a reminder of just how fragile the boat is when under spinnaker power. She is fundamentally unstable under this sail pattern, and whilst she can be sailed with a helm and only one or two crew making minor adjustments, at any time she might need as many as 8-12 pairs of crew hands just to control and manage her out of a tricky situation. When on watch, we pay close attention at all times to everything around us; constantly tidying up, checking the winches and gear so we always know what is where and can react quickly. When not on watch, we are never far away from our life jackets and deck gear, sometimes this is quite stressful. Occasionally when it's all kicking off up on deck, you just have to wait patiently down below in the knowledge you will be called if needed; rest is important and many hands is not always productive. When below and listening to this above decks it reminds me of a war zone recording, people shouting and calling out to each other whilst bangs and crashes rain down all around, it can feel quite scary in the dead of night to wake up to this. As the trip continues however, we are all getting tuned into the sounds and senses from around the boat and are starting to sense what are good and bad noises, instinctively reacting to some and not others. As we tune into these, we sleep better too, waking to certain noises and not others. I am sure this is how Skipper manages to rest and sleep. He has an uncanny knack of arriving on deck when things are tricky or about to get out of control.

It's Jason's birthday, and to celebrate, we dress up as him as a surprise just before breakfast. Boxer shorts, wooly hat and toothbrush in mouth. A look he has perfected on early mornings on board over the past few weeks. We sing happy birthday to him and share a card and balloons over hot chocolate and porridge.

First to ninth place in one day. We have jibed south; a 90degree turn, which to those at home following the tracker and the Yellow Brick app must have looked most odd. We sensed the winds changing and really needed some south track, so we took the hit on mileage, having calculated we would get it back once we turned east again. After a day heading south, we turned east once again and rode the surf at 15-20ktts average continuously for several days, eating our way back up the leader board in the process.

Shortly after the race halfway point, we pass south of 40degrees and into the southern ocean. Sailing in the southern ocean is a first for everyone on board, including Skipper, and almost immediately we see our first albatross gliding along behind us effortlessly. We celebrate all of these occasions with a fancy dress party at evening watch changeover. Some most imaginative costumes. Crocodile Dundee, complete with crocodile made from a hank of green rope and a piece of wood. A pint of Guinness. Skipper as a Rastafarian. Susie as an ambulance. Oleg, not sure what he was actually supposed to be, but dressed in fluorescent sports bra filled with apples and skin tight white jeans made for much laughter and fun. We toasted the half-way point, had some laughs and then set about a sail change almost immediately whilst still in fancy dress, the party cut short for racing.

We passed by Gough Island, a landfall, just south of 40degrees and 9degrees west, I had not heard of before. A small island of around 7miles by 7miles of South African territory, around 1,000m high at its highest point, we passed around 30 miles to the south but had a great view of its silhouette on the horizon. Wyatt, our watch leader, a 6'6" tall, man mountain of a South African who now lives in Derry, sailing with us for legs 1-3 all the way to WA. A straight spoken guy, with a wicked sense of humour, truly infectious laugh and a wealth of sailing experience which he gratefully passes to the team sharing and teaching all he can. He calls up the weather station on Gough and has a brief chat with them was we pass. They show a great deal of interest in our race and can see us on their AIS. We share some stories and pleasantries, have to interrupt them when they start to give us weather updates, which would be outside the race rules, much to their amusement. We sign off letting them know there will likely be other CV yachts showing up on their screen at some point, and we ask they make a point of telling anyone they subsequently speak to, please overtly mention the fact they have already spoken to CV30 a few days ago! We all spend the evening laughing about this on board.

Now only three days out from Cape Town and all to play for. Less than 60 miles separates the top nine places on the sheds and the positions jostle and change with every update. The fleet is now in a kind of formation and, for the first time since Rio, we are all heading in roughly the same direction, albeit on different latitudes. We spot Switzerland on the horizon and set to with chase, overtaking them in around 16 hours. We have a few spinnaker wraps and wine glasses (when the spinnaker wraps around the forestay in the middle, forming the shape of a wine glass), but escape them all. Then two rig disasters in the next 24 hours. The first is a lazy sheet getting caught around the forestay and whilst we free it, the remainder goes in the water and wraps around the rudder, temporarily disabling the steering. A mild panic ensues as we try to free it, for a few minutes we are in grave risk of crash jibing which could destroy our code 1 kite. Some heavy heaving from many hands frees the sheet sufficiently to engage steerage again, but not enough to retrieve the lines. We agree it is best left alone now, so tie it off, coil it aft and hope that it does no further damage until we can dock and free it underwater.

Our second minor disaster occurs when we accidentally engage the main sheet to the primary winches whilst double grinding a spinnaker sheet. No one notices, despite several of us standing right next to it. As we grind away, all watching the spinnaker, we place ever increasing pressure on the main sheet rig, the winches attached to it can exert massive loads, 8 tonnes plus of pressure per turn, and the main sheet currently has 6 turns on it. Eventually it is too much, and with a nerve shattering explosion it all gives way, sending the boom & shards of the broken gear wildly across the deck at great speed, over our heads and out to the side. Miraculously it misses everyone on route.

We make VHF contact with GREAT Britain who lead the fleet currently around 45 miles ahead of us, they are concerned about the wind hole we both find ourselves in, which makes us more nervous with the extra mileage ahead. A slight adjustment further north means we might exit the lighter stuff more quickly, so we take the chance and adjust.

We run into the southern oil fields and are surrounded by rigs and support vessels. Every time we venture even remotely close to a rig, its guard ship comes out to meet us with search lights ablaze and occasionally a horn to boot.

Next day it is as though the hole never existed, we power along at 15 ktts and start to catch OneDLL and Switzerland not far ahead of us. We are in seventh place now and catching at least Switzerland becomes our focus as the leading boats make port and finish. OneDLL maintain their lead and we cannot possibly catch them, but we have Switzerland right in our sights as we enter Table Bay on a glorious sunny late afternoon. Table Mountain's wind shadow however catches us both and we drift listlessly in the bay struggling to make any movement at all whilst we watch the most amazing sunset behind us.

Both boats drift towards the edge of the breeze and Switzerland somehow manage to gather pace just ahead of us. We finish just twenty minutes apart and a shade over 5 hours behind the leading finishers; not bad after 3,800 miles of ocean racing. We make our way into the outer harbour and start our arrival preparations, flags and banners rigged and ready we make our way into The Victoria & Alfred marina.

We slip into our space, moor up and file together on our best behaviour, alphabetically into a marquee for customs clearance, closely followed by a cold beer from the ubiquitous cooler provided by Clipper race at such occasions, then it's off to a bar close by for some food and drink. Many of us are still dressed in foulies and boots when arrive at the bar and take up an ever growing table outside. The table eventually becomes 20+ crew, friends and family, alongside a table of Old Pulteney crew, who have been in for a while and are already settled & well oiled. After well-deserved food and drink consumed, most of us slept on board overnight before a thorough deep clean the next day which takes most of the day.

Our time in Cape Town is super busy. The deputy mayor of Derry and his team are in town with delegates from invest NI and the tourist board. We entertain them on board with a day's corporate sailing, where the deputy mayor gets wet whilst hoisting sails, much to everyone's amusement. They reciprocate and take the team out for the evening. We all manage a couple of half days off and visit Robben Island and Table Mountain. We are all tired after the first two big ocean crossings and everyone is trying to get some rest, which is proving really difficult in between corporate and sponsor responsibilities and boat maintenance.

Cape Town to Albany
Southern Ocean broach and serious injury

Cape Town had been a most gracious host and an amazing stopover destination. One of the nicest cities I have ever visited; should the occasion ever arise, I would very much like to live in Cape Town. Our boat was fully stocked, loaded with victuals, rigged and set ready to leave by late morning on the day before race start as we set off to our pre-race briefing. Transport was arranged for us to get to the Royal Cape Town Yacht Club; our venue for the race 4 briefing. I was really looking forward to this as there is much affinity and a long history between Sir Robin & the RCTYC so I was expecting a bit of a show and some fuss. We were dropped off outside the front, with expectations rising as we entered via the front members' entrance. A beautiful entrance lobby & trophy cabinets all around. We were told of a start line crash in a previous race and warned of the desperate consequences of this happening again. Followed by a weather brief, a safety brief and some media updates. The main part of the briefing added to the concerns around southern ocean sailing, the dangers posed and precautions we should take to stay safe. Justin recounted a Clipper race yacht spotting an iceberg at 45deg south in a previous race, reporting this to the ice monitoring station who confirmed back they could see nothing on their charts, but then adding that they don't actually track anything under 5km square! We were given an absolute south latitude permissible of 46deg, warned of monitoring sea temperatures and to keep look out for ice at all times whilst this far south.

We went on to our team race briefing which was held in a private room in the basement bar of the Cape Hotel, a beautiful and luxurious facility decked out with wine racks and whisky collections, leather furniture and luxury wall prints and lighting. We stayed here for over an hour with Sean discussing our race tactics and approach. We would stay safe first and foremost and we discussed safety aboard, refreshing our clipping on procedures and MOB drills together with some discussions around ice and bulk head protections.

From the statistics of previous races, we had almost always been the fastest boat, but we appeared to have always also travelled the highest mileage. So on this race we would proceed a great circle route as far as possible with the weather patterns throughout the race. We buddied up the new comers with round the world crew members and allocated each specific roles on board, navigation, weather, scheds and engineering. We had found previously this approach worked really well to keep the team tight and integrate new crew when they join for their legs.

There were still some questions around watch allocations and these would be confirmed tomorrow. Later we discovered this was due to crew drop out for this leg. Two of our new crew members were struggling with various medical backgrounds to make the race, and both unfortunately would now miss the start.

We made our way back to the boat for final pack of our gear and to replace and re-rig the now fully repaired main sail. Charlie, Jay, Susie & I spent the evening catching up on final communication via free wifi in the V&A bar, then went on to Den Anker, the bar we had eaten in the night we arrived; a fitting place to end our stay in Cape Town. We had a dry, but quite delicious dinner, discussed the race ahead and our feelings about the conditions we were facing. All of us were prepared and ready for this, but an air of trepidation and nervousness was very apparent. We discussed the use of dry suits, personal AIS transmitters and Susie explained just how quickly the cold sea would kill you, thanks sooz!

The mood across the whole fleet over the last few days had been subtly different to that of previous race starts. The Skippers, race office staff and crew all knew this was a big one. The Southern ocean and its reputation was weighing heavily upon us all. Everyone appeared slightly preoccupied when talking about the race ahead and what to expect, some avoided it altogether and changed or avoided the subject. As we approached race start day we wished each other well and safe sailing. I hugged some of my closest friends across the fleet and one or two of us shed a tear whilst wishing each other well for the journey ahead. I had a real deep concern about this leg, I had felt this way from the outset, both the southern ocean & North Pacific races specifically concerned me a lot and inside I was really not looking forward to either of them. I got stressed and knotted up over the last few days in port and felt progressively more tense as race start arrived.

Like climbing a high mountain or running a marathon, circumnavigating requires approaching with a 'long game' mind set. It is fraught with risk and requires supremely high levels of commitment and strength, both physical and emotional. The next few weeks would really test both of these to the outer limits and I knew this for sure already. I felt nervous for the crew, both ours and those on the other boats, I really hoped all would be safe, whilst knowing only too well that someone would almost certainly get hurt and a boat would probably be damaged along the way. I just hoped and prayed it would be minor and repairable in both cases. The night before race start I really didn't sleep, I got up many times and sat on deck in the dark. I thought about Family, I thought about Siobhan and how much I had to lose if I got hurt, or worse still. I felt her with me, my monkey on my shoulder, keeping me safe. Eventually I woke early, watching a great sunrise from the deck with tea before taking a last hot shower and a full cooked breakfast in the Aquarium cafe on the dockside.

We pushed off the dock at exactly 10:34, turned to head out of the marina. There were great crowds there to see us off and a few familiar faces of other crew friends and family. I exchanged a few words, some great eye contact smiles and a few blown kisses and waves along the marina exit which added to the emotion of the day. Michelle's parents are here to see us off; I hug her Mum and she says *"stay safe"*, I promise to and she cries as we all get back on board. We pass Bertie and salute him one more time as we exit. All twelve boats form up with sails and banners awash with colour; we settle ourselves into a double chevron formation as the now ubiquitous RIBs and helicopters buzz around trying to get the best shot of us in front of table mountain, only when we get to Australia in 4,800 miles and about 22 days' time will we know if they did or not.

Breaking formation, we make our way down to the start line. I take up my position in the nav station, commencing a structured and constant call of position, direction and distance up to Skipper on the helm above. Continually calculating our directions and distances is stressful for the next hour or so; we have a start line followed by two marks to round before we head out east towards our rhum line. Skipper has several sail changes to manage plus avoiding collisions with other boats and selecting the fastest line to wind. He calls for specific directions and bearings pretty much all the time and each time I try and respond as quickly as I can. It's not always quick; sometimes I need to recalculate the figures and he asks again, it's a stressful time and we respect each other but it does get a little fraught at times. I have a note of all the visual signs I can think of, so I can at least give some reference to buy some time whilst I calculate the marks and I constantly check and recheck the stats between conversations so I have as much data to hand as possible at the very moment it's called for. It's an exciting time and a responsibility I really enjoy. Skipper obviously trusts me with it too as he continues to rely on me for this contribution.

We round the marks and head off out west, in third place to GREAT Britain and who else but Henri Lloyd again! We settle into our routines and split into watches, cruising out east comfortably at 15 ktts plus. The first few days are comfortable sailing, steady breeze of 20+ ktts and a moderate sea make for some great mileages, all the fleet doing likewise, we hold our position in fourth place.

The wind and sea starts to increase in size and power and for the first time we start to experience southern ocean conditions again; cold, wet, big gusts, high seas with waves 8m+ surfing us along. The crew have established the new team integration really well and it feels like a good atmosphere is aboard for this race down to WA. The seas pick up further to occasional 10m waves and gusts of 30+ ktts, only the strongest helm are now 'driving the bus' and watches are starting to rotate within watch to maintain some warmth amongst the teams whilst on watch duty. We receive news that Team Garmin have returned to port with a rig problem. Bad news for them yet again.

Early morning watch changeover 7th November. 05:30 wakeup call from the on watch, 20 minutes to get dressed and on deck, 15 if you stop for a cup of tea or use the heads. We all make it up on time and take over sailing duties just as any other day. The conditions are generally OK, by southern ocean standards, which does reset your levels of what OK refers to.

The boat is heeling regularly to 45deg, with a steady 25-30ktts gusting 40+ occasionally she is bit of a handful to helm. Nick & Neil doing a great job as Jay, Kristi, Michelle, Clodagh and I review the cockpit and work area. We agree all is good and sit chatting on deck together. We debate who is going back down below for breakfast, all have eaten already except Michelle & I, she is feeling queasy and really doesn't want to eat yet, so after a short further debate about it, I go below where I remove my life jacket, stand in the galley and make myself some muesli with honey and dried fruit, chatting to the others sitting on the low side in the saloon having breakfast.

At just after 07:00 a massive rogue wave catches us from behind, it lifts us up and forward onto surf, this happens with some regularity so no initial concern is shown by anyone. However this wave just keeps on rising up, it is up at around 45ft high and pushes us into fast acceleration again perfectly normal, then it grows more and shifts too, sort of turning as a beach surf wave might do. This appears to grow from nowhere, to at least 80ft high, the bow of the wave full force hits us on the port side stern, it pushes us further forward and sharply round to starboard, with no chance whatsoever for the helm to correct this.

Racing yachts, especially those 73ft long, are really not designed to slide down the face of big wave sideways and we roll over, the whole boat is pushed over and down sideways onto its side. First the sail, then the boom and finally the mast buries in the water ahead. This is first stage in the exact process of how most boats get rolled right over by the sea, the mast digs in to the water, the main sail fills with water and it just pulls you right over. Miraculously for us though, just as our mast is buried in the wave, pushing us over to at least 110 degrees and starting the inversion process, the wave passes slowly underneath us, there is a short pause and we slump back upright with a crash, not rolling over fully. Pure luck for us, and a very lucky escape from a greater tragedy than that which we already face. The boat is still sideways however and rolling along at a severe list to starboard, it takes a few minutes for the helm to get back onto their feet and correct us back onto course.

Down below in the galley where I stood this felt like slow motion. At first we list over slightly and accelerate; a perfectly normal sensation. The acceleration part is actually quite a pleasing feeling as it means we are going faster and we all like this. The heeling over is also perfectly normal for us, and occasionally this does go further over than one expects, and we normally just wait for it to correct. So as the boat lists, at first we do exactly this, waiting momentarily for it to correct. Then the slow motion seems to stop and we go to fast speed, wham we are right over, people fall from the high side, I see Andy flying past me landing in the wet locker backwards, there are stainless steel rails running across this and I briefly hope he has missed them with his head on his way in. The remains of our breakfast falls over onto what used to be the starboard wall and is now the floor, a box of muesli and a bowl of cereal with milk in explode as they hit the wall, jars of Jam and peanut butter smash, missing those sitting there by little, but showering them in food and glass debris.

All the storage areas in our galley have rubber retaining straps to stop things falling out at sea, most of these now fail under the full weight of the storage contents and I am joined all around me by jars, tins, pots and pans all bashing off me and around me as they fall and crash around. I sense something warm against my arm and by the time I realise its actually roasting hot and now burning me, boiling water from a kettle is emptying all over me after I inadvertently caught it upside down. I let it go and it falls into a corner. I watch the contents of the sink empty, at first over the side, then across to the wall and then towards what was the ceiling and is now fast becoming the floor. I use this as my only reference point, I am pretty convinced at this point we are going right over and I pay close attention to where things are falling. The floor boards lift and fly across the room, they crash down around us, missing most of us by nothing. Then the boat pauses again shaking and juddering slightly, this is the mast vibrating in the water, I feel it lift and realise we are now righting ourselves as I fall back down from the ceiling.

As we start to level out, Skipper appears from his bunk pulling on a jacket and life jacket at the same time, he spots Andy in the wet locker as he grabs his life jacket and does a double take, exiting the galley area and onto the stairs. Just quite how he moves around so quickly, I do wonder at sometimes. We start to check each other and asses quickly our numbers on board and check if everyone is OK. I do a quick head count at the companion way with Jay who is on deck and we agree all are still on board topside. He thinks some are injured and we call for medic whilst he does a quick triage update and calls back with an update, *"all up and OK except Michelle, we need medical assistance right now please!"*

Susie, our medic, steps up from the saloon wall where she ended up, steps towards retrieving her life jacket and disappears straight down into a bilge, no floor boards! I lift her out and check she is OK, she takes another step and falls into the wall hurting her arm really badly, we suspect later it might be broken and over the next few days it hinders her greatly.

Helping Susie don her life jacket we both exit the stairs onto deck. Susie goes to check Michelle and I do a quick review with the others; all fine and in control now on deck, Sean and Susie are with Michelle, the others are clearing up the decks, so I go straight back down below to assist.

We are still in very big seas and with no floor boards in place around most areas this is a really dangerous place to be. Wyatt & I gather them and get them back down in double quick time, during which Susie reappears down the stairs looking grey and cold holding her arm tightly. She thinks she may have broken it in the fall a few minutes ago and I help her to a seat. Skipper passes Michelle down the stairs to me, I can see she is in a bad way, she looks grey and ashen. I speak to her asking what I can and can't hold as I help her down, she just stares back. I look her in the eye and shout again *"where can I hold you?"*, Skipper replies *"left shoulder, stay away from left shoulder"* I can see now how she is holding this, its badly out of shape, I help and carry her to a seat next to Susie and return to assisting with the cleanup.

Susie & Skipper treat Michelle in the saloon for the next few hours, whilst the rest of us get the boat back into shape and sailing straight again. I switch between deck and below, helping out wherever I can and organising the clean up around our watch team. Some of it just gets bagged for sorting later, some gets stuffed away safe. We assess the rest of the team, everyone is badly shaken, some cuts and bruises but nothing serious anywhere else.

We get sailing again, whilst Susie & Skipper monitor Michelle, all the time in contact with shore medical support teams. The media blackout continues for a few days. After a few hours we start to drift our course north in anticipation of a possible medivac towards South Africa. We agree to make the final decision after 12 hours, but in truth we know this is highly likely now. Michelle is going downhill fast and in a lot of pain.

Susie decides it's time for a morphine drip and we prepare to set this up. We discussed this earlier, when I broke my ribs on leg one. Opening the morphine box is the final step towards medivac and pretty much decision made if you do this. We all know this and Skipper makes the call. We arrange to meet the coast guard off the coast of Port Elizabeth some 300 miles to our north. We set the new course and communicate to the crew. Everyone is calm and in full agreement, there is no debate or discussion, just concern at Michelle's wellbeing.

Susie, Conor & I prepare Michelle's morphine drip. I help Susie, who is struggling with her arm in a sling now, herself in much pain. I have always been squeamish with needles, but in this instance it bothers me not and together we put Michelle's line in her arm. It's not the most delicate and professional of medical procedures, but it's my first ever, and it is in and set ready now. Whilst Susie settles Michelle, I clean the blood up off the floor with antibacterial wipes. Susie needs help quickly again now as Michelle is going to be sick, I grab a sick bag and help her whilst she is lying down and being sick. She repeats out loud over and over again *'make it stop, please make it stop'* which is really quite upsetting. I wipe her forehead and exchange sick bags for a fresh one. Susie hands me some wet wipes, I now have Michelle's blood, sweat, sick and tears on my hands all at the same time, enough is enough for us all and we settle her down with some more morphine. She sleeps on and off for the next few hours and all the time Susie and Conor stay with her throughout.

After a wash, clean up, a hot drink and a short rest, I take up my position in the navigation station for the approach into Port Elizabeth. We make contact with the coast guard who are ready and expecting us. We agree a final rendezvous point and I set course to steer, all the time liaising with the helm up on deck. The coast guard sends out a cutter with a rib to transfer Michelle. They meet us exactly as agreed and to some of the crew's dismay as they approach us they light us up with the spot lights from the media crew on their foredeck! Conor, Susie and a coast guard help Michelle up on deck and onto the rib, we watch as they cross to the cutter and transfer onto it. We turn and head back out to sea, all the time I am navigating us clear of the shipping lanes & islands off the coast line and through the Aghulas current via the narrowest point possible. It's pretty tight in places and makes me really nervous at times. Skipper sends a radio call to the coast guard, wishes Michelle well and thanks them for their support and assistance.

We later make a public donation to their fund as a gesture of goodwill from our team. As we head back out to sea I monitor their radio calls back to their base and follow the communications all the way to Michelle making it to the ambulance on shore. I transfer the updates to the crew on deck. Kristi arrives with a video camera and asks me to comment on the last few hours, I can't remember what I said, but it's very emotional and I ask her to stop filming half way through whilst we both cry and reflect.

Next morning the mood is a little down on board, Skipper arrives at breakfast with some early news that Michelle has made it to hospital and all is well so far. We talk about rejoining the race and regrouping as a team. At first this seems futile, but we all agree and it takes us little time to get motivated again. We agree being last is an ok place to be, no pressure and no expectations, let's just enjoy the sailing and get to Albany as quickly as possible.

And so we settle back into the routine of our watch pattern and get sailing back to the race, we are at least 600miles behind the lead pack and still have over 2,600 miles to sail. We sail for a few days under spinnaker. It's a beautiful time, 25ktts downwind sailing, back on course and making great headway, on one day we are the fastest boat in the fleet which massively lifts the mood on board.

We continue down back into the southern ocean making great progress, regularly we are fastest boat again and again; the surfing is amazing and the seas gradually build as the temperature drops. We receive the latest weather ahead, there's a hurricane brewing to the east of us and it's coming our way. We start a continuous monitor of this and prepare the boat for the worst. The scene on board over the next two days resembles that of a disaster movie where the cast have lots of time to prepare for the impending disaster, and discuss the possibilities and risks openly. Kit gets stowed away, everything gets tied down and secured. I do a complete safety audit of our safety kit and we have some briefings on where everything is and how it works. I rig a permanent search light ready for use just below the companion stairs, I attach it to the stanchions with wool so it can be torn off and ready to use in an instant, if we were to loose anyone over board this would be a key part of our rescue kit required to retrieve them. I double check the dan buoy, horseshoes and throwing lines. We recap with each watch how to use the MOB tracker on the radar/AIS, this places a way point at the push of a button, which would enable us to get back to the point of loss. Susie checks her med kit and the deck bosun team of Jason & Conor secure everything and double check rigging and sail tie downs.

I can feel a sense of nervous anticipation, we know the storm is coming, we have done all the prep and are absolutely ready for this. However, there is no escape, there is nowhere to hide and no safety net. We are out here alone again and looks like we will be in the centre of this storm once it lands. And it's getting bigger by the day, now a full hurricane category storm warning ahead of us. I reflect upon the preparation we have done and make sure I am ready too. Checking my own kit. I check and grease my safety knife. New batteries into a high intensity torch in my dry suit pocket. And I double check and secure my personal AIS into my life jacket. When on deck, in between manoeuvres, I practice getting these in and out of pockets and using them with one hand. With practice I become quite adept at opening and securing the safety knife with one hand and my eyes closed. All this helps my mind state. Finally, I place all my personal kit into a grab bag, just in case. Telephone, credit cards, cash, torch, seasick tablets, spare knife, spare batteries, and some cards and photos of Mum & Dad and Siobhan. I feel ready for anything.

The storm is building and gradually it's becoming more and more difficult moving around the boat. The noise of the wind and waves is getting louder and louder. We register winds of 50 then 60 then 70 ktts. On one late night watch, I can sense the storm is upon us, I lean out from my bunk and glance at the instruments in the Nav station next to me, the wind instruments say 70-80ktts fluctuating with the gusts but registering well over three figures regularly. At home, nobody ever goes out in more than 20ktts. I take a deep breath, get up & get ready for deck.

As I exit the companion way my head breaks cover and it's like getting hit by high pressure hose. The salt spray stings and the noise is incredible. I pause and step back into the hatch, take another breath and look towards the helm where I am heading. I can barely make out the dim glow of the compass light at the rear of the boat and nothing else. It's absolute black dark. I clip onto the nearest jack stay and slowly make my way out. Fingertips searching out handholds and trying to keep my feet steady, I gradually and slowly make my way down to the helm. Neil, my watch helm companion is right behind me all the time; we check in on each other as we go.

After a detailed handover from the other watch, Neil takes the helm first, and I take up a position behind him to spot compass for him. It's extremely hard work, the sky ahead is black, there are no reference points and even the waves cannot be seen before they crash over us. All the time the boat is swinging from one side to the other and it's a very active helm to keep the boat on course. The steering is really hard work, and it takes every ounce of concentration and strength to stay on top of this. We agree after around 30 minutes that 40 minutes is probably the max we should each do to maintain this level of concentration. We switch out and I take over the helm. For the first five minutes I am not sure I can do this. The waves are massive, crashing over the bow. Occasionally we take one full in the face and have to cling on to not get washed off my feet. When this happens it takes a few seconds to gather yourself and clear your eyes of the salt water, which stings like mad. Then I settle into my groove and find my way. All the time watching instruments and feeling for wind direction concentrating fully and heaving the helm left and right to keep the boat on course.

My 40 minutes passes in a heartbeat and we switch back again. We continue this for four hours, then change over back to the other watch. We make the journey back down below and strip off top dry suit layers, take a hot drink and then a couple of hours sleep before repeating this all over again on the watches that follow.

The following night it's a full moon and we have stars to guide us, which makes course easier. The downside to this is seeing the waves before they crash over us, which is pretty daunting. Some of these appear to be 30-40m high and break as they crash down. The troughs in between waves are cavernous and even more daunting, as we roll of the top of each wave it sometimes feels like the boat will roll over forwards down the steep face.

The storm continues in its full intensity for four days and nights. The boat and crew take a real pounding. Meals are difficult and we are all wet, tired, sore and hungry as it starts to ease. We all feel down and beaten, it's good that its passing now as tiredness and energy levels are very low. 40ktts breeze and 20m waves feels like an easy day and we start to clear up. There is kit everywhere down below, the galley is grubby and trashed and the ghetto where we sleep is wet, smelly and messy. On deck we have lost our dan buoy and two horseshoe life rings, some of our instrument transmitters are damaged and our SWB radio aerial has gone too, other than this the deck looks in good shape, and there is no major damage down below.

Over the course of a day or two, we gather ourselves and get the boat straight again. We check in on the scheds and the other boats. All crew and boats are safe and well, which is great news, no major damage anywhere. Amazingly we are still repeatedly the fastest boat in the fleet. Not being last is now a real possibility and we set our sights on the boats ahead, now only a few hundred miles away. Susie opens a small injury clinic for the day down below and treats cuts and bruises as best she can, we compare these and Kristi wins hands down with a bruise the size your hand, jet black and purple on her thigh, which appears to be in the shape of a smiley face! Where she was crashed up against the helm cage by a wave. I have several, the worst of which is on my lower back from the same helm cage and wave experience, it's hard to sleep and every time I lean or stretch it hurts like hell. There is no cure or repair, and Susie's professional medical advice is *'suck it up princess!'*.

Our rudders have taken a real beating and for the rest of the trip to Albany, we bail 2-3 buckets an hour from the lazerette on every watch, which is tiresome but necessary in order to maintain stability.

After a day or so the winds ease further and we get the spinnakers out for a week or so. This is champagne sailing, downwind in between the rain squalls, some of which are full on and really test us. We prepare for them constantly. Occasionally we drop sails in a hurry, other times we bear away and sail them out as best we can. We pick up a couple of beautiful albatross outriders around 43 degrees south and they stay with us for several days; a kind of safety escort we call them.

With 2,000 miles to go we sail through one of several wind holes we encounter along the way, a few hours of nothing, then straight back to 20ktts again as if nothing happened. During one of the squalls, Skipper and I have dropped the head sails and tied them off. The rain picks up and we shelter down on the stay sail up on the foredeck together to wait for it to pass. He reaches into his pocket and pulls out a big stick of biltong, and with an enormous smile he says 'fancy *some ostrich matey?'* He cuts it with the saw from his leatherman. Awesome, the flavour was fantastic and the moment perfect. It was raining like you couldn't imagine, so hard you could hardly hear yourself talk, pretty cold too at 43deg south, and we are sitting there together munching ostrich biltong. A random but great moment.

We broach many times during the squalls and break several blocks and spinnaker snap shackles in the process. Our rear guard rails also take a pounding and are damaged way beyond repair. We start a list of requirements and realise for the first time we might be into penalty points with this list now. In contrast, Skipper receives a copy of the fleet crew personal injury list, which is much longer than previous races and puts it all into perspective. Suddenly our repairs list is not so drastic after all.

We start to plan our stopover for Albany. I have volunteered to manage this one, banking some time in lieu for family in Sydney. It's going to be a busy stopover with much to do after the two long legs and a southern ocean pounding. We also have some sponsor commitments whilst in port and a schools day to host too.

1,000 miles out we start a mini sweepstake on day of arrival, it varies considerably around 3-4 days separating the guesses. It's an interesting exercise as we each explain our theory behind each guess. It helps the mood lift too, as we start to think and focus on getting in. We receive news Michelle, dislocation & muscle damage, she has been signed off fit to race again. This lifts us all even further. 900 miles, 800 miles, it starts to feel closer with each significant mark. We sail 248 miles in one day to massive celebration. Now in 10 place, no longer last and in sight of some of the boats ahead we sail fast with fresh enthusiasm.

200 miles to run, we can now see four other boats in the distance, all converging on the finish line. 100 miles out and it looks even closer, like we will all meet at some point soon. 60 miles out we get our first sighting of Old Pulteney, Mission Performance and Invest Africa. We all converge just south of Albany, Old Pulteney & we go north of the small outer island, Mission Performance & Invest Africa go south. We appear the other side right next to Old Pulteney, only a matter of 50-60 feet apart at one point, tacking together as we race north. Old Pulteney get the last tack on us and we are forced to tack once more than them, and they turn the corner into the bay to approach the finish line just ahead of us. It's a straight drag race, 3 miles and we finish only 20 seconds behind them. Mission Performance and Invest Africa get caught up in their own battle and slip back, fighting between themselves all the way to the line, finishing 2 seconds apart. Or as the Skippers called it *'a bowsprit's length'* apart.

Ninth! Ninth! After a 650mile detour to Port Elizabeth we finish ninth! It is a simply massive celebration for us, we are absolutely stoked with the result, celebrating on board as if it were a win!

Then, just as we enter the inner bay to drop our main sails to prepare for docking. A small, light black & white RIB appears out of the harbour to greet us. On board is Charlie's wife, a big cheery surprise for him, he was not expecting to see her until Sydney. Standing right next to her is Michelle!! With a massive gorgeous smile, waving and cheering us all home! A beautiful moment and the beginning of a very very late night of celebrations with the team all back together again.

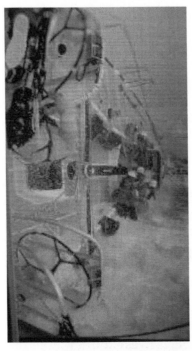

Left;
The moment we broach

Below;
Susie & I treating Michelle

Photo Credit; Clipper Ventures PLC

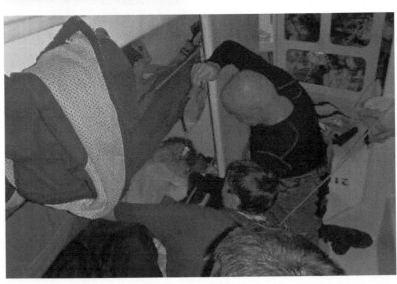

Albany to Sydney
Southern ocean sleigh ride to Christmas in Sydney

Albany was a fantastic stopover, quite different to previous ones. The Clipper race circus arriving in Albany, a beautiful small town of around 30,000 people, set into some spectacular western Australian coastline, has a different impact to that which it does when it sails into a major city such as Rio or Cape Town. As a result of this, by the time we left we really felt as though we had made some friends here, Chloe in the coffee shop, Gary in the dive shop and Sophie & Claire in the white star inn, and the whole team at Albany whale tours, who assisted us in the dock. They also took us out far offshore in the pitch dark small hours of the morning in their RIB to meet Team Garmin as they arrived. Just a few of the pleasant, friendly and most hospitable people I have met so far on the trip.

The day before departure we have our usual crew race briefing in the Albany Conference Centre, a fabulous facility which Albany should be proud of. I speak to Mum and Dad during the evening before we depart. Mum is going into hospital the day we leave for an operation she has been waiting for, for some time. Dad is going to email me with news in a few days' time, but it will be a difficult first few days at sea knowing what is going on at home. It makes me miss home and feel for Mum & Dad at times like these. We are going back south to the southern ocean again, and the mood is changing once more as we approach race start day.

For our final evening in Albany, we choose to pack and load our gear onto the boat and have fish & chips for supper at the apartment. With one small oversight, this went extremely well. All the fish and chip shops in Albany close at 20:00! So we made our way to a grill restaurant for shrimp, ribs and chicken with soft drinks, now dry pre-race start. A most delightful evening with truly excellent company. Ice cream and chocolate back at the apartment then an early night. Next morning we made a special very early trip to Kate's cafe for breakfast, poached eggs and bacon with cappuccino, a fabulous pre-race meal. Pre-race entertainment was pretty limited, but quite a few people turned out on the dock to see us slip away, which we did bang on schedule at 11:18am. We were moored next to Team Garmin, upon which I have many friends and this allowed us some close farewell last minute hugs and kisses. We made our way out into the harbour, raised our mainsail and fell into formation, line astern for a parade of sail fly past for Albany marina, all went well and we turned around to head out into the bay and beyond for race start.

Raising our selected sail wardrobe we settled into start day routine, checked out our lines and directions pre start, rounding up on some of the buoys as a pre-check on wind directions and sail trim. We were all set into specialist roles on deck, and for this race start Skipper & I had done all our navigation reviews the previous day and were happy enough to not require me in the Nav station for race start. So I took up my post upon the main grinder, really looking forward to some exercise. My ribs were really strong now and I was increasingly keen to push them harder. Be careful what you wish for some might say, I got my rewards here. Grinding on and off for several hours I ached all over the next day and felt the efforts well.

We jostled and cajoled on the start line and crossed the line fractions of a second before the gun, we were convinced we may have jumped it, but there was no recall, so all was good. We started third over the line to OneDLL & Henri Lloyd, catching OneDLL by the time we rounded the last buoy to head out to sea. The fleet put on a great show up and down Middleton Beach for the locals, all the roads around the area had been closed and we could see lines and lines of cars parked up watching the race start, like some kind of crazy drive in movie.

In the middle of the melee, PSP Logistics & GREAT Britain connect, PSP lose their pushpit, some guard rails, and their port side helm, GREAT Britain lose their entire bowsprit.

Both are required to dock immediately for repairs and neither sails out of Albany for another 36 hours, race tragedy for them both. A race enquiry follows looking at video evidence. This is not held until half way through the Sydney stopover, GREAT Britain are later disqualified from the race and PSP Logistics awarded a redress based on their average race points in the overall round the world race so far, 8 points. Later, following a protest GREAT Britain are also awarded 2 penalty points for the damage repair costs.

We turned and headed out to sea, absolutely neck and neck with OneDLL and Henri Lloyd, some great and really close racing, and I got some fantastic photos and videos of the boats so close together in between grinding our sheets. We passed OneDLL very soon after and headed on a slightly more southerly course than Henri Lloyd losing sight of them after a few hours, but knowing only too well they would still be there haunting us as always.

I have always been interested in the shifting dynamic of the team building aboard our yacht. As crew leave and join for legs the evolution continues to change pace and direction. On this leg in particular we have just 16 crew. It's a good number and makes life aboard easier with more space, even if it does at times stretch the watches and make extra work for some. We also have onboard, joining us for leg 4, a leg 3 crew member from team PSP Logistics, who wanted to add leg 4 but couldn't as his yacht was full already when he decided this. I was initially fascinated as to how this would play out with him having switched teams. On day two however, Colin was on mother duty and cooked up fresh maple syrup pancakes for the whole crew and invited us all to a barbecue at his beach house in Brisbane that was the end of any further play out for this particular team build. Welcome aboard Colin!

I receive an email from Dad, it says Mum is recovering, there were some complications with her blood pressure and diabetes etc but she is fine and well. I read all kinds of stuff into this and it plays on my mind for days afterwards. I debate with myself whether it's better not to know, or to absolutely know the truth. I can hardly debate this with anyone but myself, after all, I didn't tell them when I had broken ribs on race two! Dad is always straight with us, so I surmise all is ok, and it's only a week until we land. Even so, my mind circulates and thoughts of Mum are at times consuming and distracting. I am pointed out by some crew as preoccupied; I share some of my thoughts with those really close, and a headline only with some others to buy me back some head space.

On day three, we were already fast approaching the scoring gate, at 40deg south 127deg east, also fast approaching it were OneDLL, Old Pulteney and who else again but Henri Lloyd. Within 8 miles of the gate and the wind drops out to virtually nothing, we had been Skipping along at 10-12 ktts quite happily, then we watched it fall, 10-9-8-7-6-5-4 down to three and occasionally as low as 1 Ktt. We get the wind-seeker rigged as quickly as we can, just as we are ready to hoist, some breeze backs in and pushes us to 8ktts so we hold off on the hoist. A few minutes pass and it starts to drop off again, we all stand to and agree to hoist. Just as we do, back up to 9ktts and slowly increases to 11&12. We 'stand by to stand by' as we often say on board. We get to within a mile of the gate and Henri are now in such close proximity to us we can see their sail plan, previously they had just been a faint red light on the horizon.

We pass the gate at around 00:15 and we all cheer & clap, we are pretty sure Henri were close enough to hear this, so we cheer again! A short while later Eric, Henri Lloyd Skipper calls us on VHF and congratulates us, oh sweet victory, sweeter still as it's against our friendly nemesis. We bare away and switch sails to a code 2, which takes us bang on course at 135deg, and within a little over 10 minutes Henri are already 2.8 miles away, a great way to end a 10-2 watch, we have hot chocolate, real chocolate and head off to bed for a few hours with smug smiles and a good mood circulating aboard.

Next day was spectacularly beautiful, we were now below 40deg south and into the southern ocean once again, the morning was clear and bright and it gradually warmed up with crystal clear blue skies and sunshine all day. The breeze picked up and by lunchtime we were slicing along at 12 ktts under a code 2 spinnaker. Helming was delightful, once settled and finding your line it was quite relaxing just helming to the breeze and sky line. I turned the compass binnacle lid over so I couldn't see it and changed the instrument panel out to a different setting so it was blank to me, helming for around an hour on just the wind, with the very occasional double check of course just to make sure. The first steps towards a blindfold helm perhaps. Ahead of us were OneDLL around 6 miles away on the horizon, I set them just over the pulpit and followed. It was a truly memorable few hours racing for me, and my confidence levels were increasing day by day. The next night again we followed OneDLL and as the sun rose we were only a 2 miles behind them with Henri Lloyd just 5 behind us. We rotated the helm every 30 minutes on the night watches, Neil, myself, Susie, Wendy and Alan all taking turns.

We receive a warning from the race office of a storm coming. Our race meteorologist reports it will peak out for 24 hours at around 70ktts. Acutely aware he greatly underestimated the last southern ocean storm, (where he said 60-70 ktts max, and we subsequently recorded levels of 130ktts!) We consider whether he might be erring on the side of caution for this one? We prepare for the worst, agreeing our storm sail strategy. Down through the gears from Yankee 1 to 2 or maybe straight to 3, with stay sail away, reefs as required. Then, when it peaks, Yankee away and stay sail back up in lieu of a storm jib. The wind and seas build all day as we sail within sight of OneDLL and Henri Lloyd. We watch OneDLL raise a kite late afternoon, discuss if we might cover this and do the same, but agree we are happy with our plan and what they might gain in flying it just now they will inevitably lose later, changing it out or worse still wrapping or damaging it which could cost them hours to resolve as we sail past. Around late afternoon we get caught with our pants down, or more specifically with our Yankee up! The winds start to gust at over 40ktts and we are way over powered, it takes all of us around 45minutes to drop and pack the Yankee 1 (the biggest sail in our wardrobe) which by all standards is actually pretty good. We change tactics, put the stay sail up now, and maintain 15 ktts+ bang on course with this pattern.

Throughout the night we push on through the storm, the night is inky black with absolutely no reference points anywhere, we helm by instruments and wind feel. Only two of us on our watch are confident helping in these conditions so we rotate at 30 minute intervals, which is about all we can concentrate for. For a while, a few times, I close my eyes whilst helming, there is nothing to see anyway! And I start to get that, 'by feel' as Sean called it. It becomes intense as the hours pass by, 30 minutes is a long time to concentrate sufficient to helm in this, and is barely long enough to warm up below, hot drink and a heads visit and its back out to helm again. I fall asleep several times during helm changeover and have no trouble sleeping at watch change. I get around two and a half hours, but it is solid good sleep and I feel great for the first session of the next watch. Then the cycle repeats itself over and over.

Next morning the storm passes and by around 08:00 am we are already seeing patches of blue sky opening up. The high wind and heavy seas stay with us all day, and by lunch time, as the wind shifts to the north we have poled out a Yankee 2 and are surfing at 20-25 ktts all afternoon, awesome in the sunshine with the southern ocean resplendent in its unique shade of grey. The night is clear and bright, fantastic stars and moonlight. I see a wonderful long and bright shooting star, I give it to Mum, wishing her a speedy recovery and thinking of her for the rest of the watch. I get upset at watch change and make for my bunk. Sometimes being out of touch really hurts.

A little over 300 miles to the way point south of Tasmania, we decide our "boat Christmas" starts when we turn the corner and head north for the 600 mile run into Sydney. None of us feels remotely festive and we forget Christmas is but a couple of weeks away. So it's Christmas music only, and 24 hours a day for the next 600 miles, once we turn the corner. We push on with white sails through stable winds and great conditions. The scheds are pretty much good news all the way and we discuss using stealth mode for the wind shadow of Tasmania. We are thinking if we arrive at Tasmania first, as we enter the wind shadow we go stealth and don't give away any clues as to its effect upon us. We agree it's a go, and request it immediately.

9th December: Our last day before the way point, and probably our last day in the southern ocean. We are treated to the most amazing sunrise, and we pause to enjoy what will be our last southern ocean sunrise. An absolutely enormous albatross outrider joins us for us for a few hours, we joke he is there to see us off the premises 'time gentlemen please!' Later that morning we spot land, a great shout of *'land ho'* from the deck and we all gather to look. Seeing land after only a week at sea is still a great feeling. It's the mountains of Tasmania away in the distance.

Then around 15:00 some more shrieks from the deck, then a call of *'dolphins, lots of them'*. I slip up onto deck from down below. The water to the starboard side of us is white, with huge flocks of birds flying and swooping down onto the surface. Then a few dolphins jump, then a few more, then 20-30 all at the same time, randomly all around the same area, one jumps right in front of us and slips into our bow wave, he slides along and porpoises with us at speed. There appears to be several hundred dolphins feeding; they continue to jump and splash, more and more of them join us alongside coming to have a look at us and see what we are up to perhaps. Some of them are enormous, all of them spectacular, dark grey, some with almost pure white markings. They stay with us for some time. After a few minutes of ooh and ahhh and oh my god this is amazing, we realise now nine of us in deck and not a single camera between us! Susie and I agree, you could never photograph this anyway. Several hundred dolphins over a square mile or more of ocean, how and what would you photograph? It's a life moment, we are privileged to have witnessed, very very few people would ever see this in the wild. Fewer still at 44degrees south as there is little reason to come here. We pass some remote rocks off the south coast of Tasmania; spectacular formations, awash with sea birds, some smaller rocks around these are potentially dangerous and are watched for with extreme caution. Then we turn around the waypoint and start to head north.

Below deck, Christmas starts for us. We play Christmas tunes loud over dinner and all sing along. Tinsel arrives and we colour in Christmas trees and stick them on the walls. All kinds of colour styles are created. Bright & colourful, black & white, I create a yellow & black one in the style of a dry suit. Neil creates a black one, with a skeleton and skull & cross bones, all very dark and black, Kristi suggests he add some colour, so he adds some blood dripping off it! Not exactly what she was thinking! I make some paper mistletoe and we stick it above the galley, it makes many of us laugh and we kiss for Christmas under it a few times.

Our racing becomes fraught now and Christmas is bought to an abrupt halt! We are stalling, cannot make course and need some quick action. All hands on deck, sail change, Yankee one up, Yankee two down and away. Very shortly afterwards, code up and Yankee down, this fails spectacularly and we ditch it within minutes for a Yankee two again, shortly after this we tack and then tack again. This continues throughout the night and we make slow painful progress, increasingly worried about Henri Lloyd and OneDLL behind us, catching us whilst we mess about with these light winds. We have at least another 2-3 days of this forecast too! So we fight with the lighter stuff for another 36 hours, then it builds steadily and once again we get caught out with a Yankee up for too long, after pushing hard going for speed! The wind builds to a steady 20+ktts from the north and we find ourselves beating into the current & wind. Below deck this is hard, the boat thrashes up and down and side to side with no pattern or warning of where it will list next. Occasionally it crashes down off the top of the biggest waves and shakes everyone & the rigging violently. Chatting to Skipper I ask, *'when does the crashing become dangerous to the rig'*, *'on the way up to Qingdao, wait and see'* he replies, thanks Skipper, dry and humorous as ever.

200 miles to Sydney, OneDLL right on our shoulder, only 2-3 miles away, we are holding position, but only just. We hoist a Yankee and prepare to shake reef 2. We really don't want to do this too early, so we watch them closely to see when they shake theirs. OneDLL and Henri start to head out offshore, big decision time, our strategy has always been to stay inshore. We discussed and agreed this a while ago and the weather still points to this as a good plan. We discuss this as a full team and agree to stick with it. 12 hours later, OneDLL and Henri have pulled away and are now making good progress. Qingdao overtake us too, Switzerland are closing from behind fast. Too late a decision, but we decide to make our way offshore now, we have lost too much time now and it will be difficult to catch the leaders. The mood subdues a little on board, it's tough to lead for so long and then lose it now, seems to have been a theme for us so far on the race. We get our heads down and race hard, we gain a little but head for fourth place, then right at the last minute Switzerland gather wind and overtake us on the inside, bugger! Loosing first to third was one thing, but loosing forth now is hard to take. We do however fly past them after the finish line, congratulate and cheer them magnanimously, it is the Derry way in defeat, and will be so in victory too at some point later in the race, we are all sure of this.

Sailing into Sydney is awesome, the coastline is amazing, I have been here many times before, but never seen it from this angle, it is truly beautiful. We navigate our way up through the outer harbour, past the 'sow and pigs' rocks and on into the inner bay, I jump between the Nav station and deck, calling direction and distance for Sean, but not wanting to miss the spectacle of arrival. A RIB comes out to meet us and escorts us into the dock, where we moor up and proceed through the normal arrival procedures of photos and immigration.

Next morning Jackie Ford, leg 1-4 crew member has received some really bad news from home and is required to fly home. She is clearly distraught by this in many ways, both the news and missing the end of her leg four race having come so far are troubling her. She is cheerful but clearly distressed as she leaves us. We wish her well, and next day I post her a Sydney-Hobart race polo shirt and a short note of gratitude for her contribution to the team and boat.

Next morning early, my elder brother Sean, his wife Diana and my two awesome nephews, Jack & Patrick arrive and we have a great lunch together, before showing the boys around the boat. It's a great opportunity to catch up and I stay with them, commuting back and forth for boat work over the next few days. Our first few days in Sydney are really busy, with deep clean and maintenance. Followed by a lifting the boat out of the water into dry dock and replacing the anti-foul. Four of us take on this task and it's very hard and hot work in the Sydney summer sunshine. It's rewarding to complete though and we take extra care of the application, convinced it might give us an edge or fraction of a knott extra. Anthony, Mike & Angela host the most amazing early Christmas dinner in their apartment overlooking the marina, for a few of us gathering together. Then a few days later Diana & Sean do likewise on Christmas Day, a welcome respite and beautiful family celebration. After a corporate sail, more boat maintenance and eventual completion of the mammoth Sydney to Hobart pre-race boat audit. We prepare for race start.

Sydney to Hobart
Epic, just Epic!

The atmosphere is electric on race start day, I can feel it almost immediately as I step early morning from my brother's car outside the marina. The build up to today has been manic, every day the marina and surrounding areas getting increasingly busier.

It is just after 06:00, and I make my way down to the boat with my kit. There are a few people around busy already in the marina. The whole bay is awash with green & yellow Rolex flags and the park next door is turned into a temporary car park for the day, everyone on the dock is wearing team colours with boat names and race logos on. It feels great, feels like we are part of something much greater than a normal race start, which if course it is!

I drop my kit onto the boat, greet those stirring and waking up on board, then head back to the marina for coffee. The club house is buzzing, they are extremely well prepared for the day with a double coffee station and lots of extra staff, all of whom are pleasant and welcoming. The marina club house has been excellent, good food and great service at reasonable prices too. We have spent a good deal of time in there as a consequence and have been very warmly welcomed by them. I grab some coffee and a bacon roll, shortly joined by Neil, Colin and Tony. We chat about the race ahead and reflect on the atmosphere around us, everyone is feeling it and we all agree upon feeling a huge level of nervous tension ourselves. It feels a lot like a cup final day or Formula one Sunday morning for me, I know this feeling well previously from work, feeling really nervous about the day ahead as a manic, busy and important day is about unfold around me. I like the familiar feeling and it feels comforting and familiar.

We gather ourselves and by around 08:30 all crew are busy on board preparing for final departure. As always there are many people to see before we depart and I make my way occasionally back and forth on the pontoons to say farewell and wish people safe travels. This feels like a lesser wish than previously, I guess safe travels in the southern ocean is a little different to the 680 or so miles we are racing to Hobart. But all the same we wish each other safe travel.

The boat is looking great and we are ready for departure quickly which gives us time to take in the surroundings. The temporary car park is now rammed full, the walkway around the outside of the marina awash with spectators and the pontoons which are not closed off to public access are extremely busy, with flags and banners. As we slip our moorings, the boats around us applaud and cheer, as do the spectators. Some final waves and blown kisses to the well-wishers and we exit the marina into the melee of boats gathering outside. The bay is mental with boats everywhere, spectator and competitor, we make our way quickly out to the rendezvous area and assemble with the fleet. Main sails and battle flags raised we all head off up river to the harbour bridge and around past the opera house in formation with a police outrider boat escorting us all the way. Awesome spectacle and I can't wait to see the photographs from this one.

As we approach back to the bay, we head for the competitor start area to give ourselves some space to prepare. Flags and banners away now and sail plan ready, it's time to go to work!

I take up position on the forward grinder for the start sequence. We tack round and round again to get some practice and all is going extremely well. We are working well together as a team on deck and our manoeuvres look great. Once or twice I drop down to the Nav station to confirm and reconfirm headings for Skipper on the helm. There are so many different marks and sequences, and three different start lines, it is very important we get these absolutely right with no penalty.

As we approach the start line under the ten minute marker it gets really serious, boats in all directions passing really close quarter. Skipper reminds us, he will steer and we must concentrate on our specialist jobs, facing inwards not looking out. Easier to say than do in this instance. This is by far the biggest event of this kind many of us have experienced, or perhaps will ever do so, it is quite awe inspiring, being on the start line competing against Volvo 70's and Maxi 100's. The colours and noise are amazing too. All around us we can see thousands of spectators on the cliff tops and in the bays.

I try hard to remember roughly where Sean and his family are watching from. I wave in that general direction but suspect they don't see this. The start gun sounds and we are positioned pretty much mid field, safe spot and comfortable place to be. We follow the pack out to the marks and it gets tight as the boats jostle for position through the harbour exits and out to sea. There is a radio call for a high ranking local boat called 'Brindabella' who has jumped the start, they will need to return and re-cross the start line. We cruise around our outer mark with plenty of room to spare and head out to sea. What an amazing experience; we reflect upon this together as it calms down a little on deck. Everyone has a big grin on their faces and is filled with excitement. We split straight into our watch patterns and grab a quick dinner.

During the first night, the winds start to build and we make excellent progress. I am surprised at how little traffic we see. With over 100 boats effectively all heading the same way, there are still times when we see nothing; I would have expected to see more. Gradually the weather closes in around us as it was scheduled to, and by late on day two we are already changing down the gears rapidly. We start to prepare for the storm worsening, we stow everything below, rig the deck for storm mode and prepare a storm jib just in case. During the night it gets pretty tasty with gusts of up to 55ktts and we hold course as best we can riding it out.

As we head south towards the Bass Strait the seas build and the wind eases a little. It's a rough ride, but we have been here before only a couple of weeks ago so we all know what we are dealing with. We watch closely the water temperature and depth contours to avoid the currents as best we can. We start to see other boats around us and helicopters buzz overhead regularly. We joke about doing stuff and looking professional when they pass for photos. Some of the results we see later on the web site look great and one or two of the crew buy prints of these photos in Hobart.

Through the bass straights we see the coast line of Tasmania, it's quite beautiful and rugged, reminds me a lot of Scottish coastlines, with temperatures similar too; it gets chillier as we race further south. The winds change and we have to tack back and forth to get around Tasman Island which adds to our time and slows us down a lot, we monitor the fleet as best we can, but there is so much data coming in sporadically from different sources it becomes quite difficult to do. We think we are either first or second in the Clipper race fleet at this point.

Around the south of Tasman Island and heading west along the south coast; again we need to tack back and forth to make any progress. We try to stay offshore further to give us a better line into the bay. I spend increasing amounts of time in the navigation station now, calculating the angles of tack and distances best sailed for final approach to storm bay. It takes us almost 20 hours to sail the 12 miles west along the south coast and on deck it gets frustrating at times. We eventually turn and head into Storm Bay, north towards the Derwent River. There are no other boats in the bay as far as we can see, but we know CV10 with Sir Robin on board and GREAT Britain are now closing in somewhere very close behind us. Old Pulteney also show up on AIS for the first time, at around 25 miles behind, but we know this just took us almost a whole day to sail, so no real pressure from them just yet. We watch them closely all the same.

CV10 is one of the Clipper 68's from the last fleet which competed in the 11-12 race. Two of these 68's, CV10 & CV5 are now based in Sydney as part of a new Clipper training base, and both are in the race. CV10 is Skippered by Sir Robin Knox Johnston and Jim Dobie, head of the new Sydney Clipper operations. More importantly we recall, CV10 was also sponsored by Derry Londonderry in the last race 11-12, so we really do need to beat it, and to be fair, if it comes in second to us, that would be a pretty awesome result.

Our sail across Storm Bay takes us around 2 hours for the 11 miles or so, then we enter the Derwent River estuary, with 10 miles to the finish line. Wind angles in the estuary mean we have almost continuously tack back and forth. Our frustrations and nervousness on board now is extreme. We are looking over our shoulder, monitoring radar and AIS constantly, convinced someone is out there after us. We have lead races so many times before and lost position in the last dying miles, we know how this feels. But this one is different, we are as close as we will ever be to winning our first Clipper race, and winning our division of the Sydney Hobart race too. This is huge for us and the tension on board is now almost unbearable.

Everyone goes really quiet and concentrates on sailing. Skipper is at the helm calling the shots, no one questions anything, they just do as he asks quickly and efficiently. Back and forth we continue, it seems to take an age. We really struggle to sail the winds towards the finish line and at times it seems like it is getting further away! All the time we are looking around for competitors, it is electrically nervous. Eventually we get to cross the finish line, an escort boat immediately collects us and we oblige in controlled professional discipline, following them into the marina, dropping our sails and preparing our colours for arrival. But where did we finish? Some of us are still sceptical about success and don't celebrate too early.

We turn into the dock, it's around 06:00 and there are huge crowds all around to welcome us in. As we approach the pontoon it is confirmed, we have won our division, also winning race 6 collecting 12 points and then they confirm 29th overall line honours. Wow! We are absolutely ecstatic, everyone on board goes totally mental, and the celebrations are huge. We just won our division of the Sydney Hobart race!!

I keep saying this over and over again out loud. Cheers, hugs and many tears on board too. Champagne spraying, jumping around and all of us trying to take this in. I turn on my phone and it lights up with texts from home, so many people have been glued to this as it played out. Family & friends have stayed up throughout the night waiting for the yellow brick race tracker to update. I call home and speak with Mum & Dad, then speak to Siobhan and she laughs at me for being so excited. We pack the boat down and head straight out for a champagne breakfast, still in our sailing kit. I am really not sure what time we get back to the boat later that day, or in truth even if it was the same day! But we didn't make it back for a deep clean, and many of us never changed clothes either!

Over New Year we attend four separate prize givings, including the main official one with the Premier of Tasmania, at the Royal Tasmania Yacht Club. We have all our spare stopover time sucked up by media and PR. Our normal team approach would be to play down and celebrate magnanimously, but we take 'all' of this one and enjoy every minute of the celebrations, whilst applauding all the other boats and teams as they arrive too. I have never experienced anything like this. The Sydney to Hobart race is one of the premier race sailing events in the world, we are so very lucky just to have been given the opportunity to enter and take part. But, to win it too is still sinking in. This is one of the very highest moments of the journey so far, the crew have grins pinned to their faces at every hour of day & night. As I grow old and grey, I shall bore future generations with these amazing stories forever more.

2013 Rolex Sydney to Hobart Yacht Race
Division One Champions!

Hobart to Brisbane
Bass straights for the third & last time

Race start day in Hobart, starts pretty slowly after our New Year celebrations. The extra days rest, and delaying race start back to 2nd January is most welcomed. Without this, many of the fleet might have struggled to sail, or sail sober anyway!

We are not due to slip until 16:03 so the morning is spent preparing our own kit and tidying the boat ready for departure, then we meet for our race briefing with Skipper over lunch at T42 restaurant on the dock.

Our team briefing is pretty informal, we talk about navigation and weather mostly; it's going to be a bit tasty for a day or so, then some lighter westerlies becoming southerly as we head further north. 'Champagne sailing' we call this part; downwind straight and level with a spinnaker flying. It's hard work on deck, often taking up to six people to control and sail the boat, but it's a joy down below with only a gentle rock to contend with, making life on board a little more comfortable.

It's a relaxed morning on the dock and I get to see most friends as always around the preparation. Even some of the local *'boguns'* come out to see us off. These guys have been a constant pest to us since we arrived. A cross between village idiots and local drunks they hover around the dock and boats looking to get involved. One of them latches onto Mark Light, deputy race director. Everywhere he goes, this guy follows him with his arse hanging out of scruffy jeans and lace less shoes which we are pretty sure don't match. Mark can't shake him off and it's becoming a real pain. We ask Mark to come aboard and he escapes his shadow for a while with us. Mark was Skipper of the previous Derry LondonDerry boat in the 11/12 race and secretly we know he is a really big fan of ours. We had some special Derry branded Sydney to Hobart shirts made to commemorate our taking part in the race, and quietly one day he asks if I can let him have one. I check with the team, as we previously agreed these were for race crew on the race only. We all agree but I still charge him the full $40 for the shirt to remain totally impartial.

We slip bang on time, we are the last boat out, a consequence of being first one in! There is a pretty good crowd to see us off too. Many Sydney to Hobart teams are still here, and turn out in race colours to wish us well; much appreciated and a nice touch. We motor out to the bay and start preparations for racing. Main sail hoisted with one reef, we review the fleet and see who has what sail plan. Most have gone for one reef, Switzerland and Old Pulteney have two. No one has a Yankee up yet and we swing round past a few boats to wave & wish them well, whilst really just trying to look and see what Yankee they have on deck. Qingdao hoist first, it's a two, then OneDLL two also, Switzerland go with a three, we have to decide right now, no more time, Sean hesitates and goes around again, we all get edgy *'C'mon Sean, no time left, what are going with?'*

120

'Two' he calls back, and we retrieve this from below and hoist it in double quick time, just in time for start line up.

We round the buoys and swing along the line as the one minute gun goes, then bear away over the line as the start gun is fired. Second over the line to Old Pulteney, but GREAT Britain and OneDLL have a better set up and pull away. By the end of the first bay, we are fifth placed. Across the Derwent River we pick up the pace and round into storm bay in third place, catching OneDLL and Old Pulteney fast.

Around 2 1/2 hours out of Hobart, approaching the end of storm bay, we are discussing course and weather for the next few hours and days. I have just arrived back on deck having checked the navigation details and given Skip updated course to steer around the headland as we leave Storm Bay and head out to sea proper. I just catch in the background from the VHF the word *'mayday'* Skipper catches it too and switches helm to be closer to the deck mounted handset. It isn't totally clear communications, but we definitely hear the word *'mayday'* again. I give a clear hand signal gesture to Skipper that I am go down below to listen in, he nods back with a thumbs up and continues to helm course.

I make my way quickly back to the Nav station, grab a pen & paper as I turn the VHF volume up. I hear the voice again and in a split second I recognise it, it's Matt, Skipper of Mission Performance. Matt is one of Sean's mates, they always socialise together and communicate regularly throughout the races, he is reading his MMSI number and repeating the previous message details. It is clearly a full proper mayday call and I wait as he runs through all the specifics, position, boat ID etc. I am scribbling down details and facts of importance, like his position, but still don't know as yet what his mayday call emergency is. By now I am already sensing it, his voice is slightly choked and he is clearly emotionally stressed. I become ever more anxious as I wait the repeated details. Then he says what I really didn't want to hear *'I require immediate medical assistance for a serious injury on board'.* Oh Shit! My heart sinks fast and I become tense, I know lots of people onboard Mission, many close friends too, and I start running through who it might be.

He continues with his call details and then closes off again with the words *'mayday, mayday, mayday'.* Then next call is from Gareth, Skipper of Qingdao, he is on route to his position, Simon from GREAT Britain jumps in, he doesn't have a doctor on board, but is standing by. Hobart Port Control respond and Matt explains further the situation. A crew member fell from one side of the deck to the other, landing on his head, he is unconscious, unresponsive but breathing. He has serious head trauma and probable neck and back injuries. Now I feel really cold and continue to write down the facts and track the times of the conversation in a detailed log. Matt continues, his voice is really choked now, and he stops every now and then taking a breath and composing himself. It sounds awful and I feel physically sick listening to it. Hobart Port Control (HPC) sign out to relay details to Tasmania Police for assistance. Gareth jumps back in, he has a GP on board and is positioned ready to transfer him if required. *'Not just yet'* says Matt. HPC come back on and confirm Tasmania Police will respond with details shortly. They do so quickly confirming the Heli medivac is now launched with an ETA of around 15 minutes, they are also launching a tender with paramedics on board as backup, but it will be at least an hour or so before this can get anywhere near them. Matt agrees to head for 'Wedge Bay', a small sheltered cove close by, and prepares to drop all sails and start the engine. A little while later he comes back on VHF, his day just got worse, his engine won't start! The control panel is locked out and does nothing, there is no override to this either. Gareth jumps in again; he has an electrician on board and prepares him ready for transfer.

There are some periods of quiet now, looking back at my notes, only several very short minutes at a time, but it feels like ages. HPC are back looking for more details and Matt starts explaining again what happened. HPC request the casualties name, I expect Matt to decline this over the radio, as we would normally avoid broadcasting this at this stage, but he comes back on *"Derek Furness"* he says.

Bugger! I was with Derek only this morning, I did my level two training with him and we always catch up in port. I saw him at breakfast, *"alright fella"* he always says in his Manchester accent with a cheeky grin and smiling eyes. We departed as we always do on race start days, we hugged and high fived, *"stay safe and see you in Brisbane matey"* his last words to me. Matt continues, *"We have a second casualty with broken ribs, she may stay on board"*. In conversation with HPC he says *'she'* fell on top of Derek in the fall. So we know it's a female, now we worry again about who it might be. Matt discusses with HPC about whether she will also evacuate, she is not a mayday or critical, but could probably do with medical support anyway. Later I learn she was evacuated too.

I feel really sick now and Matt's voice is cold. The Heli arrives on scene and calls on the VHF *"CV23 CV23 CV23 this is Yankee 9, Yankee 9, Yankee 9"*. They can see lots of yachts and wish to know which one he is. Matt responds quickly setting off a red flare, and they confirm visual. They go on to discuss a medivac, the Heli however is really concerned about Matts rigging and isn't sure they want to lift directly off the boat, they try and convince him to use a tender. We only carry small soft dingy tender and this is far from ideal for this sort of injury, Matt declines. The Heli makes a low pass to evaluate the situation and review possibilities. Then they come back on VHF, they have an engine warning light, and need to put down immediately, they leave the scene, really! You couldn't write this script for this.

HPC jump in again, the police tender 'Relentless' is on route, ETA around 35 minutes now. Relentless is an amazing vessel, I went to see her yesterday as she had won a couple of special awards at prize giving the day before for gallantry during this year's race, she rescued several yachts in difficulty and towed one 30 miles to safety.

The satellite phone rings, it says on the screen its 'Gillian' from the race office, I wonder briefly if this is a call for assistance, I take the call, but it's just to request and confirm a full external media comms blackout is now in place across the fleet, this is standard practice to avoid any news going viral and causing panic back home. Jason is close by the Nav station listening in, I ask him to go and collect the crew lap top, our only means of external comms as crew. He retrieves it, and we lock it in the Nav seat for now, just to be sure.

We are getting further and further away now and the VHF transitions are getting weaker and weaker. HPC repeats back all of its conversations with everyone so we can keep up with progress for a little while longer as their radio signal is much stronger. Every now and then the Heli crew join in with updates and info, they are grounded close by and trying to affect repairs themselves. Matt & Gareth have a conversation about transferring doctors and electricians, then Matt leaves the conversation, Gareth calls him a few times *'CV23 CV22'* silence *'CV23 CV22'* silence again. It seems like an age and I start to worry about where Matts gone and what he is dealing with, the minutes drag on and on. From my notes afterwards, this is only 2-3 minutes, but it seemed like forever. What's going on, how is the casualty? At last Matt breaks radio silence *'CV22 CV23'* *'yes, go Matt'* comes the reply, Gareth dispensing with radio formality at this point. Matt says *"casualty regained consciousness, and can feel his extremities"* the words are broken and forced through a dry throat, he sounds like he is just about to cry. *'Good news mate'* says Gareth. *'Yep'* is all that Matt responds with, I imagine him and his sense of relief at this point. I almost cry myself and spare a moment to take this in.

Relentless transmit to Matt, ETA 15 minutes, how does Matt want to play the transfer? We miss the response as transmission strength is fading fast now. I catch a few calls after this, but it's mostly static with only the odd word comprehensible, and after about an hour and half of monitoring the call, I decide we can decipher no more so I close off my notes and inform Skipper I have closed our monitoring. He agrees and we discuss the last hour or so. It clearly hurts us both and we go back to sailing the boat quite soon afterwards. We later hear that both casualties were evacuated by Relentless and Mission Performance returned to port for engine repairs.

We exit Storm Bay in third place to GREAT Britain and OneDLL, as we turn the corner around Iron Pot lighthouse and out to sea we crack open the first of three spinnakers to be used for the 11 mile sprint along the south coast of Tasmania and around Tasman Island. It is a frantic hour or so as we trim constantly and peel to different spinnaker to gain speed advantage. It works for us and as we round Tasman Island to head north we are in first place, albeit by a small margin. As we start to position ourselves for the run north, outside of the Eastern Australian Current which is running south against us, the weather closes in as promised and we beat into hard waves and wind for a few hours. As the wind starts to back, we gradually drop down through the gears, leaving every down change to the last minute. By doing this we gain much speed advantage, the only downsides are the strain on the rig and boat, which so far have not caused too much damage, other than the sometimes extreme difficulty with which we have to drop sails. On this occasion, the storm is gathering pace with around 25-30ktts hard on the port beam, we need to get a Yankee three down as we are now over powered, even with reefs in already.

Nick, Susie, Charlie and myself head up to the foredeck and prepare for the drop. Even in the preparation phase we are tossed around by the boat bucking underneath us. Once or twice we are completely submerged by waves crashing right over the bow and over the top of us. We start the Yankee drop and manage to get most of it under control quickly, with the last few bits a real struggle for all of us. By the time we have finished all four of us have fully inflated life jackets, set off by being submerged again and again. We laugh all the way back to the cockpit and have a photo taken for good measure. We spare some thoughts for Derek too; we are wet, bruised and tired, but we are all OK and are laughing, it could be a lot worse and we hope he is OK.

Our run north is now well underway and we review the scoring gate tactics. The gate is positioned well offshore and it's an extra 30miles if we go for it. We review everyone else's position and agree we stand a great chance of getting it, and even if we lose two places, with three points for the gate we would still be ahead. So we set ourselves a course to the gate and set our sail plan accordingly. We scream northeast at amazing speeds, averaging 15ktts with occasional surf of 20/22, covering the 220 miles to the gate really quickly and efficiently, we bag the three points and celebrate only briefly before turning north to Brisbane.

The next two days are hard. We beat hard into wind, wave and current, making good progress but creating very tough conditions on board. There are a couple of falls down below and many minor injuries whilst we beat this course. Eventually it starts to ease and on day 4 at around 07:00 we go from a full beat, crashing down wave fronts to flat calm, followed by riding a code 2 spinnaker bang on course to Brisbane at 11 ktts boat speed with a great smooth ride along. Old Pulteney, Switzerland and OneDLL are right on our tail and we can see them on the horizon, at times only a few miles behind us.

We helm the code two through the night under the dim light of the forward steaming light to help us see what we are doing. It's a beautiful clear night with acres of stars and a thin slip of a moon. We can make out the coastline around 15 miles away. With just over 200 miles to run, we settle in and gradually pull away from Switzerland again, it's a slow process but as night falls we turn up the heat. A Derry night raid; absolute concentration on deck, no discussions, no food and drink just racing. Helm is rotated frequently and we trim and tinker with everything to squeeze out extra pace. By morning we have a 10 mile lead and are well positioned for a sprint finish.

100 miles to run and we are still making average 13 ktts. Then disaster strikes, the second sheet gives out on the code three and its flying loose, no choice but to drop it this time, in the process it gets torn, at least 8-10 feet, and a really bad tear. We bag it and dump it below, hoisting the code two as quickly as we can. A major repair job now for Brisbane, extra pressure on the team during what is scheduled to be a short stopover and we already have much to do. But for now we have 65 miles to go and a 5 mile lead over Switzerland. This is the first time we have raced this closely with them and if anyone were to get max points and take the win, better them, than one of the front runners. They are six points behind us in the leader board after 6 races, but we still have the scoring gate three points bagged on this race already too.

We settle down with code three flying and all is good, dinner is about to be served and morale is high in the early evening sun and warmth. Then disaster two strikes us. The sheet gives out on code three and its flogging wildly, many of us are down below eating and grab life jackets and jump up on deck to help. Between us, we grab the lazy sheet and start the same process as before, but it's too late, she is already torn and we go ahead and drop, bag and put her away, another big repair job for Brisbane!

We raise white sails, Yankee one and the stay, it's enough to stay with Switzerland, now about 4 miles ahead of us with about 20 to run, but we won't catch them now with this sail pattern. More worryingly OneDLL are now only 8 miles behind and closing fast. For the next three hours we squeeze every single last knott out of Derry and cross the line in second place. Given the damaged spinnaker we are pretty happy with this result, and with the scoring gate three points to boot we are actually two points up on Switzerland. Or at least we are for a few hours anyway, when we learn they won the ocean sprint, two points to them, so all square again.

After the finish line we heave too and make our way slowly around the corner into the shelter of Moreton Bay. We still have a spinnaker sheet under the boat and we are not sure what it is wrapped around, until now we have been going too fast to deal with it. So we slow down and drift under lowered sail and start to retrieve it. It takes an age to shift, but at least it is only wrapped around the keel so no prop damage. I take up my position in the Nav station and we start a five hour motor across the sand bars and narrow channels into the Brisbane River. It's extremely tight and we negotiate a fair amount of tanker and cargo ship traffic leaving Brisbane in the early hours.

Once the boat is packed down most of the crew go to their bunks, until it is just Conor on helm, Skipper on deck and me in the Nav. We have a laugh for the next five hours talking rubbish and remembering stories from Sydney and Hobart. Nav is tricky and very tight in places so it's serious at times. This makes me really nervous sometimes, watching the crazy video game version of sailing events down below, the scale sometimes makes it look much tighter than it is above deck in reality.

We arrive at Rivergate marina around 02:30 to a small welcoming committee of around a dozen or so people, mostly family and leg 5 joining crew. We dock at around 03:30 and go on to celebrate for a few hours until daylight with Switzerland and OneDLL. By now however I am really tired, the best part of 36 hours awake for the end of the race, then the motor in, followed by celebrations, I have been awake now for well over 48 hours, and it's too much even for a hardened round the world sailor! 2-3 hours' sleep then off for breakfast at a local cafe. Most welcome cappuccino and massive full cooked breakfast, feels good and sets me up for the days deep clean ahead. This goes well and we leave the dock around 17:00 to go to our apartment in the city. Michelle and I check in, shower and go straight back out for a glass of wine and some food. The others, from Mission Performance and Team Garmin get to the apartment around 21:00, we go out and get pizza and more wine, then sit on the balcony through till the small hours sharing stories of our respective races. Then it's back to the boat again early next morning for more repairs and maintenance.

Next morning I meet Derek on the dock, a great big hug and great to see him fit and well. Doctors suggested just a really bad concussion with no lasting damage, he can just about remember the fall, but many memory gaps are now getting filled in by others. He jokes about having a great story to tell now, and how it will get bigger better and more traumatic through the years ahead. We laugh and chat about the risks of the race, which we well know and both have had reminders of this, his more serious than my ribs, but we equally know just how quickly being on the boat can turn into serious injury. We brush this off and joke some more together, it's really good to see him.

The rest of the stopover is centred on boat work, no corporate, no sponsorship, no fuss and circus, just maintenance and repairs. I take a half day out and stay at the apartment, update my Facebook, website and do all my domestic stuff. I catch up with home on Skype, chatting for several hours with Siobhan about all kinds of rubbish. It's also Mum & Dads golden wedding anniversary this week and I share some quality time on Skype with them. I am feeling really badly homesick and I take some time out to reflect on home, what & who I miss. We discussed on the boat one evening whilst sailing against a backdrop of sunset, moonlight and stars, where would you rather be now? The more I think about this whilst away, the more I realise the 'where' is actually irrelevant to me and it's much more about 'who' I might be with that really matters.

Brisbane to Singapore
Extreme heat & the frustrations of drifting

In addition to our normal race briefing, course instructions and racing rule updates, we have a lengthy presentation and discussion about pirates. The Indonesian waters we are heading out into are renowned for pirates and the fleet is to be on its guard at all times. There are some official updates circulated from the marine coastguard agency and handouts for us to read on board. The tactics we are briefed upon include, a show of force, all hands on deck, dressed in team colours to show unity. Using VHF and communicating with other boats or adding handhelds & different voices on VHF just to portray we are talking to other boats in the area. Ultimately, though the message is don't fight if we do get attacked or boarded; we are to back off and leave them to it. This may be difficult for some people on the race, possibly faced with losing their iPads, iPhones or what few personal valuable positions we carry with us.

09:00 on the 12th January we slip out of Rivergate Marina and onto the Brisbane River. There is no ceremony, no music and only friends, family & race crew here to see us off. Race start is not until 17:00 and it doesn't feel like a race start day, the mood is fun, relaxed and calm. Normally on a race start day there is an air of pressure, we feel none of this today.

The 12 race yachts form up line astern with our flags and banners flying high, we head off down river, scheduled to circle a OneDLL spectator boat half way out. We are however required to break formation and head straight out into the bay as an enormous inbound tanker gate crashes our course and spoils the show.

We motor out into Moreton Bay, where we spend a few hours doing drills and a familiarisation sail for our five new crew. Normally there would have been a familiarisation sail as part of the stopover, this however was pulled from the schedule to allow for our much needed rudder repairs to take place. With five of the 17 crew on board, new joiners for this leg, the largest changeover we have had so far on the race. We have lost some real strength in those whom left us and we all know it is important to rebuild the team as quickly as we can, so we drill the important parts of our sail rotations and talk through how we manage trim and deck work. It feels strange to be doing this again and so long since we needed to, but the new guys settle in really quickly. We relax for the second half of the familiarisation time and make sure we are fit and ready for race start, plenty of time to work hard later, save some energy.

Around 15:00, after a light lunch, we motor across the flats and out to sea, meeting up with the other yachts. We hear on VHF Mission Performance have gone back to port with an electrical fault, what a shame for them after losing out on the last race too. I know they only have 12 crew on board and were in for a pretty tough race anyway, morale is not so high on their boat right now and this will really not help. I feel for Anthony whom we shared accommodation with in Albany and Brisbane, he was hoping for a better finish on this race and was feeling a bit down after their luck on the last few.

We line up in formation for a Le Mans start. This is where the yachts line abreast in a pre-agreed 'lot drawn' order, the duty Skipper acts as starter with a 10-4-1 minute countdown, followed by a 10-1 second countdown. All the crews must be aft of the grinders on deck, head sails can be hanked on but must be down on the deck. At the gun, the crews rush forwards and hoist their head sails. Traditionally in the last few seconds of the countdown crews edge forwards and it all starts on the 4 seconds to go mark. But for this one, everyone is remarkably well behaved and it goes right to the 'G' of go. We rush forward to pre agreed, practised positions and set about hoisting our head sails, stay sail first then Yankee immediately afterwards. We hold our course and sail pattern for 10 minutes, as dictated by race rules, but as soon as 9 minutes has elapsed we make a start on changing out the Yankee from two to one, we get this done in double quick time too, 12 minutes from drop to trim. We lead the fleet as we head out into the Coral Sea and morale is high again. It's a glorious sight to see the fleet behind us at this stage. We sail reasonably close formation for a few hours as we head out to sea, then lose sight of the whole fleet after the first night. Just the occasional light flickering on the horizon for us to monitor and speculate upon who it might be.

After a day or so with white sails we launch the first of many Spinnaker for this race. We hoist a code two and after only a few hours peel to a code three. This is a great opportunity to show the new joiners how we peel kites, something we as a team have worked really hard on mastering. If we get it right, it can save as much as 3-4 miles advantage, by maintaining momentum.

It basically requires hoisting the second spinnaker outside the first one, as soon as it inflates, dropping the first through a letter box drop, via the gap between the main sail and boom. Using a tack retrieval line rigged specially for this purpose, attached to the bottom of the sail and rigged via its drop route to a primary winch to grind it in double quick time. When it all works smoothly it is a beautiful sight to behold and we get quite excited about the manoeuvre as we have made it one of our own.

However it is intrinsically dangerous and several people, including me, have been hurt at various times whilst doing it. Conor broke his ribs doing just this manoeuvre. Neil, once got a sheet caught under his arm, which snapped tight and lifted him clean from one side of the deck to the other in a fraction of a second, he was extremely lucky to escape with just bad bruises. Kites are extremely powerful when inflated and can pull you off your feet if you get into the wrong place or don't let go quick enough. They have the strength to pull the boat right over sideways too, so we are all on our guard when doing this, and almost always do it double handed, with both watches on deck.

132

We make our way out across the Coral Sea and north towards the edge of the Great Barrier Reef, where we turn northwest to the Louisiade Archipelago south east of Papua New Guinea. We turn northwest again across the Solomon sea, along the north coast of Papua New Guinea and through the Vitiaz straights just south of the island of New Britain.

The heat sears to a pretty severe level; it's blazing and burning hot sunshine all day on deck, and below deck there is little respite. In bunks, it reaches around 40 degrees, and sleep is a luxury, sweat is full, like a sauna. You sweat all over when below decks. As we cross the Soloman Sea, Old Pulteney tack right across our stern at one point, and OneDLL are seen clearly on the horizon. We love this kind of close racing and it generates an excited focus on helm and trim on board, every little helps make the boat go just that little bit faster with each hour that passes. We tack back and forth and at one point it seems as though both tacks are working against us. Whatever we do, neither tack seems to take us in the right direction, all yachts at one point, on the same tack, are all going backwards, the wind just works against us.

It takes an age to make our way to the straights of Vitiaz and by the time we eventually get there we all run out of wind and for a whole day. We bob around with a limp windseeker, trying hard just to get the boat moving. It provides an opportunity for crew to wash themselves and some clothes. Most of us take this chance for a spring clean, we eat on deck too which is a rare treat; both watches together in the evening. North of the straights of Vitiaz there are a group of small islands, including Long Island, which we end up looking at for three days as we drift and bob without wind. When we get moving again, Old Pulteney have caught us and for the next two days and nights we tack and gybe alongside them. At one point we stop a VHF conversation with them and just shout across, as they are now close enough to hear and reply! We sail overnight out into the Bismark Sea, and head offshore way farther than we had planned. All the time we watch sea temperature to monitor possible currents as there are some pretty strong ones in this area we need to avoid.

We are making really slow progress, and with 2,700 miles still to run and around 17 days to go, time is now getting tight for this race to finish in time for the next one to start. We always knew there was a chance this would be split into two races, with a motor in between and we had agreed at pre-race briefing to accumulate time from both legs for final results, should this happen.

However, with several boats at least 2 days behind us and an average speed of just 8ktts when motoring long distances, the race office are rapidly running out of time to call this one. There is much speculation on board as to how and when this will occur. Some stopover maintenance jobs start to get done now, deck work and rope work especially become our priority to complete. The boat is going to be out of the water for at least two days when we get to Singapore so it would be good to be ahead of the game before we arrive.

By the time we reach the Bismark Sea, it is us, OneDLL and Old Pulteney out in front in a group of three with the rest of the pack around 30nm+ behind us and the back markers some 280nm behind. We catch OneDLL slowly over the course of a day or so. On one tack we catch the wind early and pull out a small lead, for the next 30 hours or so we tack back and forth covering each other's moves in a very slow race game of chess, we pull out a lead of around 6 miles during this, then loose it again easily as the wind dies.

In between the blistering heat and baking sunshine we experience some amazing squalls, during the day these can be seen building and approaching, at night however it is a different story. We monitor our radar which picks up storm clouds and rain, or at least it did until it registered *'error code #3362'* whatever that means! For now at least, it means it doesn't work. So we occasionally get caught out at night by a storm we haven't seen approaching. They bear down upon us very quickly, the temperature drops, wind decreases at first, sometimes only very briefly, then increases with rapid acceleration, sometimes to a point where we can be massively overpowered in just a matter of seconds.

On one such night storm, we see the thunder and lightning approaching in the distance, in a matter of minutes it's over us and the rain crashes down. I have never experienced rain like this, almost as though the drops are joined up, it's like getting fire hosed, it's really hard work just to see and stand as its pounding us so heavily. After a fashion, we get the sails under control, the lightning continues and the thunder resonates through the hull as it crashes directly above us. At one point, two bolts of lightning strike the water either side of the boat, so close you can feel and smell them! This continues for many minutes. Skipper drops down below and checks the AIS; there's a cargo ship dead ahead and heading directly for us, and we are sailing in full anti-pirate mode currently which means we are not transmitting our position so the tanker won't have seen us on his radar or AIS. Skipper plugs back in our AIS transmitter, grabs a hand held VHF, calls the ship, as he starts the engine and issues and immediate *'all hands'* call. Those sleeping jump to it and soon everyone is on deck. Skipper calls the cargo ship again, still no answer, which way to steer? We still can't see him as visibility is virtually nil in the thick of the storm. The ship responds in very broken English. Skip responds and our worse fears are confirmed, he's doing 15ktts and cannot see us either visually or on any of his electronic systems.

Skip goes back below to check AIS again, rebooting it to transmit and waiting the 30-40 seconds or so for it to burst back into life, which seems like an age. As the screen clears the ship shows up on screen, calls us on VHF again and confirms he can see us now. He is around 15 miles away dead ahead, he will alter course to port. Skip looks at the scale again, it's been left switched to 30+miles and so the ship had appeared on screen much closer than he actually is. It is a really easy mistake to make in the heat of racing and depth of a night, but a very frightening experience for us all. We stand down, wash in the rain some more and as it passes we get back to sailing again. Skipper smokes a cigarette and watches the ship pass. He recounts this several times over the next few days, it's the first time he has ever been scared as Skipper and continuously apologises profusely for the mistake. It's a good lesson for us all though, it is easy to become complacent out here, apparently thinking we are on our own.

The race office confirm via email, although we are making good progress in line with previous races, they are issuing a shortened course notice to manage our time and our pending corporate commitments in Singapore. The new finish line will be the next way point, just south of the Sulu Sea around 900 miles ahead of us. We calculate with the current weather patterns this could take us 10 days. It's a frustrating time and the mood sinks on board. This is becoming an endurance test for the crew. We are all feeling the effects of dehydration, fatigue and the constant severe heat.

We have been sailing upwind for days too now and it is difficult to sleep, on the low side you are pinned hard up against the wall and can hardly move, on the high side you cling on to stop yourself falling out of your bunk. We tack every 8-10 hours, so wherever you sleep, you experience high & low side sleep, or lack of it. On one night I fall out into my lee cloth (the sling we tie up around our bunks to prevent us from falling out) I awake with a start, facing downwards incased in a sort of 'lee hammock'. I'm totally disoriented and confused, it takes me a second or two to realise where I am, and a few more to realise which way up I am; it is most disconcerting. My next move needs to be really careful to get out if this safely. I reach out and can just about get a good hand hold inside a cave locker, before rolling slowly and carefully back into my bunk, relieved to still be in one piece.

The days of beating into wind continue, one day blurs to the next, I sometimes forget what time it is and what meal we are about to eat. On one day I ask one of the watch to put the kettle on ready for breakfast, only to be informed it is 9pm! Ahh righto' Maybe not then?

I helm for at least 2 hours on each watch and spot for others doing so in between. I have blisters on my thumbs from helming and a sore head from hours on end out in the sun. We get splashed all the time on deck, nothing ever dries and even if it does, you will sweat it wet again. I am now suffering a kind of nappy rash from the constant wetness around the nether regions and my lower back. Many of the crew have the same, it is most uncomfortable. I take a break from deck work as my mother duty day comes around again. It's a real challenge, heeled over at 45degrees, pounding through the waves and baking hot temperatures. I make banana bread and spill the mix twice, then it heels over in the oven and makes a mess again, the sink splashes out all the time, I burn my leg from a kettle water splash. Then, in a massive boat crash on a big wave I lose a third of the bolognaise sauce I just made, all over the stove, and all over the coffee and tea jars too, it's another big clean up job. Ohh what a day!!

After what seems like way too many days in a ground hog circle, the wind drops and the skies clear again. It's frustrating as we slow right down, but it's a slight respite from the pounding we have been taking. Still 500 miles to go to the way point at Sarangani straights, just south of Mindano Island which is part of the Philippines. This is also the location of the shortened course finish line. At our midday briefing, we pass the 500mile point and celebrate this. Late that evening when come onto watch at 18:00 it's down to 498! 2 miles in 6 hours and right now we are drifting backwards on the current. At this speed it will be July before we reach Singapore. Overnight, the race office request a fuel audit; this could be the early signs of another race shortening call off. We still have 1,700 miles to go to Singapore and, even with a fair weather run, that is 8 days motoring. It's now the 1st February and 9th is the end of our current arrival window, we also have a boat lift for rudder maintenance scheduled for this stopover, so there really is no time left to spare now. Race 9 start date is put back one day, another indication that race office are onto the detail of this now.

We calculate, if we hold the line with the wind ahead we can just about make third place to the way point behind OneDLL & Old Pulteney. The boats to the north of us will have a steep southerly course to follow and the winds, which will ease for them over the next few days, will be at the worst possible angle for them. This plays out exactly as we suspect and we fast approach the way point in what we consider to be third place. Well when we say 'fast approach' it's around 4-6ktts with occasional 7/8ktts bursts, with regular wind holes where we just wallow and wait. It's painful and takes us days longer than anticipated to reach the way point. Then for the final 50 miles, we hoist a code 2 spinnaker and cruise at 10-13ktts all the way to the line, eventually crossing it at around 02:30 in the morning, after a really tiring 23 days and 3,900 miles.

The final results are cast the next morning we finish seventh. The guys in the north get favourable wind after all. It's been a lottery of a race all the way and we really feel as though we have done our best. Seventh place plus our scoring gate points is a good result through, we are happy to celebrate this.

Overnight, we motor on through the straights, out into the Moro Gulf, part of the Celebes Sea. This is a total desert of a sea and we experience absolutely flat calm with no wind or wave for the next three days. Despite the frustrations of the heat and not being able to sail, it's absolute bliss however and we all take the time to rest and recuperate in between working on boat maintenance during the day. The blistering heat does slow us down at work somewhat. It also happens to be my birthday, which so far I haven't mentioned to anyone, it passes unnoticed, which I quite like actually, it is a really deep contemplative and reflective day for me and I really enjoy it.

We motor for three days across the gulf, together with OneDLL and Old Pulteney for company. On the second evening we do a crew swap for the evening with OneDLL, it's a great opportunity to catch up and watch our own boat on the water, which we never actually get to see!

As we exit the Moro Gulf through the Basilian Straights, past the Sulu Archipelago and into the Sulu Sea the wind picks up and we sail a code two spinnaker with winds from directly behind us for around 36 hours, absolute bliss, beautiful sailing and a delight to helm. As we pass through the Belabac Straights, north of Sabah, part of Malaysia, the wind drops again and after some fresh fuel calculations we motor at an increased 9ktts towards our fuel stop at Kota Kinabalu.

We continue with our boat maintenance which is progressing well, and by the time we reach the fuel stop, all the winches are serviced, most of the sail repair is completed and all our rope and line repairs are done. We also strip down the main grinders and repair all of our stanchion bases which are leaking. The bad news is, once we reach the refuel point it's too late to refuel, we end up spending a night offshore and waiting 17 hours for the fuel dock to reopen next day.

We are close enough to shore to get a phone signal so I text Siobhan, I get a really nice birthday text back from her and agree a time to call her on her birthday next week. This all makes me feel really good, I really am starting to miss her a lot now and it hurts a lot when I get her text, I go into my bunk for a cry and to be alone. She is with me all the time though, my monkey sitting quietly on my shoulder.

We drift around for while contemplating either a drift night or anchoring up somewhere sheltered. Skipper hails a hotel taxi over and we bribe him with US$ cash to take two of our crew ashore for supplies, in a remarkable feat of negotiation from Skipper he agrees and we dispatch Carmen and Nick who return a few hours later with beer, wine and crisps! We anchor in a sheltered bay as the sun sets, Susie and Skipper host a quiz night on deck and we stay up laughing until the early hours. In the morning we swim, bucket wash and have a late breakfast, raising the anchor to get to the fuel dock by around 10:30, we wait outside for another few hours, then get in and dock.

It takes around 3hours to get fuelled, so in groups of two and no more, dressed only in civvies so as not to attract attention we visit the nearest hotel which has wifi, air conditioning, a coffee shop and a small gift & sweetie shop. Most of us buy sweets and ice cream. By the time we slip away from Kota Kinabalu in the late afternoon, our fuel stop has turned into a massive morale lifter and we are all feeling refreshed and ready for the four day motor sail to Singapore, past Brunei and Borneo, across the South China Sea.

I awake on 11th of February full of fear and trepidation, I have absolutely dreaded this day for a long time. It is Siobhan's birthday, and I have not been looking forward to being this far away from her, having not seen her for so long. I had made a point of telling a few of the crew this, just in case I seemed pre occupied in any way on the day. I snooze for a little while. When I next stir and wake, Michelle comes by and sits on the edge of my bunk. She is half smiling half crying and asks how much I must hate her for forgetting my birthday? I tell her not to be ridiculous, I wasn't expecting anything and actually I had a really great day. She apologises profusely and I continue it really doesn't matter. *"Anyway"* she says, with a massive smile and tears still on her face, *"I know it's Siobhan's birthday today, so I thought we would celebrate them together, look"* she says pointing down the ghetto towards the galley.

It's fully lined with coloured balloons all around tied to bunks and lee cloths. She grins and says *"I baked a cake too!"* *"Wow, awesome!"* I reply, and so for dinner that evening, we celebrate the birthdays, I insist it is for Siobhan not me, the crew sing happy birthday to us and present me with a really nice card they have all signed and written some nice things in.

We have a really nice dinner with jelly and cake for desert. Many of the crew ask about Siobhan and we talk about her a lot all day. Just before 01:00am next morning (17:00 UTC) I call Siobhan from the satellite telephone, straight to voice mail! Typical! I wait a few minutes and call back, she answers straight away. *"Hi Monkey, happy birthday darling"* I say, there is a slight satellite delay and then she replies *"Dad!!! How are you? Where are you? What are you doing? Are you on the boat? What time is it?"* We chat for around 10 minutes or so and she updates me with her news including her first job now successfully secured. She sounds really happy. We agree to speak more at the weekend from Singapore and sign off.

I stay in the Nav station for a little while and have a short cry again. It is so good to hear from her after over a month at sea, and great to hear her so happy too. A very great day it actually turns out to be after all.

Next day we finish the deep clean with the galley floor boards and bilges, almost everything now cleaned and serviced ready for arrival into Singapore. With just over 180 miles to go, we will be in next morning. We eat the last of the meat from the freezer for dinner in the form of a beef stew, followed by cake and custard. We set up a convoy with Jamaica Get All Right and Invest Africa overnight as we are now passing the highest risk area for pirates. We have a short recap on our pirate tactics and ensure everyone is alert to the risks.

Singapore to Qingdao
*The coldest & most uncomfortable sailing
you will ever encounter*

The afternoon before race start I check out of my hotel with clean kit packed and sorted into to small dry bags, one for warm weather and one for cold. I take a taxi down to the boat and stash the dry bags under my bunk. As I wait for the taxi, a message comes through from Sean *"would I be OK to take over as watch leader for the next leg?"* Wow! I hadn't expected to be asked. Conor has been suffering with a severe tendonitis in his wrists, and has been signed off; he will miss the next race. We have all suffered a little with this; it's a kind of RSI injury from gripping all the time, but Conor has it really badly and will do lasting damage if he doesn't get it sorted. I had really enjoyed the responsibilities of assistant watch leader on the race so far working with Conor. I thought about it for few minutes during the cab ride. It is a massive responsibility, it takes up much of your time and is pretty tiring. This was going to be a tough race already. Was I ready for this and did I want to take it on? It was not an opportunity I would want to turn down and having been specifically asked, I felt I really should do so. I messaged him back, saying it would be a pleasure, thank you, and I was stoked to be asked. I thought more about the race ahead. *"The hardest sailing you might ever do" "look after the mast when slamming" "be prepared for the extreme cold"* just some of the phrases used by Justin in our race briefing. I tried hard to prepare myself, but the intense feelings of nervous anticipation were well and truly mixing it up within.

After we finished drinks and dinner, I cleared the last email and made my way to the boat, I didn't sleep at all, getting up several times and sitting on deck. I had way too much in my head. The deep nervous feelings about the race and the excitement of a recent job offer for after the race all mixed up together. Next morning, the dock came to life really early, the first teams to clear immigration did so at 06:00. I took an early shower and joined a few others for breakfast in the hotel bistro next to the dock. We talked about the race ahead and it was clear we all felt similar feelings of nervous anticipation. Our turn came for immigration clearance checks and there was the usual fuss and palaver whilst we got ourselves together into alphabetical order, which you would think was easy! Then, back to the boat for last minute checks and prep. I made my way slowly chatting and hugging friends on other boats as always with stay safe wishes. The same mood was evident around the fleet; you could really feel it. We had felt this on the dock at Cape Town, but this seemed deeper still.

Almost ready to slip I took the bow line and waited final instructions from Skipper. We slipped and made our way out to join the fleet. Meanwhile, all this time, a frantic race behind the scenes was going on to get us new battery chargers, ours were completely shot and needed replacing. We finally got the call to say they were on their way, and as soon as the media shoot was over we were to come back in to have them fitted. We lined up for the photo shoot, flags and banners flying in glorious colour and with our new team shirts looking great too. Half way through the photo shoot, the media RIB broke down, the shoot was abandoned, and we towed the RIB back in with us. We moored up and waited what seemed like an age for the chargers to arrive. It took the shore crew only around an hour to fit them and eventually we are out and on our way. The fleet had been instructed to wait for us, delaying the race start. We had a 55 mile motor to get to them. We motored out through the incredible shipping traffic lanes and dodged our way safely out offshore. By the time we reached the fleet it was dark and duty Skipper, Pete Stirling on Jamaica had decided to delay race start till next morning and motor overnight. We set into formation and motored for the next 13 hours until first light. At just after 06:00 the one hour notice was given and we set about making our sail plan and getting into position. We set a Yankee two and agreed positions for the Le Mans start procedure. We had nailed the last one in Brisbane, and we felt a little pressure amongst us to do well again. As we lined up and prepared to start all was clam and Sean was calling the shots and keeping us clear. One minute to go, all goes quiet and we wait. VHF countdown out loud from Pete, *"10-9-8-7-6-5-4-3-2"* .... and we are off, we didn't hear the *"one, go"* straight into our positions and hoisting head sails, from where I am on the grinder, and in our position as boat eleven in the lineup, I can see most of the fleet. Qingdao have a problem, at first it looks as though they have a stay halyard on their Yankee, so it won't go all the way up, they have to drop it and switch which costs them dearly and they back right off. We are away in the lead again. Brilliant! Two out of two Le Mans starts for Derry. We really put ourselves under pressure by doing this, but it makes us work harder and boy does it feel good.

As the fleet sails on forward over the first few hours we share the lead with GREAT Britain and Henri Lloyd. It is hard sailing into the wind on a really close haul. As we pull away during the first day, we are pushing hard. The boat feels a little sluggish and slow, we cannot seem to find why, but to all of us it feels slow. We hear a few days later that Jamaica have broken their forestay and retired from racing, they are rerouted to Kota Kinabalu for repairs and will rejoin us in Qingdao. A broken forestay is pretty big and possibly very dangerous occurrence for one of our boats and the fleet is instructed to add safety lashings to the bottle screws in the forestay where the break has happened. I am standing in the companion way hatch, talking to Jason who's down below, when there is a loud crack from above us, sufficient to make me flinch and duck. We look at each other, then exit and look up, it's a noise that is unfamiliar and doesn't sound good.

It's interesting as we have got to know the boat over the seven months to this point, we know her moans and groans as she shifts and twists under pressure. She is always talking to us and gives us audible feedback. The water sounds outside the hull whilst down below give you a really accurate sense of actual speed. The creaks and bangs from above let you know where the pressure is on the rig, and consequently how she is sailing. Each winch and block makes a slightly different noise, one can often tell what is being manoeuvred, just from this sound.

This loud crack from above however is not good, we look each other in the eye briefly with a puzzled look, we don't have time to discuss it when again from above, this time louder and more a crunching crack, which resonates through the boom and mast giving us the first clue as to what it is. We both look up again, this time to be met by the entire main sailing falling down around us.

There are many calls on deck for people to move and the crew scatter. Everyone gets out of the way and no one is hurt, but we have no main sail hoisted now, so our main drive forward is compromised. We can see a small tail of main halyard left on the head of the mainsail so we know this is what let go. Quickly, and without fuss, we all know what to do and just get on with it. Sean from the helm keeping us straight and motivating us with direction. I jump up onto the boom end and Jason eases the topping lift. As soon as I have enough, I untie the lashings and pass it forward to him, he jumps up onto the mast and ties it onto the sail head. Meanwhile, Michelle has already loaded it back onto a primary winch and several others jump straight away onto the twin grinders. By the time Jason has tied it off, they are already slowly grinding it out of his fingertips. Before you know it we are full main hoist and back underway again in double quick time. We barely loose a half mile during this whole manoeuvre and we congratulate ourselves accordingly with high fives as we tidy up the cockpit.

The fleet splits around some Indonesian Islands in the Palua Palua Archipelago, we head south and east with Jamaica, Henri Lloyd, Old Pulteney and Qingdao, with the rest of the pack going north and west. We are pretty sure our route is better, it gives us a faster route east and a better angle back to the North West up to the scoring gate. We tack back and forth making as best VMG as we can, on one day we fly past both Henri Lloyd and PSP Logistics on the opposite tack, shortly afterwards they both tack and cover us from behind, confirming what we believe to be the right course. I am really enjoying the sailing on this race so far, it is very hard living again at 45degrees plus of boat heel, slamming into waves constantly though.

Perhaps you get out what you put in, as I am also enjoying the watch leader role. I have never found responsibility a chore nor a burden and am happy to stand up and be counted when required. We have a really strong watch too and all the shared helming we did on the previous race is paying off now. Everyone is confident to take the wheel and the course and speeds we are getting are consistently high. The boat behaves upwind really nicely, when she is set up and trimmed she is beautifully balanced and a real pleasure to helm. It's really quite relaxing and mesmerising as you cannot let your mind wander at all, concentration levels are high and the rewarded pleasure is a delight, the hours pass really quickly, everyone I am sure would be happy to stay and helm for longer, but we stick to our one hour maxiMum to keep it fresh and fast.

We spot some lights in the distance in the middle of a pretty dark night. They gradually appear to come closer. It is so difficult to gauge distance and speed on the water at night, almost impossible to do so. They start as just a white light, then two can be seen, sometimes brighter and sometimes feint. We have nothing on AIS so believe it is probably just another fishing boat, but we keep a close eye on it. After a while it splits again and has three or four orange lights too, at times it seems close but we really can't tell. I am unsure as to whether it is a risk or not, but err on the side of caution and wake Skipper anyway to check out what he thinks. We come back up onto deck together, he's slightly bleary eyed having just woken and we watch the lights together. He can't really tell either and we watch together for a while discussing it might be this, it might be that. He agrees it is worth watching and after a while says he's going back down below and for me to call him if we see anything clearer. As he says this the lights rotate and shine directly at us, and we clearly see the wake on the front of a boat way too close. He jumps over the traveler, asks politely to take the helm as he takes it anyway from Richard. He pulls us over hard to port and calls for traveller right down, I grab the winch and let it right out, as we turn and head around I slowly bring it back up and we power away from the fishing boat as it passes us and sprays the side of us as it does. We settle for a moment then set back up onto course.

Skip passes the wheel back to Richard and we laugh about nearly having fish for supper. *"I was going back to sleep"* says Skip *"but think I might have a tea and smoke first and calm my nerves now!"* We laugh and he heads down below. We talk about this the next day and share it with both watches, it really is sometimes impossible to tell how close a vessel is, so ask everyone to be extra vigilant with lights, especially potentially blind fisherman!

We have set up the run into the scoring gate nicely from the east, which gives us a great head to wind. The breeze is picking up from the north east for the next 24-36 hours and with just over 120 miles to run we are in with a real shout at this one, with the rest of the fleet further out east. We focus in on the helming, driving every last knott out of the boat, each and every one of us taking our turn and concentrating hard. Closer and closer to the gate and you can start to feel the tension and anticipation build on board. Around 70 miles out from the gate and at around 04:30am, I am awake in my bunk. We are crashing hard over waves still and the boats creaks and cracks as she always does.

We drop down really hard over one wave and she gives out a really loud kind of chink/bang unrecognisable noise. Immediately I can feel sails flogging and a loss of drive. This is not good, but quite what it actually is, I am unsure. I jump up, get dressed and make my way quickly up onto deck. The forestay has completely broken off, the Yankee is now down on the deck. Skipper is already frantically tying off loose ends of forestay and rigging temporary forestay supports with spare halyards. A couple of us climb over, tie off the Yankee head and pull it out of the way so Skip and a couple of crew assisting him can work with more space on the foredeck. I call to him, *"what's the priority Skip?" "Drop in another reef quickly"* he replies, I make my way back to the cockpit, there are four other crew there poised and ready to help. I tell them that's what we are doing next. Several ask me to call it off and I check back that everyone is ok with that, *"absolutely!"* is the response. So I position everyone with jobs and together we prepare to put the reef in. Reefing is a regular manoeuvre and pretty much everyone knows the routine so I work on this basis and try not to be detailed in any way with my instructions. It is however complicated and requires everything to be done in a very precise order. Once everyone is ready I check back with a quick run through before we start. The reef drops in and is completed in minutes and we tidy up behind us quickly and neatly, awaiting next instructions. Skip appears to be getting on well on the foredeck so I rally a team together; we drag the Yankee back, flake it away into its bag and drop it down below as quickly as we can.

In all it takes us a couple of hours to fully stabilise the boat, during which time Skip makes a few calls to the race office. We hear back that PSP have broken their forestay too, that's three boats now all with the same break. The race office call the whole fleet, suspending all racing. The fleet is instructed to motor sail making best time, rendezvous at Hong Kong for repairs and safety checks. We get ourselves set with a stay sail and three reefs, I take the helm to get us moving again. It is a really nervous next two hours. Like driving a car with three wheels over sheet ice, the concentration to ensure we don't slam over a wave is immense and I feel like she is super fragile to helm. I think about the potential for lost confidence in the boat as we sail on. Up to this point, we have had so much faith in her and trusted absolutely everything she did. I really hope this does not damage that in the team.

We receive further updates from the race office with details of the exact destination and repair plans. Race restart is now scheduled for 2nd or 4th of March. It will now be a time trial with all boats to start as soon as they are repaired and ready. This gets some of the boats to Qingdao quickly so we can still deliver on our corporate and sponsor agreements; but could be a weather disadvantage to some if we are starting days apart? Arrival in Qingdao is now expected around 12th.... ish, with race start held at 16th for race 10 across the North Pacific. That is barely anytime at all to recover before the biggest race so far, across the mighty North Pacific. We motor for the next four days to Hong Kong.

On arrival we are met by Sir Robin, who has flown out with the repair materials and sets about the repair with our assistance. In simple terms, the repair is to loosen the backstays, flexing the mast forward. Bind the forestay back to the deck with new shackles top & bottom and a dyneema binding. Dyneema is a technical line which is much stronger than steel. We tension tighten the binding with the primary winch before binding off the ends. Then tighten the backstays to tune the rig back into place. After the work is finished Sir Robin stays for a cup of tea with us and we discuss the 6 nations amongst other current topics with him. He sets us a challenge to get to Qingdao in time for the next game on the 9th, if we do, he will buy the drinks! We accept and shake on it. After a test sail out in Hong Kong bay we return for a further rig tune up, then head round to the next bay for refuelling. The refuel bay is located right next to Jumbo the floating seafood restaurant, which I visited last time I was in Hong Kong. This brings back some cool memories of a great trip with a very special person many years ago.

Once refueled, we head back out, do another test sail and some final tuning. All looks OK so far, so we set off out to the start line with Mission Performance around 20 miles ahead and GREAT Britain a few miles behind. As we approach the start line we call up GREAT Britain and agree to wait for them and start together to make our time trial racing a little more interesting. We cross the line pretty close together and set off north. We very quickly head straight into wind over tide again and we slam hard over every wave, bang, bang, bang; the relentless slamming. It is possibly the most uncomfortable sailing you could ever do and really tests the boat and crew to new limits as it continues for days and nights. It is almost impossible to sleep and every move has to be carefully timed and thought through to prevent injury. Using the heads is a traumatic and equally dangerous experience, many of us start to dehydrate as a consequence, reducing our liquid intake to cut down visits! The first few nights are long and arduous, helming is a real challenge, trying hard to reduce the impact where possible and maintain a straight course. There are walls of white water ahead. At one point whilst in the Nav station I miss time a change of grip and fall a long way out and into the wall and bunks on the low side. It hurts like hell and I sit still for a quite a while whilst I slowly check everything still works. This is exactly how Alan broke his shoulder on leg 4. For me it turns out to be lucky and I escape with nothing more than an enormous pair of really painful square bruises and a stiff shoulder to show for the trauma.

We face the additional challenge here of increased cargo ship traffic and the massive Chinese fishing fleets. We install a permanent Nav presence. We steer as best we can to avoid these, calling on VHF the ones we need to for safety. The fishing fleets mostly just ignore us, but the cargo ships generally are really helpful and obliging, with the odd one showing a real interest in the race and wishing us well.

I break out gloves for the first time since the southern ocean a couple of months back. I prefer not to wear gloves on deck, my hands have toughened up as a consequence and it's only the intense cold this time that drives me to do so. We wear huge mittens for helming and in between jobs just to rewarm hands.

As the scheds come in, they become increasingly difficult to follow. The fleet all started at different times, this race now working on time elapsed, so all the different times are difficult to calculate. We do however know we are pretty close to Mission Performance who started around 3-4 hours ahead of us, and GREAT Britain who started at the same time as us are just in front, so we at least have some competitive spirit in full flow and chase them down.

Being watch leader on this race has its moments. Such as, in the middle of the night when three or four things are all happening at the same time and you have to make a decision quickly. The Skipper is asleep, as are a dozen or so other crew, and it's your call to keep the boat fast and safe. I guess you get out what you put in, and I am certainly putting in on this one. It is much harder being watch leader than assistant. I try to be out of my bunk 10 minutes earlier and always last off deck. Plus the constant awareness and nervous tension of being responsible. Much more than responsible in a work sense, this really is life and death at times in your hands and occasionally I do really feel this. I count to myself the watch teams on and off deck, especially at night, when it would be easy to lose someone as people move around the boat. This would surely be our worst nightmare. If you fell off the boat behind the helm, you might not be seen, it could be hours or even next watch change before someone noticed. These thoughts sometimes really haunt me.

The cold continues to take hold of us and we wrap up more and more. I am now wearing almost all of my thermal layers. They are working well, so far I have not really been very cold. My boots are amazing, never once, even with thin socks, have I had cold feet. They are wet, but not cold. Gloves however is another matter altogether. All the gloves I have tried fail, and I rarely wear them. Actually preferring the dexterity of bare hands and deep pockets for warmth. This does however mean very cold and very sore hands. During these supremely cold and wet times we describe the surroundings as black and white, with shades of grey and no colour at all. All around us, grey sea and grey skies, dark nights follow dark days, and when it rains it stings your face like being shot blasted.

We continue to beat, tack after tack up the Taiwan Straits, sailing in excess of 200 miles a day, but only making VMG of never more than 110 miles a day; boy, it's frustrating and uncomfortable. We tack whenever the speed or course drops, which turns out to be quite often; anything to make better headway. On one of the tacks, GREAT Britain appear to have missed a way point. After an hour so when we realise we call them and point this out, all agreeing this is the decent thing to do. They reply that they already knew, and make a detour to round the mark; we gain a few hours as they do. Our sporting approach has always been thus and it is absolutely the right thing to do to point this out to them.

As we head into the last 24 hours, we are still tacking all the way north into the Yellow Sea, which incidentally is also black and white. On one afternoon, I am going through the weather grib files for the next 24 hours with Skipper. The weather colour coding, which is shown as shades of blue and purple for very low numbers, or low current and tide, with progressively yellow, orange and red shades for higher tides or currents. Without thinking I ask, "*Is the Yellow Sea always blue?*" We pause and smile then laugh together, recounting it for others later. As we sail past the Shanghai port entrances, the shipping increases as do the fishing fleets. At one point we have 1124 AIS targets on our radar, each one is a ship or boat moving and each one is within an AIS range of around 20 miles! I ask the helm at one point if he is comfortable aiming at the two ships ahead whilst he is helming? "*It's ok he says, there are no gaps to aim at and I'm hoping someone will move shortly!"* In amongst the ships are massive fishing fleets dodging around and dragging nets behind them, and showing little or no regard for us.

Eventually, we arrive at the finish line, a marker buoy just off Qingdao outer harbour. We arrive just a few minutes behind Mission Performance, we get the race honours after the adjusted time elapsed, but the line honour bragging rights belong to them all the way and we are really pleased. Mission Performance are one of our sister teams and we are thrilled they have beaten us on the last sprint and it's a provisional podium for them too.

GREAT Britain beat us both by a few hours, galling though it is, we are pretty happy with a provisional second place to GREAT Britain, and congratulate Mission Performance on their first potential podium place. We drift slowly and motor at a slow 2-3ktts for the final 20 or so miles to the bay as we are not allowed into dock until morning. We set to on our deep clean and complete the sail locker and galley, getting all the food bags ready for taking off and packing our own kit. By the time we arrive at the bay, we have all our branded banners and flags up, are kitted out in purple and ready to dock.

The final 3 miles, we pick our way through a bizarre chequer board of polystyrene fishing floats, some with nets attached and none more than 1 1/2 boat lengths apart. It proves a real challenge and takes us ages to manoeuvre through without snagging. There must be a sea route through but we are dammed if we can find it!

We wait outside the harbour entrance and listen to the crowd noise as GREAT Britain and Mission Performance dock. There are fireworks, drums and music followed by speeches. We get the general gist of what is in store but nothing prepares us for the actual experience.

As we are called in to dock, immediately we are surrounded by media boats, tv cameras & photographers hanging off them on all sides. One of them is flying a drone with a gyro camera taking arial shots. We later see the results of the arial camera in a bar owned by the cameraman. Awesome footage, and over a glass of wine, he gives me media access to it to post and share on my Facebook page. As we get closer, the fireworks go off and the crowds can be seen and heard. Thousands have turned out to see us all around in every direction there are flags waving and people cheering. On the dock ahead of us there are several hundred drummers playing in tune to our boat song 'Hall of Fame' by The Script. A surreal sight. After our song has finished they revert back to Chinese rhythm, which is much more fitting.

We walk up the dock in between the drummers waving and taking it all in, having been semi crushed already by a media scrum as we tried to get off the boat. We are ushered to the stage by security guards and wave as we are presented to the VIP party. The British ambassador, the president of Sailing China, the Chairman of this and Secretary of the other. I can't remember them all; there were a lot! Sir Robin and William Ward are amongst them too. We are presented with red scarves and red stuffed horses with the Clipper race and Qingdao logo embroidered on *(it is the Chinese year of the horse)*. Skipper is presented with a bright red brushed cotton Cape, with gold embroidered Qingdao logos. Speeches are translated into Chinese in an instant over the PA and Skipper gives his 'quality rather than quantity' speech as always. He actually says hello and welcome in well-rehearsed Chinese which gets massive cheers. We get stuck into another media scrum as the speeches finish and we are ushered towards the yacht club building some 100 meters or so away. The security guards start escorting us there, but most of us break ranks to greet to friends and family on the dock side. We subsequently get caught in the crowds and it takes us forever to get to the yacht club, signing autographs and stopping for photos, once you stop it is impossible to move again as the crowds close in. At one point I am handed a baby and a crowd gathers to take pictures of me with it; I feel responsible and nervous until it is taken back. Eventually we reach the yacht club where there is food and drinks laid out for us. Before anyone does anything we all strip down in the middle of the room; all of us still have full sailing thermals and ocean foulies on and we are burning up now indoors!

We sit down and take a breath, then we do what we always do when we first get off the boat. Hoover up as much food and drink as is put in front of us. As the calm starts to dawn we all look like we are going to fall asleep; everyone has been up all night and is totally done in from the trip. A friend from the shore support team of Mission Performance wanders over, and hands me a hotel room key, it's from Anthony whom I was going to share a room with, with a note attached *"sorry I missed you mate, I had to leave early, room all sorted, square up in San Francisco"*

Anthony shall forever be a legend for this, such a perfect moment, made even greater later that morning when I check in and found a really nice bottle of red wine for me in the massive suite he has upgraded me to, legend matey!

The hotel turns out to be a much needed sanctuary for a few days after the race; breakfast is excellent, the pool and sauna amazing and I get some really well earned rest in between the normal boat maintenance workload, corporate sailing and events we are required to attend. I get out for a half day into the city and see a couple of sights, but mainly use what little free time we get for some welcome R&R; I swim every day and walk everywhere. The next race is by far the biggest one and I want to be as fit and ready as I can.

The food we experience is excellent, chicken feet, some unrecognisable fish and meat which is varying in degrees of delicious. I have a couple of really good Skype chats with Mum and Dad and a really long chat with Siobhan too, she is struggling with becoming a teenager and I really miss being around at home to help her through this. Her Mum is doing an amazing job with this as she always has done, but it would be nice to be more involved right now. I talk to her straight and as an adult, I have done this since she was really young and I think she appreciates it. I share what advice I can and tell her to just be happy in whatever she does. The sense of missing her is deeper than ever now, I have been away for nearly seven months and it's getting harder each time we speak. I hadn't expected it to be this hard.

At the prize giving, we are treated to a mixture of Western and local food & drink, and as always the Clipper race fleet crew make pretty short work of this. The prize giving has the same level of ceremony as our arrival with wall to wall VIPs and speeches, media scrum all around us. We collect our second prize trophy and pennants; much welcomed and we are justly proud of these. We are presented with beautiful gold boxes each tied with equally beautiful ribbons. It turns out to be thermal underwear! A random prize giving gift, but excellent quality and almost all of us wear them when we leave for the next race. Sir Robin is presented with a magnificent bronze bust of himself as a seventieth birthday present; the sculptor and the British ambassador present it to him and he is visibly moved. There is an excellent reception for this, much applause and cheering from the crews and the race office team. I chat with him about it later and he still looks clearly touched. It's great to see such a well-travelled and worldly wise man being totally human and emotional.

Qingdao to San Francisco
The big one

The night before race departure, after our race briefings and final boat prep, I pack and sort my kit and take it to the boat to save some time and hassle in the morning for an early start. We are treated to the most amazing sunset which I stay for a while and enjoy; I take a couple of great pictures and share them on Facebook with a departure note. I can feel the tension really building once again. You can sense it in conversations with other crew. I can not sleep; I listen to some music, drink tea, and eventually I drift off and sleep soundly for a few hours. I feel slightly sick when I wake; it's time for the big one now. North Pacific. This has always bothered me since I signed up for the race. All the big incidents and accidents on previous races have happened here, many people have been very badly hurt before and the boat crew numbers taking part in this race are reflective of this. Some boat race crews are as low as 12 or 13. We are lucky to have 17, which includes a sea cadet trainer guest and a media cameraman. I think about the race ahead and it fills me with dread. Why should I feel like this? I am trained, experienced and fully prepared for this. I am a stubborn person so I am highly unlikely to back out, so they are slightly irrational thoughts really. But even so, it is still a tough one to commit to. I get up, go for an early swim to think more clearly about this before a 06:00 breakfast. I am at the restaurant at 05:50 and they graciously serve me coffee as they finish the buffet preparation. I grab a table for 12 and it is not long before it is filled with crew friends from several different boats. We have a sociable chat over breakfast but no one is really looking forward to this race and most of the worlders just want to get it over with. I have by now sorted this in my mind. I have convinced myself I am actually now looking forward to this race. Nothing adventurous & rewarding I have ever done before has been easy, climbing mountains, running marathons, completing triathlons are all hard, but that's why I do them. The work and career I chose, was intensely hard at times, but again that's one of the reasons I enjoy it so much. I enjoy the feeling of stress, personal achievement & success that goes with it. Always having adventure stories to tell afterwards. I signed up to circumnavigate, which is extremely tough, which is why so few people achieve it. This particular ocean crossing is one of the reasons many who set out fail to complete the circumnavigation. So I have fully sorted this now in my mind. I am here to circumnavigate, I want to have an epic crossing with many stories to share as part of this great adventure, let's bring it on and get going.

I say my goodbyes to crew friends early as we prepare, leave the hotel and make ready the boats. Once the massive start ceremony starts here there will be no time to socialise, so I make a point of seeing as many of my friends as I can before the music starts up. We are running around a little too with some last minute repairs. Our main sea cock, which allows sea water into the boat, to feed the heads, engine and generator, without which, we cannot use any of these facilities, is still on its way back from being repair welded, but has not yet arrived at the boat. It's a five minute job to fit it, but without it fully fitted and tested we don't sail. As we set off to the stage, the engineer with it in his hand passes us on his way to the boat, talk about cutting it fine with this one!

The teams assemble and file up to the stage in the crew colours to a serenade of Chinese drums and battle music. Each Skipper wearing their red cape and scarf, carrying the good luck pennant flag staffs we were given on arrival. We are wearing red foulies and purple team fleece. The sun is out and in a group protected from the biting wind it's really quite warm and we are opening up our tops to vent the fleece where we can. There are massive crowds all around and the drums and music really get things going. It feels quite emotional, with the build up to this race we are about to get a good luck farewell and send off. I am feeling nervous but really just want to get it on now and feel tense with the time we take standing around for speeches etc. This isn't fair really and I try to take in the moment some more. It is all well-choreographed with staged arrival and welcome of the various VIP guests and speakers, there are many speeches with the British ambassador, the Chairman of sailing events China etc etc. Mid-way through the ambassador's speech there is a commotion off to our left. A call for a medic goes out as someone has fainted in the heat. It turns out to be Pete Stirling, Skipper of Jamaica Get All Right. Not a great start to his race campaign, but we sympathise with him. We are struggling with the dress code and sun, he was wearing a Cape and scarf too!

The Chairman of Sailing China starts us with a green flare from the stage to massive cheers and the music starts up again. We file back to the boats, feeling really emotional now and a bit tearful as we get back on board. We are first boat to slip, our battle song strikes up and we reverse, turn and head out of the harbour. We quickly drop the lines and fenders down below to stash for the trip as we always do.

All around, on the harbour walls and dockside the crowds are massive, waving and cheering, it is a fantastic send off. Still feeling emotional I high five Richard Dawson with a big smile, he hugs me and bursts into tears, *"what is it matey?"* I ask, *"we're going home"* he says. This is a massive turning point in the race for him, heading east, across the date line and back to the western world it's too much build up for him. Everyone on the race has differing horizons and ambitions, for RD this is one his emotional horizons. We both have a really good cry. One or two other crew take the piss, Michelle & Suzie come over and give us both a hug and we share the stories of going home. We all agree we are most looking forward to getting this one over and done with as soon as possible. Roll on San Francisco.

We await the parade formation, when we receive news that Team Garmin are still on the dock with yet another problem, we cruise around in circles for an hour or so frustratingly awaiting them joining us. Such a shame for Team Garmin, they are on their forth Skipper already and have had way more than their fair share of bad luck. They are a fantastic team, so strong and together, just continually plagued with bad luck. Eventually they come out to join us and we all set off along the shore around the various media, chase, race and spectator boats in our formation. This part of race start is always a spectacular sight and great fun, but frustrating and time consuming too. It's incredibly difficult to concentrate on racing during this, I really feel for professional sportsmen and women, suffering the massive demands which the modern media fuelled world puts upon them. The start line is laid and we start to round & circle each other as the countdown starts, this is the really exciting part of racing. These big boats Skipping around each other within touching distance at times, all vying for best position. We nail it once again; Sean is a tactical genius at start line sailing. GREAT Britain second and Qingdao third over the line. It's only by a few meters, and on a 6,000mile race it is pretty irrelevant really. But it's a moral victory and we allow a moments celebration on board. We are beating out of Qingdao, directly into the wind, we tack a few times holding onto our lead. The fog closes in, the wind dies off, and as we approach the VTS traffic separation scheme, where there is an enormous amount of traffic today, the race office call off the race, suspended until the weather improves for safety reasons.

We motor for the rest of the day and overnight in a sort of planned formation, Qingdao slip back from the group as they pick up some fishing debris which takes them several hours to free out from their rudders. We awake to the most beautiful red moon and sunrise. Duty Skipper Pete Stirling calls the one hour start line warning and we prepare for the Le Mans start, which we nail again. Off the line, away smart, a few boat lengths ahead after the first few hours. We have a code 1 spinnaker up after the 10 minute compulsory sail plan hold at the start. We peel this to a code 2 after a few hours, which is easier to handle and gives us better speeds, around 14ktts right on the money and on target for our first way point across the Yellow Sea, to the bottom of the Korean straights, just off the southern tip of Japan. It's very choppy across the straights with some tricky navigation around Japan and I get a few sleepless off watch sessions, keeping an eye on this. We are in the lead group with GREAT Britain, Old Pulteney, Switzerland and Qingdao as we turn the corner and head north. We settle into the 'black snake' current which runs up the eastern side of Japan and pretty soon we are doing 15-20ktts, surfing hard all the way, it's good to be back doing these speeds again, first time since the southern ocean.

Conor has rejoined us back on board, but is still really not fit & well and so I am back as watch leader again, with Kristi working as my assistant. We discuss and agree to switch Kristi and I for the second half of the race for her to gain watch leader experience too, which I am really pleased about, she has worked extremely hard since we left London and really deserves this opportunity. I am really looking forward to supporting her as assistant during her first gig as leader too.

We enter the first of two really tasty sessions of weather and for 36 hours or so the breeze is 70+Ktts with some gusts of 90+ in between. We switch between Yankee only and stay sail only as the wind changes. On one of the big sail drops, I get my finger caught in a hank as we remove them and I'm thinking it might be broken, I just strap it up for now and try to be careful. It's a tricky helm and there are only a few of us keen to helm in these conditions which makes it quite tiring. After an hour in big seas you are exhausted and ready to drop, then sometime less than an hour later you are back on again. There is nothing to hold onto, only the helm which you cannot let go of. I fancy a piece of chewing gum on one session but cannot get to it in my pocket for over an hour. On tip toe on the helm board it is like standing on an upstairs windowsill hanging onto the curtains, with little or no stability. I push against the wheel occasionally and set my back into the protective A-frame, but this hurts too. I remember off road driver training about not putting your thumbs in the wheel, which is useful here too, to save them from the retching they might otherwise get. My finger hurts like hell still, it is swollen and very badly bruised now; I can't quite close a grip on that hand and struggle with zips and fastenings.

We lose the lead to GREAT Britain overnight by only a few miles. We start getting short on numbers with a nasty bug on board, Jason, Nick, Suzie, Richard and Keith are all down and not on watch. Skipper joins my watch and Tristan the media cameraman traveling with us on this leg also joins the other watch to make up the numbers. Next day on his first watch back on deck, Richard strains his back and can hardly move, we get him into his bunk, he is in real agony and stays there for several days. When he does appear he sits carefully in the saloon and has mad conversations with people several times over, repeating himself with the strong pain killers he is taking.

We receive news that PSP and Jamaica Get All Right have both had medivac evacuations of crew to the Japanese coast guard. One with a shoulder injury from a fall on deck and one with severe chest pains and possible angina. It reminds us of the fragility of our environment as we head further offshore, I spare some thoughts for the angina sufferer, another week and we would have been several days miniMum from medical help and could be very tricky place to be with that condition. We are lucky so far with our injury lists on this one, apart from Richard we are still in reasonable shape.

The second storm hits us and records winds of well over 100ktts at one point, it blows itself out pretty quickly in a little over a day and half we are back into lighter stuff again. The temperature drops and on night watch we spend maxiMum 45 minutes on deck and rotate down below to stay warm. I have really cold feet, possibly for the first time ever in my life, my toes are frozen and even my now damp sleeping bag cannot warm them. When they do warm a few days later they really hurt for a whole day.

162

After the storm passes we have the most amazing star lit night followed by an awesome sunrise, still biting cold but spectacularly beautiful. We have gained more mileage on GREAT Britain and OneDLL are closing in on us, but overall we still think we are in a good place, leading the northern pack on route to the scoring gate, six boats all lined up almost astern, with the balance of the fleet spread out to the southern end of the gate approach. We feel confident, but it is going to be close for gate points on this one. We shift our clocks, the first of many hours forward to adjust our boat time to best fit the daylight hours for working on deck. Generally we just ignore time zones and make boat time work for us as best we can. At one watch change over, we inflate Susie's dry suit with her inside it and she dances to Rizzle Kicks, Mama do the Hump, we laugh until we cry at this over lunch and it lightens the mood. One of the funniest thing I have seen in a very long time, and the tune for me now will always be her in the moment. It makes me smile every time I hear it now.

Qingdao have been struck by lightning overnight, it sends a flash of light through their Nav station, along the boom and takes out all the lights throughout the boat. It has knocked out all their electronics and most of their comms systems, which takes them several days and a very slow talk through on the one surviving satellite telephone by the experts to repair in a fashion.

Injury and illness is still keeping our watches painfully short. We switch out back to the code 2 and spend the day whooshing along at 20+ktts with some absolutely amazing surfing experiences. She is a real handful to helm and Skip and I helm through our watch at night, with Nick and Charlie helming the other watch. When the scheds arrive next day, we achieve our first ever 300 mile day. We have sailed 300 miles many times before, but not VMG on target, this one is ratified by the race office and is a small but very significant victory for us. We still search for the elusive over 30ktts max boat speed achievement which has evaded us to this point.

As is often the case, we push the limits of the code 2 for a few days again to maintain speed. We broach a few times and it gets really exciting; at one point we reverse broach whilst I am helming and we recover in what seems to be only split second. I check with the deck to see everyone is ok. My hand and finger are incredibly painful though having tried to hold this tight with both hands. On the next watch, we get a loose spinnaker sheet trapped under the boat and it takes 9 of us over two hours to free it; we are really properly cold and dog tired after this one. Throughout the recovery, most of us are on the foredeck, the boat is still racing along at full chat and the waves are crashing over us. Chris climbs out onto the bow sprit once or twice, with me in support in the pull pit, hanging onto him tightly. Whilst he is out there, the bow dives underwater several times and it is all we can both do just to hold on. It's truly exhilarating and not in the least bit scary, we know what we are doing, we work together closely looking out for each other and we are both clipped on at all times. Nick, the opposite watch leader and I shuffle our watches around and shift the watch times to try and give everyone a little rest where we can.

Checking the scheds, we appear to have a 30+ mile lead now, so we go back to a Yankee to give ourselves a small break, even with this we are still flying along at 15+ktts. We take around 24 hours rest, whilst still sailing hard under white sails it is none the less easier on the crew onboard the boat when we don't have spinnakers up.

When we go back to code 2 again, immediately we run into difficulty, getting a lazy sheet stuck right under the boat and around the keel. It's key we get this back out quickly before it gets anywhere near the rudders. We assemble two teams one for each side and we work the sheet forward under the boat. It is incredibly tiring work and takes every ounce of effort each time we call for a haul upwards and forwards. The weight of the water flowing under the boat against the sheet is immense, as we Skip along at almost 16ktts. We rest briefly in between each lift. As we near the front of the boat, we free up a loop and pass it out to Chris on the bowsprit again, with me back in the no1 position as before. As the boat lifts up between waves he tries to swing the sheet out from under the hull. It takes three or four attempts and, as it comes up, we let a small cheer go. Now we feed it back down the lazy side and let it go back into play. All the time, we have been watching the loops and twists around the deck making sure no one stands on or in them, one slip could easily break your leg as the sheet lets go.

The wind builds as the day progresses and we enjoy ever increasing speeds over 20+ktts regularly. We are well into the grey area for flying the code 2 now, on the extreme of the wind levels it can cope with, but the speeds are immense and it is giving us great mileage. We stick with it until after dark. Then, disaster strikes. Minutes after I hand over the helm to Skipper, the code 2 flogs and, in an instant, it disintegrates like a tissue in the wind. It almost explodes open and is clearly very badly torn into several pieces.

We go straight to an 'all hands' call for an immediate Yankee hoist and code2 drop. The Yankee is very quickly rigged and ready to go, then the spinnaker retrieval line is missing; it's played out over the side and running in the water. We retrieve the lazy sheet and run it around to use as the recovery line, it takes us a few minutes and confuses the deck teams slightly. All the while, the Yankee is being rigged and ready. We call for a 'go', everyone is ready, agreed? Yes, go! We hoist the Yankee and it's going well, half way up in the hoist the sheet is rigged the wrong side of the preventer. Bugger. Immediate re-drop; I grab the sheet, untie it, pass it to Wendy who runs it back around the outside of the preventer and hands it back, I tie a super quick 'bowline under pressure' (everyone's favourite knot!) we go back to the hoist and it's up in double quick time. All this while, the code2 is flogging away and tearing further, one end of it is now in the water and another big piece is wrapped around the forestay. We go for the drop and it takes ages, splitting the deck teams Nick & I liaise together and call the positions; teams move around the boat working on different pieces of the spinnaker at the same time. Eventually it's inboard and looks a real mess. We reckon its trashed way beyond repair, but there is no way we can really tell this whilst still on the water so we just stuff it into its bag and down below out of the way. Everyone is really disappointed; we have done so well with spinnakers so far on the race. We have had some big nightmares, but this one was our first real proper 'kitemare'. We later discover several other boats have trashed their code2 on this race too, in similar circumstance. OneDLL already took a 6 point penalty to replace theirs, it looks like we might now need to do the same. We go back to white sails again for a few days and lick our wounds.

We don't have long to lick them, the next storm is approaching and it's a big one this time. 55ktts constant, gusting to well over 70ktts. We prepare as we have done so many times before and change down our Yankee sails early. It passes without major drama. I get washed down the deck at one point into the Yankee car, badly bruise a knee and cut the opposite shin, it's reasonably painful, but it's minor really and I just carry on. The storm gives us some really tasty seas for a while and makes for some hard work night shifts. I really enjoy helming in the storms, but getting to and from the helm along the decks is a real challenge and for a while on our watch there is only Chris and I who will helm in the storm at night. We alternate and work together, rotating in 30-40 minute sessions, spotting for each other in between. It's exhausting but rewarding work.

We approach the gate from the north as the storm passes and the win abates a little. The boats in the south have had a great final run into the gate, with the wind on their backs and their spinnakers up. We watch the scheds as they creep up and grab all the points. We end up 5th through the gate. Bitterly disappointed and really down after working so hard. Sometimes the winds are a lottery and just play out that way. You make a certain amount of your own luck, but sometimes it's just not enough. We settle into the remainder of the race and head for the 'date line,' our next navigational horizon.

As we approach the date line, with the weather still building, we have settled into a starboard tack on top of a big low pressure system. We know it is going to pass and we prepare for the wind shift. We wait an agonising 36 hours, expecting it to happen at any time. It's an extremely frustrating time as we want to change course on the new wind. When it eventually happens, it happens suddenly. One minute we are Skipping along at 12ktts, then the wind shifts and tacks us over almost instantly. We pull the main across and tack the head sails as quickly as we can and proceed on the opposite tack. It's the most amazing sensation to be absolutely on the edge of a weather system. We look at them on the charts and see their shapes and interaction. But here it was playing out for us in full view, switching from one weather pattern to another like a road intersection. The weather patterns continue to build and another violent storm is fast approaching us, we will need to change down head sails again very soon, and this sail change will be very difficult in these conditions.

We cross over the date line. It takes our navigation electronics a moment or two to settle back down and we joke about millennium bugs. It's now the 30th March all over again for us. A truly weird sensation. I can just about cope with understanding the date line on an airplane, but in a sailing boat it is even more pronounced and takes a little while to get our heads around it on board. It throws our rota into disarray and the food day bags now work one day behind! Calculating time difference to UTC is strange. From +12 to -12 hours but now on a different day! Yesterday I was preparing for it being my Mum's birthday tomorrow. Now today is tomorrow and her birthday is still tomorrow, really! This is confusing?

Later this day, the absolute unthinkable and everyone's very worst nightmare happens to us.

Man Overboard

Early morning, Sunday 30th March 2014, mid-way across the North pacific. We are around half way through race 10 from Qingdao to San Francisco. Having sailed over 2,500 miles on this race already, there are well over 2,000 miles still to go. Our nearest land is probably Midway in the Hawaiian Islands, over 1,700 miles due south. Whilst we had been in Qingdao, the Clipper race media team had been using the line *'where the astronauts are your nearest neighbours'* to describe this race. Right now, with the possible exception of anyone exploring the Arctic this is probably true as they pass over head a little over 300 miles above us.

Sean, Kristi & I are standing together around the port side helm discussing the merits of shifting to a polled out Yankee. The wind is around 40ktts coming pretty much from behind us. It would probably ease later at some point, but the sea state was still rough and actually seemed to be getting worse at the moment. Waves now well over 8 meters high are breaking over the deck occasionally. The air temperature was around 11degC. The salt water frosted wind chill however, takes the real temperature on deck considerably lower than this. The sea temperature was below 09degC and every big wave and wash of water over the deck takes your breath away.

There had been some massive squalls beating over us throughout the night. The last one, a few hours ago, had been extremely cold & ferocious with terrific, battering hailstones. We knew there were many more of these still to come on our race to San Francisco. We had been tested hard already today. We were all cold, wet & tired. It had been a busy morning in challenging conditions. We had been working hard, had not had any hot drinks for quite a while and were all really looking forward to getting back down below for a hot lunch in a couple of hours' time.

After a short discussion, we settled to go for the polled out Yankee and set about preparing to rig the pole. The wind speeds were consistently too high for anything else and we could easily get into trouble in the next squall. The whole crew were tired & cold, and we reckoned we could make better speeds with less effort with the Yankee on a pole. The first task was to remove the Yankee 2 from the forestay, replacing it with a smaller and easier to handle Yankee 3. I was watch leader for our watch, with Kristi as assistant watch leader. It was the first time we had worked together in these roles and I had really enjoyed working together with Kristi. We were due to swap our roles in a few days' time. It would be Kristi's first watch leader opportunity. Her infectious, youthful enthusiasm and energy were contagious on deck, and her physical strength for one so slight was truly admirable. I was feeling confident and happy on deck too right now, moving around the deck quickly and confidently.

In discussion we agreed I would go forward and work with Sean. There was no great debate about it, I felt pretty good today, Kristi was feeling the cold and was happy to helm. I felt really happy with Kristi helming at this time whilst we went forward. It gives you a much greater sense of confidence having someone in control of the boat you really trust whilst you are in an exposed position right up on the bow.

Sean and I made our way carefully and slowly up onto the foredeck together; both clipped on. We set about un-hanking the Yankee. Just getting to the bow had been tough, we were bouncing along amongst some really big waves and getting proper wet as we went forward. It's times like these you really need your wits about you, just moving around the foredeck and staying on your feet is a workout, before you even start the job in hand.

Sean stepped out into the forward No1 position, on the outside of the pulpit, I was directly behind him assisting in the no2 position, just inside the pulpit, right at the very front of the boat. Sean & I had done this job together many times before and each of us had operated in either position. We didn't discuss what we were doing, we just got on with the job in hand. Sean was there first so he got out onto the bow sprit. I am pretty sure, had I arrived first, I probably would have done the same and the day may have turned out different for us both. In truth, I was happy Sean had done this though. Today was a pretty big one and we wanted to get on with this quickly. He is much stronger than me and we would get this done considerably quicker this way. The Yankee was already down and tied off. I shifted the head of the sail as far over to starboard as I could, trying to make myself some space on the port side of the foredeck. There really wasn't much space left for me, and I shuffled my left foot around to find somewhere secure to put it. I stepped out over the guard wire with one foot, wedged it into the fairlead on one side. The other leg, I kind of wrapped under the sail as best I could, shuffling my foot around finding some non-slip to steady myself on. With one hand around the forestay I started to heave the head of the sail forward so Sean could unclip the hanks, taking as much of the weight of the sail to allow him to do so.

Right away we ran into difficulty. One of the first of the brass hanks which fasten the Yankee to the forestay, was twisted and refusing to open. We fumbled, yanked, heaved and pulled it around between us as best we could, both of us straining and swearing at it, we just couldn't shift it. The hanks are under enormous stress. They bend and twist, wearing around the edges and are exposed to extreme levels of salt corrosion in this super exposed position. They are actually designed to fail, made from brass so they become the primary weak point, wearing away slowly in order to protect the rest of the rigging. In every stopover we scrub and lubricate them. Replacing any that even remotely don't work properly. It is inevitable however to have hank trouble mid race, given the exposed, rough, salt encrusted life they lead. I gestured to Sean I would go back and get a hank claw tool to assist with this, which he acknowledged, clearly understanding what I was doing. Kneeling down and unclipping my safety line, with one arm wrapped around a stanchion to steady myself. I turned on my knees on the port side just below the stay sail to retreat from the foredeck and get the tool. Chris was right behind me and asked what we needed, I shouted close to his ear in the wind, *"we needed a hank tool"*, *"OK I'll go dude"* he shouted back, turning as he heads off to get it.

Sill kneeling down I clipped back on to the starboard side jackstay on the high side, turned around and stood back up really slowly to continue working with Sean removing the head sail. It was freezing cold and wet. We had already experienced a few massive soakings in the short time we had been up on the foredeck. Our hands were sore with the cold, we just wanted to get on with the job in hand quickly. The pulpit is no place to delay, mess around or work slowly. It is a torrid and uncomfortable environment. As the boat lifts and bucks on the waves, the bow takes the brunt of the crashing. Every move the bow makes below your feet is massively exaggerated. Usually you see the waves coming or feel the roll of the boat. It's like standing right on the very end of a see-saw as its bounces up and down beneath you. Sometimes it takes your body longer to come down than the deck your standing on and you crash down upon it as it comes back up to meet you. You need to really hang on tight occasionally, just to stay connected. As I stood up, I looked down to search again for my foot holds where they had been previously.

Almost immediately as I turned around and looked down, the boat lurched violently over to starboard. There was no warning of this, just a massive wave I hadn't seen from the port side throwing us right over onto one side. I saw the head sails and forestay pass me by to one side. In an instant I was thrown over the side and into the water. The Yankee acting as a slippery slide for me to slip right over the top of. It happened so unbelievably quickly, there was no moment's loss of balance to consider first, no time to think about holding on or grabbing hold of anything. One second my feet are on the boat; the next my head is in the freezing waters, closely followed by the rest of me in a fraction of a second as I dive underwater into the ice cold and reach instinctively for a breath that isn't there.

I cannot begin to believe just how quickly this happened. It was a flash, a fraction of a second and an instant dunking. Sean recounts to him it appeared like slow motion. He reaches out his hand instinctively to perhaps steady me as I fall, or as a futile and instinctive attempt to catch me with one hand. It is absolutely futile though, and my heels clip his hand as I rush past him head first.

The fixed CCTV cameras on the boat cannot see me at the very bow behind the stay sail where we are working and where I actually go over from. There is however a go pro camera on the helm frame facing forwards which was running at the time. We had been having some fun earlier, using this to capture some great footage of us working hard helming in the really big seas. It captures the actual moment. If you look really carefully at the footage, you can just about make out me going out over the rail, and see the first stages of the man overboard procedures unfold on deck before the battery dies a few minutes later. The first part of the footage shows Sean rushing back to the helm, passing almost over the top of Chris whom is now absolutely transfixed on me, pointing a full arm outstretched, calling range and direction. As Sean passes the companionway he ducks his head down the hatch and screams as loud as he can *"man overboard! All hands on deck!"*

All Hands on Deck!

Sean continues at double quick speed back to the port side helm. As he wings past the backstay his face changes as he sees me out in the water already 80m+ away from the boat. Up until this point he is sure I am still clipped on and hanging off the bow on the high side. His face changes dramatically as he looks back and sees this. A video footage image which I have since seen many times and shall never ever forget, his face in this image still haunts me slightly when I think about it.

Chris starts to make his way back slowly along the rail. He has one hand gripping the guard wire tightly for balance, the other outstretched pointing clearly. He can see me in the water and has started shouting distance and direction. He is absolutely fixed upon me and stands tall and fast. *"Thirty meters, seven o'clock"* he shouts, the guys back in cockpit can barely hear him above the wind. *"Sixty metres, six o'clock"* he shouts again almost straight away. Sean jumps onto the helm, all the time he is looking out to the port side to where Chris is pointing. The wind is 40ktts, gusting occasionally to well over 50ktts. Waves of more than 8m in height start to consume me as I drift away from the boat. A few seconds later, two really big waves pass over me. *"Hundred metres six o'clock"* Chris shouts. *"Don't take your eyes off him!"* Skipper shouts back. Sean's experience working as lifeboat crew in Derry is about to stand him in good stead managing this situation. He knows only too well more than most just how quickly one can lose sight of a casualty in the water. A few seconds later, Chris drops his arm briefly and shouts what nobody wants to hear *"lost visual"* then with a slight air of panic he adds *"I can't see him Skip!"* Charlie climbs up joining him on the rail. Even the climb up is hard work. They both concentrate hard on the spot where visual was lost which Chris continues to point at. Both hard glaring; still no sight. Chris is pointing all the time, and continues to do so for ages. *"Still no visual!"* he shouts, his words now slower & strained.

Down below crew feel surreal, we have only ever heard an MOB shout called in training or during a drill, never for real. Everyone takes it seriously, jumping to action in double quick time. Some crew are eating, they jump up, dropping their food bowls in the sink, some grab wet weather gear, all grab life jackets and safety lines, pulling them on as they exit up onto deck. Some crew are sleeping and just grab a life jacket on their way up onto deck.

In our training & drills, a full MOB drill from start to finish lasts about 20-30 minutes. The boat makes a figure of eight course back around to the spot where the MOB went over. It closes in onto an upwind drift approach from the windward side, a rescue swimmer goes over the side, lowered on twin halyards with a recovery strop. He places the stop around the casualty and is winched back up over the rails. Realistic but quite straight forward in training.

Wendy is first up on deck, only seconds after the call. She is on mother watch and was in the galley serving lunch to the off watch. She is still bare foot, wearing only a thermal top and leggings, Michelle is next on deck, right behind Wendy seconds later, she is dressed in leggings too but with boots on, she pulls on a foulie top as she exits the companion way carrying her lifejacket. Charlie is close behind them in trousers and just a lightweight waterproof jacket. Between them they immediately start to prep for a stay sail drop, and start to bring the main sail in square. The stay sail is not on a winch; we were in the process of switching winches around with the work we were doing on deck when I went over, so this causes a delay. It is rectified with minimal fuss, in a few seconds and is down on the deck before you know it has even happened. Down below, Jason grabs a climbing harness, rigging himself to go over the side. He has done this many time in training. In fact, Jason & I have done this together many times. At this point, he has no idea who is in the water or what the conditions are like up top. Nonetheless, he prepares to get wet. No discussion; no debate. As far as Jason is concerned, he is getting wet. A totally selfless act of extreme bravery. He knows how this works, he knows he is good at this and just gets on with the job of getting ready.

Skipper shouts for the button to be pressed and engine started. Both are well underway already. Down below, the button is already pressed and the engine is already running. The 'button'. Is a marker control button on our main navigation system. It marks an exact way point onto the electronic charts, which allows the boat crew to navigate right back to it, or around it, using it as a control point for a search pattern. It is critically important, in this situation, to know exactly where the casualty enters to water, to stand any chance of calculating where you might find them later. Conor is eating lunch as the call is made, he makes his way straight to the Nav station. Pressing the button and starting the engine, before he takes up a position in front of the screens and communication systems. He opens our ships log book and starts to write a log of details. As the boat is prepared for a search & rescue, he calls back up to Sean on the helm distance and bearing back to the way point. Sean is shouting all the time, calling for sail drops and winch grinding. He shouts to be heard clearly, with an air of confidence in his voice, not panic, all the time emphasising the urgency of his requests. He shouts back and forth to Conor, asking him to repeat almost everything. Its clear Sean can't hear him above the wind up on deck. Michelle steps over and takes up a now vital position by the Nav station hatch, acting as a critical communication relay between Sean on the helm, Conor in the Nav station and the crew on deck.

On the aft deck, Kristi is fighting trying to untangle the danbuoy. Every boat carries one of these. We refer to this and the life rings as 'toys'. Part of MOB procedure is to 'throw the toys out' into the water. Regardless of time and position, just get them out as quickly as possible when a man overboard is called. The theory being they would drift at the same rate as a casualty giving the search team a bigger target to look for. The dan-buoy is basically a floating flag pole. Ours is carbon fibre and around 10ft tall. It is attached to a horseshoe life ring with flashing lights reflective tape adorned all around it. The fluorescent purple flag on top of the pole, sitting high above the water line, would be much easier to see than a person's head down low in the water. The reflective tapes would be easy to find with a search light at night. In some respects, although considerably more traumatic an experience, had I gone overboard at night, it might have been easier to spot me, and I do mean might, with lights and reflective tape on both me and the dan-buoy. I was also carrying several high intensity torches and a waterproof camera with a flash, all of which could have assisted with signaling my position back to the boat.

With the main sail now pinned square and stay sail down on the deck. Skipper swings the boat hard around, to motor back on an immediate fast fly past just downwind of my last known position. At this point, he realises too this is going to be harder than he previously thought. Derry's engine is huge, but in these conditions heading straight back into wind, it is straining hard just to get the boat moving through the waves.

Nothing seen. Almost the full crew are now up on deck, with only one or two injured exceptions still down below. Skipper calls for all eyes to sea, marking an area for the next search. Everyone is glued to the spot, concentrating their view hard out to the waves. At this point, only a few of the crew actually know who they are looking for, some others start to work it out. *"Who's missing?"* someone asks. Word goes around that it's me and the search continues. I'd like to think it's totally irrelevant who you are looking for, you look just as hard and just as fast. On the other hand, being clear on the colours you are looking for will be a great help for sure.

I was wearing a bright orange Henri Lloyd dry suit, with a fluorescent yellow hood. Even in these colours, visual contact is lost at considerably less than 150 meters. Visibility is good, clear easily to beyond 500 meters. However the white water breaking wave tops, grey skies and occasional sunshine make for a really difficult sea state to spot anything in. The enormous waves continue to shield me from view.

Skipper requests Chris climbs up onto the A frame, at the back of the boat to get more height for searching. He climbs as high as he can, clipping a short safety line strop around the top of the frame to lean himself against. Wendy is standing up on the rear helm guard frames, her legs braced around it to hold on. She has binoculars and is scanning back and forth across the horizon. *"Get someone up the mast"* Skipper calls next, *"quickly please"*. Kristi jumps straight to it, the same as Jason had done earlier; no self-thoughts or concerns and another selfless and immediate voluntary act of extreme bravery. She harnesses up and gets ready quickly, then is hoisted aloft, up to the first set of spreaders from where she can get a higher 360 view of the surrounding seas. She would now stay aloft for well over an hour; her hands are already cold and it's really painful for her to grip holding onto anything. She is extremely exposed here too and gets pummeled hard during the storm. By the time she gets back down onto the deck later she is totally exhausted requiring assistance from others to get down below deck.

We are mid North Pacific, over 2,000 miles from land in either direction east & west. Our closest landfall is the uninhabited islands in the Bering Sea. The closest inhabited land is the Hawaiian Island of Midway well over 1,500 miles away to our south. Two mayday calls are placed by Conor in reasonably quick succession. *"Mayday, Mayday, Mayday, this is charlie victor three zero, charlie victor three zero, charlie victor three zero, we are at 41degrees, 43 minutes, decimal 213 north, 179degrees, 11 minutes decimal 451 west"*. Followed by our MMSI number. He continues. *"We have a man overboard and require immediate assistance, we do not have a visual on the casualty, we require immediate assistance, mayday,*

mayday, mayday". He pauses and waits for a few moments. Nothing is heard. He waits a moment longer, takes a deep breath and repeats the message word for word. This time he is filmed by Tristan. Conor doesn't notice Tristan filming him, he is so engrossed concentrating hard on what he is doing. He finishes broadcasting and pauses. Silence, nothing heard again. He prepares himself for another broadcast, thinking this will be his last broadcast, when suddenly the VHF speaker cracks open loud and clear *"Charlie victor three zero, charlie victor three zero, charlie victor three zero, this is charlie victor two zero, charlie victor two zero, charlie victor two zero"*. It is OneDLL, responding to his call. They agree to switch to Channel M1 and go straight into conversation without radio pleasantries. *"Hi Conor It's Caty"* (OneDLL RTW crew member Catriona Savage) *"calling from DLL"*. She discusses with Conor the situation, marking down in their log the facts and relaying details to Olly Cotterell, OneDLL Skipper, who is on their helm. They are around an hour away, maybe more in these conditions. No-one else responds to Connors calls. This is not a busy sea area, there is little or no commercial traffic here and with the exception of the Clipper fleet, it would appear we are alone for several hundred miles all around. Tristan's footage of the second mayday call, is used in the later media coverage, it looks staged and rehearsed. It is however, absolutely the real thing; a testament to Conor's professionalism and his calm approach to this. OneDLL contact Qingdao, who are the next closest of the race fleet. They are probably still too far away to support, but go into full standby mode anyway and start to divert.

As I fall from the bow and plunge into the icy water, I hold my breath and brace myself. Waiting for the safety line to snag tight. I reach both of my arms across my chest, holding tightly onto my lifejacket. I am expecting this to hurt. I have fallen in a harness whilst climbing training before. I know, whilst this is safe, it does still really hurt as your safety lines catch you. I re-surface instantly feeling a massive rush of ice cold water over my head and face. I am convinced this is me being dragged along by the safety line as I had expected to be. This has been one of my worst nightmares; I know it would take a minute or two to stop the boat. During this time, I would be dragged uncontrollably, probably underwater at high speed, pinned hard against the side of the boat. People drown in this situation and I have had very bad thoughts previously about this happening.

Immediately, I see the side of the boat rushing past in a flash of purple. I can feel myself sliding along the hull; it's slippery and glass smooth, flashing past me at high speed. I have absolutely no control of my position in the water. Instinctively, I reach a hand out and it slides fast along the hull like ice. I realise instantly I am away and no longer connected to the boat. There is a brief moment of panic and slight disappointment with myself to have gone overboard.

Then 'bang'. In an instant, a massive thud hits me. It spins me around and puts me right back under water. It takes me a few seconds to recover from this. As I re-surface again I can see the transom of the boat speeding away from me. I realise I have just been hit by the rudder as the boat passed over me. It hurts like hell, *"fuck, fuck, fuck!"* I say out loud! This is bad.

I feel a sudden sense of disappointment, not only have I gone overboard and somehow become disconnected from the boat, it's now run me over too! And it's hurt me really badly in the process. I really didn't need this too I think to myself, bloody bad luck and I start letting more expletives out loud again! Both my legs hurt really badly, the rudder had smashed right through both of them. For the first few moments I am convinced they are both broken. The pain is so intense and I grimace and grit my teeth hard, trying not to scream and cry. I wiggle my toes, the left ones wiggle OK, but hurt a lot. The right ones? No idea, I just can't feel them and it hurts even more. OK, so maybe only one leg is broken I think, maybe that's a bit better than I first thought! I try and bend my knees, same again, left seems sort of OK, hurts but is moving, right leg, no chance, can't bend it, can't feel it, can't wiggle toes. *"Fuck! That's definitely broken then"* I say out loud again.

The rudders on our boat are massive; at least a metre and a half high, around 5 inches thick at their widest point, tapered forward to a reasonably sharp leading edge to cut through the water at high speed. They are made of the same reinforced plastic as the hull of the boat, rock solid hard, absolutely no give or flex in them at all. This is just like getting hit by the edge of steel plate at 30mph. I watch the boat disappearing off into the distance for a few seconds wondering now if anyone saw me go over. I heard no shouts, and saw no one on the way over the side. Then I feel cold as I remember the last conversation I just had with Sean, telling him that I was going below to get the hank tool. If he just thinks that's where I am now! *"Shit, now I'm in big trouble"*

My mind rushes over the facts so quickly, I can hardly think straight. Sean thinks I am down below getting a hank tool, I watch as the boat speeds further and further away. How long before they realise I am not on deck? No-one saw me? No-one knows I'm overboard? Shit this is it? I'm on my own now?

As my mind clears, I suddenly realise how quiet it is here in the water on my own. On board there is always noise, the boat rushing through the water, the wind blowing around your ears, the sails tightening, people shouting to be heard as they work together. I can still hear Sean's shouts and the conversation I just had with Chris is ringing loud in my ears. Suddenly, violently and without warning, all of this noise stopped. After the commotion of the fall, and the rudder, it's quiet now; eerily and spookily quiet. So what happens now? Chris gets back with the hank tool in a few minutes, will they realise then? Will he notice I am not around? Or will Sean and he just carry on with the job wondering where I have gone? I play through in my head their hypothetical conversations as they start to carry on with the job I was previously doing. I feel alone and totally lonely. I am really worried!

On board OneDLL, Olly calls for all hands on deck and they set about getting their sails down. They already have their Yankee poled out and it takes them a good few minutes to get the pole down & stowed away. They report in their log that the wind is 40Ktts+ and, by the time they drop their stay sail, preparing to divert it has increased to 70Ktts+. The sea state is getting mountainous. They have ceased racing and are starting to make best speed under motor to our location. Olly asks Caty if the race office have been informed or Falmouth Coastguard. She checks with Conor who confirms not yet. Caty agrees with him the she will do so on our behalf and act as a relay with the race office from here on. She telephones Mark Light, deputy race director on the Satellite telephone.

<u>This is Mark's account of the early hours of his longest day;</u>
Just before 01:00 local time, I wake up to my mobile phone ringing less than 12 inches from my ear. Since taking the job of Deputy Race Director for Clipper Ventures, I always sleep with my mobile phone switched on, fully charged and in the same position next to my bed.

Having been a professional sailor for many years and a former Race Skipper for Clipper Ventures in the 11/12 Clipper round the world Race (ironically for Derry~Londonderry), I am accustomed to being woke at all sorts of odd hours and with regularity. Nowadays, as with lots of offshore Skippers, I am quite expert at subsequently waking up very quickly and being able to react as normal as possible. As my phone rang this time, I immediately recognise the difference between its normal raucous 06:10 alarm and a normal ringing tone. I roll over reach out and answer in my normal manner *"Hello, Mark Light speaking"*

"Mark, this is Caty Savage from OneDLL. I am reporting that we have received a Mayday from CV30. They've had an MOB and have lost sight of the casualty" I can hear the urgency in her voice and can also hear the stress behind the composure flow of information. *"Fuck!"*

It takes me a few seconds to digest what I am hearing, then the sick feeling in my stomach hits me hard! Pure horror, personally, my worst living nightmare!

I am the main emergency contact for the Clipper race fleet when they are on the water racing and this is absolutely the phone call that I have always dreaded the most. I had often thought about this scenario and how I would react if, or when, it ever happened. During my time as Skipper I would always be thinking about the 'What If??' scenarios and playing certain 'disaster type' situations out in my head and I would regularly challenge my crew to do the same, particularly in the early parts of any race. I knew that this type of call or situation was one of, if not, the worst 'an MOB with no visual contact'. The chances of it happening grew with every Clipper Race, not anything to do with safety procedures, but purely the law of averages in sending more and more people sailing in the serious weather conditions often encountered this far offshore. I know first-hand from my time as Skipper, the high standards of safety and training that go into to every Clipper Race and I can honestly say with hand on heart that our standards of safety and training are unrivalled in the yachting industry and paramount to everything that we do.

I composed myself, then went into autopilot, gathering as much information as I could and as clearly as I could. I grabbed my notepad from my rucksack at the end of my bed and began my routine questions to Caty. I noted the time of call, 00:51 local time, the boats position (CV20) and noted that they were a good way away from the position of CV30. I quickly got details of the weather conditions on scene, (wind speed, direction, sea state, visibility, etc). I noted the course and speed of CV20 and quickly worked in my head how long it would take them to reach the position of CV30. My next question to Caty on CV20 was simple *"Who has gone overboard? Is it the Skipper?"*

"We don't know" came the reply and my heart sank further. I didn't' want to think of anybody going overboard in any conditions but the thought that it might be the Skipper would make an already dangerous situation even worse. I thanked Caty for all her information and instructed them to cease racing and make best speed towards CV30 to assist in the search and rescue. This was the decision already made by Olly Cotterell and the crew of CV20 but somehow I felt it necessary to enforce and make it official. We all knew the potential consequences of what we were all now fully involved in. I said that I would make all the calls to the necessary people outside of the immediate situation and that CV20 should stay in VHF contact with CV30 and keep me completely informed of any update no matter how insignificant it may seem. I asked them to call CV30 and try to ascertain who had gone overboard. I desperately wanted to know if the Skipper (Sean McCarter) was still on board knowing that the chances of a less favourable outcome were greatly diminished if the boat had lost its Skipper.

On this note, I would like to say that Caty's (Catriona Savage) composure and delivery of information to me was absolutely outstanding and a great example of how to act in an emergency situation, calm and collected. I can say the same of everybody involved in this situation but particularly Olly Cotterell and his crew on One DLL. Thanks must also go to Olly for compiling the Radio Log which very accurately captures the events as they unfolded and all communications from his boat to CV30 and to me (on behalf of the Race Office).

My next phone call was to Justin Taylor, Clipper Ventures Race Director, to inform him of the situation. As a former Clipper Race Skipper himself and like me, Justin knew only too well, the potential consequences of this situation. After a brief conversation, we agreed on the plan to move forward. As per our Clipper Ventures Incident Management plan, I was to continue handling all communications to the boats involved and any external search and rescue authorities. Justin would handle all communications to the Clipper Ventures Directors (Robin and William), our own communications & media department headed up by Jonathan Levy and any necessary communications to family members, once we had identified exactly who had gone overboard. We agreed to keep in regular contact and I would inform of any updated information as it came in. One decision that I made very early on, and that I agreed with Justin, was that I would not contact CV30 directly, simply because I did not want to distract them from the immediate task in hand, location of their missing crew member. This was very clear.

I finished the call with Justin and immediately called Falmouth MRCC (Maritime Rescue Coordination Centre) to inform them of the situation. I gave them as much detail as I could and told them that everything necessary was being done on scene and that I would keep them informed of any updates. I was asked specifically what communications equipment was available on board CV30 and to give a satellite phone number for the boat. This is something that I very respectfully denied to do explaining that any comms to CV30 could potentially distract from the search and rescue attempts and that I would keep them up to date with as much appropriate information as possible. Falmouth agreed and stated that they would inform their Search and Rescue colleagues at the US Coastguard in Norfolk, Virginia, USA. I gave them all my contact details, including house phone number and finished the call.

My partner Helen, had realised that this was an emergency situation and the whole nature and urgency of what was unfolding. She was up, lights on and making tea, and realising that this could be one very long night!! She had spent most of the 11/12 Clipper Race wondering about and dreading this type of situation when I was Skipper and it was clear that all these emotions were coming flooding back and tears started to roll down her face.

I immediately called the sat phone on board CV20 and asked for an update on the situation. I was informed that the MOB casualty was not the Skipper and I remember thinking that this was the only bit of good news that I had received this night so far. My thoughts quickly turned to exactly who was in the water?! It was confirmed to me that the casualty had now been in the water for approximately 40 mins and there was still no visual contact. My heart sank even further and amongst all my other duties I was thinking exactly how I would feel and how I would be acting right now as the Skipper of Derry LondonDerry. All my 'What If?' thoughts and training exercises were feeling quite valuable now!

I instructed CV20 to instigate a 'comms lockdown' (a routine comms blackout so that Clipper ventures could control the flow of information and make sure that no erroneous information gets passed on to anybody outside of Clipper Ventures). I also asked them to relay by VHF to CV30 that they should call me as soon as convenient and should also instigate a comms lockdown.

Over the next 60 minutes I found myself going from one phone call to another, updating important information in my notepad, speaking to boat, Race Director, Falmouth MRCC, US Coastguard the other side of the Atlantic, retrieving voicemail messages from calls that were made to me while I was on another call. So much happened in that hour but it actually only felt like minutes. I realised that I had been informing, instructing, updating, note taking and updating again and again constantly for the last hour.

During this period of time, I learnt that the casualty was CV30 crew member Andrew Taylor, a Round the Worlder, a good friend, someone who I knew personally very well. A really nice guy, intelligent, always saying hello on the dockside and always with a positive 'Get it done' attitude. This made the whole thing so real because now I knew exactly who was missing in the North Pacific Ocean, a good guy, a good friend and Andy Taylor, *"fuck, fuck, fuck"*!

Helen straight away asked me if I knew him and I confirmed that I did, I knew him more than most of the 670 or so Clipper race Crew on the 13/14 Clipper Race. She looked horrified, and immediately started looking him up on the internet. She googled Andrew Taylor and Clipper Round the World, quickly coming across his personal blog. As the events of the night unfolded, she constantly gave me personal information about Andy and his family, lots of which I wasn't aware of. I'm not sure really if this helped my feelings or not but it did give me a bit more knowledge of the person I was trying to help, albeit from the other side of the world.

I remember one of the many calls to Justin Taylor that night, when I informed him of the casualty's name, he also knew Andy. *"Oh God, I know him as a good friend as well"* came the reply. *"How long has he been in the water now?"* *"Over an hour"* I said. Silence! A very long pause, we were both thinking the same. *"We are searching for a body now!"*

Another phone call from CV20 and I learnt that Andrew was wearing a bright orange drysuit and he also had a personal AIS beacon (Automatic Identification System) that could potentially send a signal back to the boat confirming his exact location. This was the second piece of good news that I had received and although things really didn't look good at this point, there was still a glimmer of hope. No matter how bad things seem, you always have to have hope and believe.

More phone calls and frantic note taking and then the phone call that I was waiting for. Approximately 1 hour after the initial contact, CV20 called me to say that CV30 had picked up an AIS signal from Andrew's beacon and they were motoring towards this position. CV30 were 1.8nm from the position on AIS at that time but still had no visual contact. I know that I was not alone in thinking this but right now, all I wanted was visual contact to gained, the MOB to be picked up and news that they were alive, all in that order. I remember thinking that apart from the length of time Andy had been in the water, things were starting to progress in the right direction. Nevertheless, the situation still seemed pretty bleak.

Yet another call from CV20 to confirm that CV30 now had a positive visual contact with the casualty and were making best speed directly to him. At this point I had very mixed emotions. I was elated that they had found him but was deeply disturbed that they might well be too late and may well be there to recover the body. I know the sea temperatures in the North Pacific Ocean, Northern Hemisphere in March and had lots of thoughts on how long somebody may be able to last. This sounds very grim but in my eyes, and also given my very logical and pragmatic nature, this is the reality of the situation but it is still better than it was some 30 minutes ago!

This is where all the time started to go so slowly. The previous hour passed in a flash, I was so busy, but now all any of us could do was wait and hope. I am not a religious man but I have to confess that I said a small and silent prayer in my head that Andy would still be alive.

Back on board; almost all crew are now on deck. Sails are down and tied off, the main with two reefs still in, is centred. Skipper has the motor running flat out, as he circles around. Jason arrives up on deck, fully kitted and ready in his harness. He makes his way up to the mast and Nick helps him tie halyards around the harness, together they prepare him ready to go over the side. He is expecting to go over straight away and begins to get ready to climb out. *'No, not yet'* Skipper shouts. He climbs back in and hangs onto the mast to steady himself. Jason still doesn't know who is in the water and joins the lookout searching the water with fixed wide eyes along with the rest of the crew.

<u>Justin Taylor, Race Director, recounts;</u>

My mood was grim and after Mark had rung off to await more news from CV30 my thoughts turned to Andrew's next of kin and how I was going to tell them. I delayed this for now and continued with the incident management plan. I called the board of directors; Sir Robin and William Ward. Sir Robin answered the phone and I informed him briefly of the facts as I was aware of them. Then I emailed the director and media team at 00:51UTC;

'I have minimal details at the moment. Casualty is Andrew Taylor, RTW, 46. He went into the water at 23:40UTC so about 1 hour from time of this email. Yacht is conducting a search pattern. OneDLL have diverted to render assistance. No other yachts informed yet due to distance from incident. Sea state rough, visibility good, wind 35/40kts WNW. Jonathan Levy informed. Falmouth CG informed.'

I plotted Andrew's position on my navigation software. *"Bloody hell, you are a very long way from anywhere. Nobody is coming to get you out there, except Sean and your own crew"*. As there was still a chance of recovering him, I did not inform Andrew's next of kin straight away. There was a full communications blackout in force and no immediate urgency anyway. I did however retrieve Andrew's details from Clipper's crew database and discovered that he had given two contacts for next of kin. Older brother Sean in Sydney, Australia, and parents in the UK. I decided that I would call Andrew's brother due to the time difference. I also remember thinking that I did not want to wake up his elderly parents in the middle of the night.

I made plans to meet the media team and Sir Robin at Clipper Race Gosport HQ so that we could manage the incident at our end, all from one place. I instructed Mark, Deputy Race Director, to remain at home and liaise exclusively with the yacht and myself. I also made plans to inform the Crew Manager, Carol Blythe so that she and her team could call every crew member's next of kin to reassure them that the MOB was not their loved ones. This is also important as we all know that if you hear it in the media first, that you always think it's one of yours if not told specifically to the contrary.

Whilst emails and calls were being made between the various Clipper race team members and myself time flew by. The phone rang again, Mark tells me he now has comms with Caty on OneDLL. This was preferable as it did not tie up Derry's Satellite phone in case Sean needed it to manage the incident. Caty confirmed that they had received the mayday call and had subsequently suspended racing and were making best speed to Andrew's last known position. She also confirmed that Andrew was wearing a drysuit. *"At least now some hope is restored!"*

In the dark grey icy cold water, I am cold and shocked. The yacht has gone and it's very quiet now. I stop and pause for a second, telling myself to focus and pay attention. *"Right matey, pay attention, what do I need to do next"* I tell myself out loud. I reach down and grab my safety line as it was still attached to me; it was played out with the long clip in the water. When I am working on the boat, if it isn't clipped onto the boat, it's always clipped onto me. So why had it been like this? I don't ever leave it dragging. Had I forgotten or not clipped on properly? Or had it just come off something? I couldn't work out why as I was absolutely sure I had clipped back on. It was still intact and all in one piece, I really don't get this. I stared at it for a while, frowning. *"Fuck!"* I say out loud again. I say this out loud quite a lot over the next hour or so! It's as much of a sentence as I need, I know what it means, each time I say it.

I realise only now that my life jacket has not inflated! It is only the buoyancy in my dry suit that is keeping me afloat. I felt pretty uneasy at this point. It's the first time I have sensed any kind of real danger in the water at all. I knew I was not in a good place to have such little buoyancy. I needed to sort this out, and double quickly too. I felt around for the weak point in the life jacket zipper. Ripped open the zip on the left side of the jacket and checked over the canister, hydrostatic charge and all the workings inside as best I could. I check these over fully, routinely on every stopover to make sure that they are all ok. A bit like packing your own parachute. On this race I had checked them less than a week ago when I had a random inflate in the Nav station after a particularity wet shift on deck. Everything appeared in good order, still intact, I couldn't understand why it had not inflated? Looking at it again and frowning yet again? I checked the gas canister once more, unscrewed it and screwed it back in again. It was screwed in fully so again no reason for it not to inflate? I pulled the red release toggle. Bang! Fully inflated life jacket, stable in the water at last. My lifejacket is too tight and I can't move at all now. I try and adjust it but I can't get to any of the straps, and can't move around to do so anyway. I shuffle my shoulders and pull the whole lifejacket down a little and feel a little bit more comfortable. *"Ok, probably just best to leave it alone now I reckon".*

I pause again and check myself over. Talking myself through it. *"OK so what else?"* I say to myself. I run through a check list in my head; *"head, arms, neck, shoulders, back, hands"?* All seems OK, I think? I shuffle around and move gently each of these body parts as I run through the check list. Everything seems ok apart from my right leg which now really hurts a lot. I thought again about the rudder hitting me. I was really annoyed initially, this was not really a symptom or usual MOB injury or occurrence. Then I thought about how lucky I actually was. That could have very easily killed me! If it had hit me on the head, chest or back, that would have been game over! Unconscious, with a non-inflated lifejacket and a manual AIS, I would have drowned by now and would never ever have been found. At least it would have been quick I think.

My dry suit appeared to be working really well and holding me afloat. I tried really hard all the time not to put any strain on the seals around the cuffs or neck as I moved around. So as not to break the water tight seal. Whenever I turned to look around I moved my shoulders without straining my neck around to maintain the neck seal. I was very worried now about the suit leaking. If it fills with water it would become heavy, and very dangerous. I might need to ditch it, which would be incredibly difficult to do in the cold big seas. Not to mention the fact that without it I might not survive the cold for long either anyway. I ran through a plan in my mind as to how I might go about getting it off. It is very difficult to get it on and off at watch change, whilst on board the boat. After wearing it reasonably continuously now for a few weeks, I do have a fairly well-structured routine to do so. I tried for some time to work out in my head how I could do this in the water. I would have to remove my life jacket to do it and was considering somehow tying the life jacket to something whilst I took a break and wriggled out of the suit. This would be very ugly! It would take a huge effort to do too. I remembered lifeguard training in a swimming pool as a youngster. Wearing pyjamas, and how difficult it had been to get them off in the water. *"I'll have no chance getting this off"* I thought! I said a little prayer about this. I really hoped it didn't leak.

I remembered I didn't have a knife on me, which I was really pissed off about. This should be standard kit in your pocket. I even have one! A really nice proper new safety knife, which I bought specifically for emergencies only. It is in my kit bag in my bunk. *"No bloody use there"* I thought!

I thought about what else I had on me that could be useful, what other tools were available to me right now? A flare would be pretty awesome right now I thought! I did have my camera with me in a shoulder pocket. The flash could be very useful in low light, maybe if it got dark this would be a great tool. *"OK wait a minute? Dark! Bloody hope I'm not here that long!"* I wondered if maybe a couple of photographs of the boat would be good, *"must be a photo competition winner in there somewhere"* I thought? And smiled at the thought of doing so. Or maybe a selfie video diary, I thought and I laughed out loud. I reached around to get the camera out. It was difficult to reach and as I stretched around I was putting huge pressure on my lifejacket and the neck seal on my suit. I stopped, repositioned myself and tried again. *"No, I'm not going to do this"*, *"way too much risk to neck seal, not worth it just now"*.

I struggled around trying to find the whistle attached to my life jacket, to no avail. I felt around everywhere for the cord which retains it, but could not even locate that. The boat was probably too far away by now anyway, but I was really disappointed I could not find it. It might have been useful? I looked and fiddled around again many times later but never actually found it.

I felt confident and content I had my AIS beacon on me. *"OK, get this set off now" "Someone on the boat will see it" "It makes a noise on the chart plotter when it goes off right?"* I don t know! I have never done this! AIS and PLB beacons are common on the race, all the round the world crew have them, and many leggers are sharing them too. They are not however standard kit, so we don't train with them. This is stupid! I think to myself, if they are so common amongst us, we should do this, we should know this stuff! I have absolutely no idea what will happen when I set this off. I don't know what the range is either.

But it's here and so I reached around and retrieved it quickly. It was attached to the grab lines inside my life jacket. I had checked it before we left Qingdao, it was well attached, safe and sound, checked and ready to go, now I really needed it! I felt really content with myself, smug actually! Not only had I purchased this, but I had fixed it inside my lifejacket so I had it on me at all times. It was only a couple of hundred pounds, and now it was going to be worth every single penny, or at least I hoped it would be?

I pulled out the bright red pin that says 'PULL'. I twisted the bright orange knob, in the direction of the big white arrow on the side which said 'On'. It instantly started to flash a white light. I breathed a sigh of relief, *"it's working!"* I felt really pleased it was flashing away happily. I held it above my lifejacket as best I could pointing upwards like it said to do on the side. I wondered about the range and battery life of this? I had absolutely no idea. I wondered if the boat was looking for me or not, and if there would be anybody checking the AIS at their end! I didn't know what the response would be by the AIS on board, did it set of an alarm or just appear on the screen as a registered point? We should have known this, it would be useful to know and others should know this too in future. I remembered other crew who had beacons. I can remember seeing them on the boat, not attached to anything or anyone! How easy it would be to leave this in your kit bag, pointless! I knew some had done this. But then I had done the same with my safety knife, so I'm no angel either.

Although quite far away now, I could still see the boat quite clearly every time it rose up upon a wave, or when I did. I moved my legs and arms around to maintain sight of the boat as best I could. It hurt to move my legs around and I did it gently. With just enough pressure to spin around in the water. When I came up on a wave, the boat seemed to always go down and there were several waves between us. One of us was always obscured by the water. I saw the deck only very briefly once. *"If I can't see the deck then they can't see me!"* I looked around and took a rough bearing on the sun so I could re-find the boat whenever I lost it. This worked well a few times, but when it clouded over I found it slightly more difficult. All this while I was lifting up my spray hood high to try and make myself more visible in the water. After a good deal of time I wondered if this might be acting as a sail and drifting me further away from the boat so I stopped doing it.

I could see the side of the boat and thought *"this is good, it meant they had stopped at least"*. The stay sail was down, this was also a good thing too as I remembered it wasn't on a winch when I went over. The side then became the back which really bothered me. *"You're going the wrong bloody way!"* What about my AIS, maybe they haven't seen it, maybe they are all on deck looking for me? There are enough people on the boat who know I have it on me to provoke them looking for it? Surely they are monitoring the AIS all the time just in case? I was glad I had shared with people that I had it fixed inside my lifejacket. I had no idea really what was going on onboard. What I did know was that we have an awesome team on board, under the command of an awesome Skipper and they would be doing everything they could to find me quickly. I knew this and kept telling myself.

Back on board, Skipper was still following his search pattern based on what information he had. Wind, currents and the way point marked exactly where I had gone over. Circling around and around, covering concentric circles. All the time he is looking at wind and tide to try and second guess where I might be. *"Worse than looking for a needle in a haystack"* he recounts later. Crew are spread all around and occasionally Skipper asks for all eyes on a certain area. Otherwise, it is 360degree vision with no rest. After some time. One at a time, the crew go below, quickly getting better equipped for the cold and wet. Everyone on deck is now getting extremely cold & wet. No one had stopped to fully prepare for the elements when the call for 'all hands' went out. Jason had however taken time to fully kit himself out in harness and recovery kit. He is now attached to halyards and waiting patiently by the mast to be lowered over and recover me. He is going over and over in his mind what he is going to do. Checking and double checking his kit again and again. He is tense, full of anticipation & apprehension. Ready to get wet. Actually he is desperate to get wet; he wants to get on with this and the wait is horrible. He is visualising the recovery in his mind. He is thinking *"OK, any minute now he's going to pop up, we will see him and away we go with recovery"*. He didn't know it yet, but he still had a very long and cold wait ahead of him!

I continued to keep the boat in sight but was starting to get tired and lethargic now. In our sea survival training we are taught to stay still and preserve body temperature. We are taught to stay in a foetal position holding our legs and staying tight. In a rolling sea this is virtually impossible, it certainly isn't comfortable. Staying alert and retaining sight of the boat was giving me real hope and encouragement. It felt critically important to me to stay with this. I considered ditching my boots, they seemed heavy and cumbersome, certainly not good swimming gear! I wondered if they were helping or hindering? I figured they were probably a little positively buoyant. Although they were full of sea water they were probably keeping my feet vaguely warm too, so I kept them on.

A fair amount of time seemed to pass and the boat was still a long way away from me. I kept seeing the side of it, at one point, I thought it was facing me and coming my way, but then it didn't appear any closer next time I saw it. I had no concept of time or how long I had been in the water. I thought about looking at my watch. It was under my dry suit seal, so I decided not to.

I wasn't going there! I thought it's no good looking anyway. I decided it would only ever serve as a morale killer for me. I'll look at the time an hour later only to realise it has only been five minutes. It will totally mess with my head. *"It won't make any difference anyway, I need to focus on the now and what I'm doing here right now, this moment. Focus on the things you can control and manage, that's more than enough to do at the moment!"*

I remembered I had promised my watch to Siobhan one day if anything ever happened to me. I was disappointed I was wearing it, if I'm not recovered it will be lost. *"Bugger"* I thought. Oh well at least it is insured anyway, so she still gets the money. *"I wonder if she will buy one the same or similar with it?" Dad will recommend she does, he is a logical thinker, yes he is bound to suggest that?"* I bet she doesn't though, we joke about it sometimes she says people sometimes charge me more for stuff when they see me wearing it. She once proved this at a pop up shop in Cambridge, going back on her own and getting charged less than half what they were going to charge me for the same item. *"That Dad, is because I'm a kid and you're wearing a Rolex!"* she said as she returned with a smug smile on her face. I do love her sense of humour! I remembered my family gold cygnet ring is in my kit bag on the boat *"That's good news"* I thought *"Siobhan gets that in my will, it's much more precious and she will appreciate it more anyway"*. I was glad I wasn't wearing it.

"Wait a minute! What are you thinking! The boat IS coming back, you ARE getting out of this one, right look for it, where is the boat? c'mon now pay attention!" These were my thoughts but it felt like someone was talking to me. I can't see the boat anywhere! I spin around a few times, still no sign of it! Again the thoughts talk to me. *"Where is the sun, you took a bearing right? c'mon, focus, pay attention, stay with it, right there it is look, over there. OK so take the bearing from there to there"*. Nothing! Still no sign of them! I spin around again and again, almost in a panic for a few moments. I had kept the boat in sight right up until a few minutes ago. Now, drifting away in my own world of thoughts of home, I had lost concentration, thinking about other stuff, *"not bloody focused" "fucking Idiot!"* I said to myself out loud, *"pay attention"* I said to myself over and over several times out loud.

<u>Julia Wall-Clarke, PR & communications manager for Clipper race recounts;</u>

My phone is ringing. I glance bleary eyed at the clock. It is 1.30am on a Monday morning. Ugh? The name on my caller display is Jonathan Levy. This is not good I think? Seconds after I pick up and I am wide awake. Truth is I had been preparing for this moment since the race started. I just hoped I would never get the actual call. As a PR professional you always have to consider the worst case scenario in any situation and have a plan for how to act if it ever becomes reality. Whilst safety and training is embedded in everything our race crew go through. Sailing, especially ocean racing, is notoriously a tough and very dangerous sport, and whether you are an amateur or a professional sailor, incidents do occur. As the race is on 24/7, we are always on call. My phone is by my bed each night.

I will remember that phone call for the rest of my life. Jonathan and I get on very well and his tone is usually rather jovial, but this was different. He sounded very grave. *"Hi Julia. I'm afraid there has been a serious incident involving Derry~Londonderry~Doire, and it doesn't look good. I think we need to head into the office and prepare for the worst"* Immediately I felt totally sick. This was Race 10 of 16 that make up the whole circumnavigation and we were ten months in at this point. I didn't even know who was involved yet, just a male round the worlder, but it didn't matter as all our crew feel like family at this point. As Jonathan relayed the facts; *"man over board" "middle of the Pacific" "3,000 miles from land" "an hour in the water with no visual reported"* we both agreed that we would head to the office immediately. I dressed quickly and tiptoed down the stairs, hoping not to wake my parents who I was living with temporarily at the time. I wrote a note and left it on the dining room table in case they thought I'd been kidknapped and even worse perhaps, that their car had been stolen. *"We've had a man overboard in the Pacific and there has been no sighting of him since. I've gone into the office. Please pray for him."* My last thought as I headed out the door was to fill a bag with some food. I knew this was going to be a very long day.

There was no traffic on the road so between praying desperately for good news, I was hitting refresh on my emails, waiting for the ping of a new message alert to give me an update. From updates I'd had since the call, I now knew it was Andrew Taylor. I didn't actually know Andrew too well personally at this point as I didn't look after his team directly but I pictured his face immediately. He was always friendly and always made an effort to say hello and chat to us in port.

Meanwhile back in the North Pacific. I rediscovered the boat a while later. No great plan, it just reappeared. I could make out lots of people on deck whenever I caught a brief glimpse of

198

it. Then I spotted someone up the mast, this gave me real hope, and I smiled to myself *"YES!" "They are looking for me!"* I absolutely knew this now for sure now. It had been a long time wondering. Now I absolutely knew they were looking, this was great news and gave me a massive lift. It felt really good, this was excellent news, won't be long now I thought. Here they come, back on board soon, and then we can get on with the race! Sooner we race, sooner I get back home to see Siobhan. I thought about her with me, safely on my shoulder. Always there with me. I thought about the gate at St Katts too. It's still a long way off, but it's what we set out to do. Circumnavigate. *"Let's get out of the water and get on with it. C'mon guys over here!!"* Instinctively I knew it was Kristi up the mast, she was always first for this and had absolutely no fear. I knew she would have volunteered for this. I felt for her though; the conditions were gradually getting much worse and were really bad now. Very high wind, really massive waves, not a good time to be going up the mast. She would need all of her strength to hold on as the boat rocks and bucks around. Then a rush of cold hit me. *"Fuck, no!" "This isn't good at all!" "This is really bad!"* Having someone up the mast looking for me, positively confirms they don't know where I am! *"Fuck!"* I felt really very cold, I had stopped and thought about this and for the first time. I really felt for my situation. I absolutely know now for sure now they don't know where I am!

I was shivering uncontrollably & violently too. I was surprised just how violent the shivering was. It blurred my vision, hurting all of my muscles. There was nothing I could do about it either. I tried to stop and focus on the boat in the distance. I couldn't! I tried to wipe my eyes & face, clean some of the salt off. It hurt and scratched as I did it. I also realised I couldn't feel my hands at all now. I bit the end of a finger to check, I could feel nothing! I tried to clench a fist and move my fingers in and out. I couldn't do this either. It hurt really badly moving my fingers. My feet and face were numb now too! My vision was blurred and my nose really hurt, of all things! I stopped, looked at the boat and felt sick! I started to worry a lot for the first time. It wasn't a good place to be, the boat seemed so far away, and I knew right now they didn't know where I was. I felt totally helpless. I have absolutely no way of attracting their attention. No way whatsoever! I felt pretty low. *"This might be it now?"* I now need to dig really deep to gather all of my strength that's left. I wondered if I can do this.

I stopped kicking and swimming around. Started to try and settle down to conserve energy, maybe even try and warm up a little. As I settled I started to wonder if I was too far away now. Maybe I won't be found? Surely not? I couldn't think this. I felt like I was losing control. Up until now I had focused on what I needed to do. There seemed to be nothing left. Nothing else I could do. *"This is it then?"*

From absolutely nowhere, for no apparent reason. I remembered it was my Mum's birthday tomorrow. *"No!" "Not today! I can't die on Mum's birthday that would be a really bad thing to do"*. I was going to write a blog dedicated to my Mum this afternoon. I had started writing it in my head a few days ago. It was all about whether it was ok to miss your parents at my age or not? I do miss them. I hadn't realised I would miss them so much. I thought through what I was going to write, and got really upset. I started thinking about Siobhan too. How would she cope? What would it be like if I didn't come back? We had been through a tough few weeks before I went away. That would be a really bad way for her to think back and remember me. I thought through my plans at home. I had left everything well organised and in place. My will was in order, and funeral plans all sorted just in case before I set out. Siobhan would be ok, there would be nothing out of place, and everyone would know what to do.

This is unthinkable *"stop it, stop it, stop it, stop it"* I told myself out loud. *"Right come on matey, pay attention, sort yourself out! I am not going to die today, not today, no, no no!"* I spun around as best I could, but it was really hard and painful to do it this time. I caught a tiny glimpse of the boat in the distance. The sky behind it was absolutely jet black and menacing. I could see massive waves breaking all around it, a huge pacific squall rain storm which is now hitting them full on. They were getting absolutely pounded by a massive rain squall, *"oh please no!"* This is just going to slow them down even more already and take them longer to get to me. I watched the storm for a while, it was a violent and quite impressive storm to watch. A pretty amazing and quite unique perspective to have on it from here too. The sea where I was drifting had calmed a little in front of the storm and it was easier to drift in one place, keeping the boat in sight. Slowly, it dawned on me what the storm was about to do, and I realised with a large amount of fear welling up inside me, the storm is coming my way,*"oh shit!"*

"Ok, so what do I need to do to prepare for this?" I checked the tether on my AIS was secure first. It was secured to my wrist by the lanyard, and was attached to my lifejacket lifting straps too. This was my lifeline to rescue I thought, better look after this. Next I double checked all the life jacket straps and clasps. All still seemed to be well and my lifejacket was still well inflated. I thought about topping it up, then decided not to touch it as it was ok just now. I didn't want to risk any possibility of making it worse in any way. The next time I looked up, it had already started to rain. The sea was starting to increase in size again and I could feel myself once again rising up and down on the waves, progressively higher and higher. The rain quickly turned to hail stones which really hurt my hands, head and face. They were stinging hard and ice cold, I really didn't like it. This is the point at which you would actually run for shelter or go back inside if you were anywhere else. I got quite upset with this and felt like I was being kicked whilst I was down by the storm.

The sea state quickly became rougher and rougher, the waves suddenly much bigger, breaking white water too. Everything changed really quickly, from calm to storm in what seemed like only a few moments.

I turned and looked over towards where I thought the boat was and just saw the biggest wave ever. A huge wall of jet black water, easily 20 meters high. It seemed to be increasing as it came closer to me. It passed and I felt almost as though I fell off the back of it. I could feel myself tumbling and steadied myself with my arms out to stop myself rolling over as I slid down the back of the wave. There was another one right behind it, there were five or six of these between me and the boat. *"No chance of seeing me now"*. There is no way they will ever see me in this. I heard a loud rushing noise and got hit in the back by a white water breaker. It took my breath away, caught me unawares & winded me. Rolling me over several times. I resurfaced face down and had to fight around to struggle against my lifejacket to right myself. Just as I had done so and came up for air, I heard the next one. Looking up it seemed even bigger. I pulled my spray hood down, held onto my life jacket with both hands, pinched my nose through the spray hood and took a big deep breath. Boy did I need that breath, it rolled me over and over again. Like getting wiped out in the surf and washed up onto a beach. It seemed to last for ages. I came up to the surface face down again, struggled myself over, went to take a big breath and got hit square in the face by the next one. I wasn't ready for it and I swallowed down inside a whole load of salt water. When I came up from this one I was coughing and spluttering around, trying to choke and breath. My lungs screaming for air. I got only a few seconds to prepare for the next one. So it continued for a while, wave after wave, some worse than others. Some I was ready for and some not. I'm really not sure how long or how many but it was truly horrible. I really thought it was never ever going to end.

Once or twice there was a split second break and I held still, grabbed my lifejacket tight and prepared myself for the next one. Knowing it wasn't over yet. I knew the storm was gradually passing over. The hail stones had turned to back to rain. Stinging cold rain grinding on my skin. All the time I gripped tight around my life jacket determined not to lose it. I was really worried about my drysuit leaking now. Each time I came up, I took deep breaths and shouted abuse out loud. It wasn't going to help in any way but it made me feel better. I tried to control my breathing and stay calm, but it was really difficult to do. I kept on thinking all the time, *"not like this, I am not going down in a storm"*. It was truly horrible during the storm it seemed to last an age. It totally wiped me out, physically and mentally. I am in real trouble now!

Strangely the storm had improved visibility for the crew on deck. The definition of colour on the grey dark water was potentially easier to spot. After the rain passed the light seemed brighter and clearer. The conditions however were dreadful and it was tough for the crew to maintain the search, which they never slowed down or stopped. All this time, Jason was stood patiently ready to go over the side, he had put himself forward for this, and there had been no discussion, debate or second thoughts. He went and got ready straight away harnessing up and preparing to go into the water. He is now thinking *'we are flogging a dead horse here, he's been in the water over an hour now. He will be unconscious at best'*. He is trying hard to prepare himself mentally for this, talking it over to himself in his head. Preparing for the worst.

Susie, began to call for her medical preparations below deck. Ready for my treatment once I was back on board. Richard was below deck, still quite heavily restricted in his movement with a really badly damaged back from earlier in the race. Some days he cannot move at all, on others he has sufficient movement to at least move around a little. He is in agony all the time and really needs medical treatment as soon as we land. Susie gives him very clear instructions of what she wants. *"Boil and reboil the kettle all the time. Get as many water bottles and containers for hot water as you can gather ready to make hot water bottles. Gather together all the dry sleeping bags we have on board to wrap him in. Find all the scissors we have, including the big sail repair ones, sharpen them if you have to; just have them ready to cut off his kit".* She returns to the hatch a few minutes later and calls down to Richard. *"better make ready two sets of everything"* she says, *"one on each side of the saloon we are going to need one for Jason after he's been in the water".* She asks for the emergency medical kit and oxygen kit too. Richard gets busy preparing these. Hastily getting it all ready and waiting for Susie just as instructed.

An hour has passed now. All this time, Conor has been calling up periodically to the team on deck the time passed. Initially he does this every five minutes then latterly he switches to every ten. As the hour mark is reached his voice changes. With some trepidation he calls loudly up to the deck *"that's one hour passed".* Silence! There is a totally silent reply on deck. A few crew look at each other briefly. No-one speaks. Many are fearing the worse at this stage but no one discusses it. Many are thinking after an hour in the water, there is little hope of finding me now. Or perhaps worse still recovering a body from the extremely rough icy sea they were transfixed on looking at.

Skipper remains absolutely focussed. He is still confident he will find me. His thoughts however are turning to a recovery not a rescue. The silence continues for a few minutes as they make busy with their roles in hand, searching and preparing for recovery. Jason's thoughts deepen; when he does go in? *"what state am I going to be in, conscious? hurt? alive?"* He starts to fear the worse and can feel the fear welling up inside. He manages to control this, but is now absolutely convinced privately in his own mind he is recovering a body.

204

The storm subsided, the seas calmed a little. Still rough, but no longer breaking white water. I can feel myself riding up and down over the waves again. I can also feel now I really don't have very much strength left at all. I wait, relax for a while to be sure the storm has passed. The sea state has definitely eased and it felt calmer. I am still gripping my arms tight around my lifejacket and slowly I loosen my grip and start to relax a little. The waves were still easily 6m+ but by comparison to earlier, this is calm.

The sun is out and the sky clears. I straighten my life jacket and pull the spray hood right down over my face. I settle back, and get myself into a comfortable position. Taking a couple of deep breaths, I sigh and rest, still taking deep, slow, long breaths. I was glad the storm had passed. It felt happy to have survived it, I feel slightly smug and tell myself *"well done matey" "that was tough" "still here though, not bloody going that easily!"* I smiled, a wry smile of minor success and I let out a small laugh.

The sky cleared a little more and the sun was shining through the small clear plastic window in my spray hood. What little warmth was in it, felt really warm on my face. I leant my head back and enjoyed the sun for a few moments. It was lovely. I no longer felt cold, I had stopped shivering and felt content, comfortable and, if anything, I actually felt happy. I was relaxed and breathing deeply. Thoughts turned to the adventures we had experienced to this point. What an epic race it had been and how lucky I was to be doing this. For a brief moment I totally forgot where I was and drifted through thoughts of friends, home, family, work, the race. All kinds of nice things, I remember skiing with Siobhan and smiled at her sense of humour and us laughing together.

Then, my senses kicked back in. *"wait a minute, this is very bad"!* This is not a good place to be, I snapped myself alert again. Wide eyed and fully awake. I realised exactly what this meant from my training. This signifies a later, and now very dangerous, stage of hyperthermia. I have read and even discussed before how Hypothermia is actually nice way to die! You enter a slightly euphoric stage and relax. No longer feeling the cold, life slows down and you drift off to sleep. This is the body shutting itself down, this is very bad. I realise quickly and violently I am in a bad way and snap to my senses. I pulled the hood back and turned myself into the wind. I wanted to get cold again to stay alive. I tried to shiver, it didn't work. I didn't think it would, but I tried anyway! I knew now I really needed to stay with it and concentrate, this was a very very dangerous state for me to be in. I was in real proper danger now and I really knew it. *"You need to focus real time now boy"* I told myself. *"Lose concentration now and you die"*

On deck, Tristan, a media cameraman from the Clipper race TV documentary crew traveling with us for this race from Qingdao to San Francisco, has started filming. He is moving around the deck with his heavy weatherproof camera equipment, catching the best shots he can from the search operations going on around him. He wants to help in the search too. So in between shooting he is looking all around. Tristan feels torn between capturing the amazing footage and helping the crew who need all hands and eyes. He feels as he tries to do both jobs, like he is doing an average job of both filming and helping and it messes with his head a little. Wanting to concentrate on one or the other.

Tristan tells Chris that 90 minutes have now passed. *"Really? They were long minutes, ones I am in no hurry to repeat"*. Chris recounts, seeming inadequate. The sea so big we have become almost insignificant. From the top of the A-Frame to the Helm, all he can do is follow his training & Skipper's instructions. The time ticks away, far too slowly and yet far too fast. *"In training we always find the MOB faster than this?"*

206

I pulled my spray hood right back and looked around hoping to see the boat for some encouragement. I tried to remember the bearing on the sun but couldn't remember it, I got really annoyed that I couldn't remember this. I tried what I thought it was, but saw nothing. I did a 360 spin around and saw nothing still. I wished I hadn't done this as it made me feel worse. I said I wouldn't do it again. I was starting to think this might be it now and I was not going to be found. I thought about the enormity of where we are and just how remote I was. I could drift for days here and not be found. I drifted into some thoughts of home and Siobhan again, I remembered walking on the beach together, skiing, and tobogganing when she was small. I remember jumping into the ball pit with her and her mates, being mad at parties and I smiled about these moments. I thought about the magic of when she was first born and how amazing this felt. I thought about the monkey on my shoulder and felt content that she was with me. For a few moments I drifted with her, talking to her. We are together, close smiling at each other.

I looked down at my AIS beacon in my hand. *"How long does the battery last?"* I wondered. I have no idea how long it's been turned on for now. *"What is the range? Does it even work?"* I started to fiddle with it. My hands and fingers didn't work well at all, my fingers really hurt too with the cold. Every movement of them was painful. I found a small legend on the bottom of the AIS which indicated the different flashing sequences to confirm whether GPS signals were working or not. *"Maybe it has no GPS signal?" "Was it out of range? Did it not work? Did it only flash when it was connected? Was there any GPS signal out here?"* I really didn't know. I fiddled with it some more. Then, and for no reason, I turned it off and turned it back on again. It instantly flashed differently! Really? *"Oh my god maybe this might be it now?"* I thought *"It'll pop up on their screens and they will see it and be here in a jiffy"*. I played through in my mind the scene on board, signal received, full throttle, straight line, there he is! I lifted my spirits again and felt good. I knew I was in a pretty bad way now and really needed to stay alert. I knew I really didn't have long left.

I still couldn't see the boat though and I didn't know about the range of the AIS either. I decided if this was it now they would be here soon. There really was nothing else I could do now. Stay calm and stay with it. Could be my last chance. The last hope. I settled back into the comfortable position in the sun with the hood down, and tried to control my breathing. Holding the AIS aloft carefully as best I could with my cold hands. I wanted to stay with it whilst I waited so I thought about the stopover in San Francisco. I thought about lunch, I thought about family and friends again. I pictured our gate at St Katts. Created the image of walking through it in my mind. Occasionally I just counted up to twenty, then backwards to one again, back and forth. I even tried to do this in French and Spanish. Something to occupy my mind. Anything, just anything to keep me occupied and try to stay alert. I was losing what little strength I had left quickly now. It became hard work even just to think.

On board, Skipper is leaning down into the Nav station through the hatch from up on deck. Conor is down below and between them they agree the next search pattern to follow. Skipper slips back up onto deck towards the helm. There is a 'ping ping' alarm sound from the chart plotter. It says on the screen 'Emergency SART located' with two options on the screen which say, 'back' or 'go to' Conor reaches over hitting 'go to' straight away. He screams out up to Skipper *"got him Sean, got an AIS signal here, hang on a second for a course to steer"*. Skipper later describes this as an hallelujah moment. He jumps over to the helm, takes over from Chris, pushes the throttle forwards and calls back to Michelle *"give me course, give me course!"* He shouts forward to the deck crew *"we have his AIS, get yourselves ready guys".* Conor shouts back up *"086 degrees 1.5 miles, and get this Skipper he's doing 4.7 knotts!"* Skipper swings the boat around and shouts back *"distance?" "1.5miles"* comes the reply, a few minutes later Skipper calls again *"distance?" "112 degrees, 1.5miles"* a few minutes later again *"126degrees, 1 mile".* It's taking them ages to get to me as I drift away from them at over 4ktts on the current. Skipper pushes the throttle all the way down the engine screams loud, as the boat pushes on through the massive waves as fast it can. Straining against the wind. The boat has an enormous engine for its size, a massive Perkins diesel unit pushing out around 140bhp. But even with this at full throttle, it is barely enough to push the boat through the massive waves. At about 400meters distance Kristi calls down from the mast with the first visual *"got him!! 400m dead ahead"* she screams. A few minutes later, at around 200 metres, a few people on deck, including Skipper on the helm have spotted me for the first time. Skipper lines up for his first approach. *"Got him"* shouts Skipper, *"here we go, ready everybody".* Nick is forward of the shrouds helping Jason climb out and shouting back range and distance to Sean. *"I'm coming round into the wind"* shouts Sean. *"hold tight, coming round". "Come to port, come to port now!"* Nick shouts back as the boat straightens up, then *"easy, easy, straighten up".* Constantly he updates and calls back to Sean.

As the first call from Kristi comes down, they have spotted me. Tristan grabs his camera and films constantly all of the final stages of the recovery. During this time, he still feels really guilty. He says he feels like it's intruding on a friends misfortune and he shouldn't be filming it. Some crew tell him it is really important to keep filming. We all have jobs to do, and Tristan's is to document the story, besides the footage will be really useful for our own debrief afterwards and to help understand what happens during this

Jason and the recovery team at the shrouds ready themselves. Jason is out and already over the side, leaning out from the rails, hanging on with one arm. His eyes focused on me in the water, poised and ready to go in. As he spots me for the first time in the water, he starts to wonder what state I am in. Conscious? Alive? Dead? I haven't moved yet, they are looking at my spray hood down, arms locked over the top, grasping my AIS aloft. He looks at me and thinks *"I am recovering a body here!"*

Jason and I trained together almost two and a half years ago. We requested to be on the same boat and have become really quite close friends since. As the boat closes in, the crew shout my name. I turn, wave my arms and he breaths a sign of relief as he lowers himself quickly over the side and down into the icy water. As he gets wet for the first time he takes a sharp intake of breath, it's freezing and very quickly he starts to shiver, his hands hurt with the cold and are already difficult to use. Like the rest of the crew, Jason has been on deck for a long time in the cold, wind and rain. The swell is bouncing him off the side of the boat and it's really hard to keep his feet on the side. The boat lifts right up out of the water and crashes back down over the waves. Skipper is trying to bring the boat close alongside me up wind, to then drift down onto me. Jason realises this is going to be even more difficult than ever now with the cold and wave swell. His lifejacket goes off, now he finds it difficult to move around. Good news his lifejacket works but this makes working and moving around incredibly difficult. We discuss this afterwards. If you have time to do so, removing the charge before going over would be really beneficial. The lifejacket could still be manually set off with the pull toggle. It would make recovery much easier for everyone we both agree.

I think I probably lost consciousness at some point after the storm. I am really not sure, but the period of time before the boat arrives seems fuzzy and a little blurred in my memory. Almost dream like. I think I can hear voices shouting, I cannot be sure, I hold my position in the water and concentrate hard. I can hear something I am pretty sure, but check myself out of it as it's not clear. I am sure it's my mind playing tricks now. Then I hear my name called clearly. I am sure, that was definitely my name! It's amazing how you can pick out your own name from the background noise of the wind and sea. Like some kind of animal instinct or sixth sense. I lift up the spray hood and there is the boat bouncing up and down on the waves, right next to me. My first thought was *"jeez the boat is enormous!"* I try to give a clear 'OK signal' with my hands over my head. I can see Jason over the side, in the water already. With full harness and halyards all around him for recovery. This was a great sight I was really pleased to see him in the water and it gave me a lot of confidence. I knew I was in safe hands; at least almost anyway. Jason and all of us together had practiced this drill so many times before. I knew he was confident in the role of recovery swimmer. I knew he was competent and focused, we had a great working relationship too and overall this would make the recovery easier working together. I made eye contact with Charlie up on deck, his face was stern, really serious, and he looked concerned and a little scared. I still have this picture of his face rigid in my mind as clear as when it occurred. He then gave me a big smile, a thumbs up, and shouted *"we've got you now mate, hang on"*. I saw Nick standing up leaning over the side holding the halyards, another sight for sore eyes, he looked massive standing tall over the top of the recovery lines, calling the manoeuvres to the team and controlling the situation as he is so great at doing.

I felt relieved and overwhelmingly pleased the boat was now with me, I reckon my time was running out by now. I had possibly already been unconscious once. I knew we still had some hard work to do though to get back on board. I knew this was difficult and I would need to dig deep for some energy. We have done this so many times before in training. It's a difficult task even in the calm waters of the Solent where we previously drilled this over and over again. We had refreshed and drilled this in Cape Town and again in Australia several times during pre-race training on the stopovers too. In the high swells and extreme cold however this was not going to be easy. The waves were still really big, easily 7 meters plus, lifting the boat right up and dumping it back down crashing hard next to us in the water. The boat came closer and I made first contact with Jason, he said *"boy am I glad to see you"* We grabbed at each other's hands and I said *"likewise matey"*. Immediately we lost grip and I slipped back down into the water. We both reached out and sort of linked our arms to try and hold on.

Jason was holding a helicopter recovery strop, together we got it over my arms, starting to get me into it. He reached up and clipped it into the halyard snap shackle and called for the lift. The guys on the winches started to lift a little and the shackle snapped back open, *"shit"* exclaimed Jason. He had hold of the strop over his arm and was shouting up for a quicker lift. *"up, up, up!"* he shouted. He was never going to be able to hold on to this and he started to lose his grip. I really didn't want to fall back in with the strop still attached to me. I thought Jason will need this for the next attempt. So I slipped myself out of it and tried to hold onto the halyard. Splash! Back in the water. Drifting away from Jason as the boat lurched from side to side. I kicked myself away from the boat as it was dragging me under and was coming right over on top of me. As it passed by and rolled over I could almost touch hands with Skipper on the helm. He leant over with a great big smile and said *"stay there mate, I'll be back in a minute"*. It made me smile too.

I tried to stay calm; I had just used up a lot of my last energy reserves trying to get into and out of the strop, I was very tired now and knew I was running on empty.

I could barely move, my arms ached, my body felt heavy and my hands were useless. I stopped swimming, leant right back into the lifejacket to take a brief rest, whilst waiting for them to come round again. I could feel my leg really hurting too, probably from kicking out at the boat just now. My back hurt, my arms and hands really hurt from the extreme cold. I had a cracking head ache too and was really struggling to focus my eyes properly. As the boat came round the second time, looking at the side of it I couldn't read the text on the branded logos. I thought to myself *"This is bad, you are in a bad way now matey" "come on focus in mate, this is it now, you need to work hard, just bloody get on with it now, get on board, so nearly there, not long now, big effort, big effort, no prisoners on this one, let's do it c'mon!"* I kept repeating this over and over to myself as much encouragement as I could muster to myself in my head. I really did think I was done in. I was really struggling to find effort now.

The boat accelerated away, making a perfectly rehearsed figure of eight course around and back to approach me. As it approached I was right in front of it. It bounced back and forth on the big seas and came closer and closer, I was almost under the bow at one point as it was chopping up and down. I was very scared it would come down on top of me at this point. I grabbed the bob stay, which ties down and joins the bow sprit to the bottom of the bow, for some stability. I had my arm over the top of it. It jerked me right up out of the water then unceremoniously dumped me down again and crushed me under water couple of times. By holding on at least I was away from going under the bow, but this was really not a good place to be. I tried as hard as I could to get away from the bow and down the side to where Jason was in the water. I just couldn't do it and eventually I ended up the wrong side of the boat. Kicking out and pushing myself away from it again. Skipper reversed back slightly, then came hard around slowly to within a few metres of me. As it approached this time I already had my safety line clip out and in my hand. Holding it up high so Jason could clearly see it. I handed it to him as we passed in the water he briefly missed it, I kicked really hard with my legs and arms and got it back into his hand. He put it around the halyard and clipped it back onto itself. It took him ages to do this as his hands were so cold. I reached up at one point to help with this but couldn't quite reach. Futile really anyway as there was no way I was going to help with this. Once Jason had hold of this, I was getting pulled back and forth in the water as the boat rocked and moved, it jerked me forward and right underwater a few times. I took on a lot of water at this point coughing and spluttering it out. I could see the clip and I heard it snap shut. A noise I shall never forget.

Then I hear calls for lift; it seemed to take ages for the lines to come tight. I was still being dragged under water back & forth. As the mast and halyards reach us up and down. I smashed my head against the side of the boat at one point, I said to myself out loud *"wow that fucking hurt!"* I kicked the boat away hard again with lots of aggression, this really hurt too! Then I got pulled straight back up against it and under water again. Again and again I got dragged back and forth under the strain of the boat moving around. I was convinced I was going to drown at this point, I had no strength left to steady myself and in any case I was just getting towed back and forth by the boat. There was no way I was going to resist this anyway, I took in loads of water and struggled to catch a breath in between.

Eventually the lines came tight and started to lift us both up out of the water. I was immediately concerned about the load exerted on the safety line and the crotch strap of the life jacket. They are really not designed to take this kind of load and I worried I would slip out and back into the water if it gave out. I got up to the level of the guard wires and wrapped my arms over them. There was a commotion around us, everyone has been watching me and whilst I was being lifted clear, all the time above me Jason had been winched right up into the shrouds and he was now being crushed by the halyards against the shrouds. There was a call from the team around him *"ease! ease! ease!"* with much haste and stress shouted by many. Calling to ease the halyard winches. I guessed this would probably ease me down too. I was struggling to hold onto the guard wires. I am probably going back down the side now. I wasn't sure if I had enough energy to keep hold on much longer. The guard wires were cutting into me and I was losing my grip. I reached over, grabbed a stanchion and climbed right in over the wires myself. Right through the middle guard rails and onto the deck. I really don't know how I did this or where the strength came from.

I collapsed into a heap, coughing and spluttering. I really thought I was going to be sick. I braced myself and thought about where it would go if I was. I looked for somewhere to throw up and couldn't see anywhere. Michelle calls back to Skip *"he's OK Skip, he's OK"* with a hand gesture to calm him. Sean is desperate for some news. Surrounded by crew, I was wrapped and tangled with safety lines and halyards together in a ball with Ali, Charlie and Nick who had all been helping me in over the side. I tried to unclip myself to free some tension from the straps that are crushing me now. I can't manipulate the clip as I am too cold and my hands don't work at all. Frustration and panic, looking down I can see a blurred view of myself clutching at the clip. I can't see what I'm doing and my fingers and hands are just frozen solid. I can't move them or feel them at all. I ask Ali to do it. Charlie already has it in hand and has released it. I fall down, face first, onto the deck and take the first deep breath with a sense of relief. When I look up, I look straight at Skipper on the helm, he smiles, winks and says *"Hey Andrew, we're going to San Francisco, fancy a lift!"* I blow him a kiss and shout *"love you Skip!"* then collapse back in a heap on the deck breathing heavily and tying hard not to be sick.

Wendy appears and bursts my life jacket with a sharp. I am filled really quickly with a massive moment of fear as my life jacket deflates. Momentarily I worry about falling back in with no flotation. I can feel myself filling right up with a blind sense of panic, maybe I have become so used to it and comfortable with it on. I am disillusioned with it now being deflated. This is the worst sense of panic I have felt so far. *"Clip me back on?"*

I say to Wendy with a sense of panic in my voice. It's too late, no time for this to happen. As a number of the team grab hold of me and under Susie's clear and concise instruction calls, they drag me into the cockpit and stuff me, unceremoniously into a sail bag. *"Ready, two six lift"* she calls. In one move I am down in the pit and in the sail bag.

It feels really rough but strangely it doesn't hurt. I thank people and hold hands as they appear to help. Each time I make contact with another crew member, it's good to see the faces smiling back at me. I keep asking to help and trying to get up, Susie shouts back at me and tells me to stop; she has a plan. *"Just wait, I'll look after you now, you do as I say, now bloody keep still and stop fucking fussing mate"* she shouts at me. Ok, I guess I probably should do as she says, so I do. *"Alright, alright mate, I know, I know"*. I tell her. I am lifted again and the sail bag is wrapped around me, a few times my leg is manipulated and it really bloody hurts. I relay this to Susie and she asks everyone to take extra care of it. I am fully in a cocoon now, the sail bag together with me in it, is passed along the cockpit, straight through the companion way hatch and down below where another team are already waiting to receive me. *"You can do this Andrew! You can do this!"* shouts Michelle. *"Stay with me!"* shouts Susie, as she looks into my blank stare, continuing to shout at me *"look at me, pay attention, over here Andrew, look here!"* I am placed down onto the floor and several people arrive with scissors. Susie tells them, *"start cutting, everything off, as quickly as possible"*. I protest and tell her it's alright I can unzip my dry suit and take it off. *"What did I tell you"* she says *"my rules now, keep still, start cutting guys"* *"quick as you can please!"* They cut all around and start removing layers, as they do I start to feel really cold again, I start to shiver over again. This is good news but it really hurts already and I really start to feel the cold again as they remove the layers underneath my suit. Connor puts a call out to OneDLL and they call the race office.

<u>Mark Light: recounts more of his story;</u>
I received news that he had been picked up. Amazing news but I still didn't have confirmation on his status, was he alive or not? The next phone call from CV20 was less welcome. *"Disregard the last message, Andy had not yet been recovered"*. *"Fuck it!!"* 10 to 15 minutes later, another call came through from CV20. *"Andy has been recovered and is on deck. Still no confirmation on his status?!"* I asked CV20 to relay to CV30 that they must call me absolutely as soon as the opportunity presents itself. I realised that now the casualty was back on the boat and on deck a completely new set of problems are presented. Search and Rescue completed, now it is over to the immediate medical procedures and administration of first aid. Also how effective the private pleas and prayers were? I knew that CV30 had crew member Susie Redhouse on board and from a medical point of view Andy was in very good hands.

At precisely 02:14 BST (0114 UTC) and a full 1 hour and 23 minutes after I had received the initial call, the call that I wanted and needed came through. *"The casualty was alive, Andy was alive!"* It was unbelievable news and the best call I had ever had. I had a quick chat to CV20 and then finished the call knowing that I could now speak to CV30 and hopefully Skipper Sean McCarter without interrupting the situation in hand. I came off the phone and sat back on my bed next to Helen. *"My God, he is alive!"* I can hardly believe it. My eyes began to water and I blinked profusely to try and hold back any tears. Skippers can't cry and definitely not Deputy Race Directors. One huge sigh of relief and then the enormity of the whole situation fell upon me.

I finally managed to get to speak with CV30 and Sean. I congratulated him and his crew on a job well done, all very matter of fact, but I think he knew exactly what I meant, in his usual modest and understated self. They had achieved something very special in very extreme circumstance and I'm sure upon reflection would realise this. I made all the necessary phone calls now, firstly to Justin Taylor, secondly to Falmouth MRCC to inform them that all was well and no further assistance was required and then finally I spoke with the US Coastguard to inform them of the same. Justin's notes from that call read;

02:30UTC.

Down below, fully conscious
Pulled himself back on board

Justin emails the Clipper race directors and media team, his email sent at 02:34 UTC says;

MOB recovered.
Initial reports of shock and hypothermia.
More detail to come as I receive it.
Falmouth CG stood down.
US CG has been in contact and told no assistance required.

Mark Light's partner Helen recounts:

I was very used to the odd call going off in the middle of the night. It would ring, I'd half listen and hear that it was usually something mechanical. I'd roll over back to sleep and drift back off into oblivion. Since Mark had taken on the role of the Deputy Race Director, we had always talked about the possibility of him receiving an MOB call and how it was his worst nightmare. Then, the call he'd been dreading since the race began happened.

When the phone went off at about 1am, only 2 feet from me I clearly heard the words *"this is Caty on OneDLL, we've picked up a mayday from Derry LondonDerry. They have a man over board situation and they have lost sight of the casualty!"*

Even recalling those words and remembering that night, it still sends a shiver down my spine. Both of us immediately awake, faster than I've ever woken up in my life, I wanted to do something. Mark was busy on the phone taking as much information as he could from Caty. I got up and made tea. My heart thumping at the absolute horror of what these people must be experiencing. Surprisingly emotional, since I had no idea who the casualty was. All I knew was that a person was in the middle of an ocean, totally alone, desperately hoping that his Skipper and crew would find him, but not knowing if he'd ever see another living soul ever again. A tiny spec in the most vast and dangerous place on earth. I made an instinctive and desperate plea to God that he would grant the casualty a miracle. It was all I could do. I overheard Mark take the name of the casualty, so while he was still on the phone I googled Andrew and found his blog site. After reading each page, I knew he had a family, I felt for them and that at some point soon, their world might be torn apart. I carried on listening and heard that he'd been in the water for more than 15 minutes and the Derry LondonDerry team were operating search and rescue patterns. Off the phone once more, Mark's face said it all. He really wasn't hopeful. Way too much time had passed. It felt strange that although we were on total opposite sides of the world, we were the first people to know on this side of the globe.

Several phone calls later and a few more discussions about Andrews's chances out there, another 45 minutes had passed. Still no sighting of the casualty. Our hearts heavy now at what the inevitable outcome would surely be. It was a very strange period of time, much of it spent trying to get to know as much as possible about Andrew from his website. As I read, I wanted to be able to tell him that what he'd done with his life mattered because I was interested in what he'd wrote. Very strange, reading about a person you've never met but someone you know could die any moment is really hard put emotions on. More phone calls, one of them with Justin, the race director, deciding that it would be him to tell Andrew's family. Almost time now to face the awful reality.

Now 1hr 15 since Andrew went overboard. Convinced now that all must be lost. I started to imagine how the Skipper and crew must feel, having to decide at some stage soon to abandon the search and sail on without him. Another phone call this time from OneDLL. Derry LondonDerry Doire had picked up a signal from an AIS beacon, around 4 miles from the boats current location. Where they had been searching was nowhere near. *"Why had it taken so long to be set off?"* We discussed the possibility that the beacon had set itself off otherwise, why had he not done it immediately? Perhaps he'd been concussed and only just came around? Or perhaps he was badly injured and had simply been wrestling with activating it all this time? Either way, for now it was a tiny glimmer of hope.

Another 15 minutes and Mark takes the call, Andrew is back on board; my deep prayers were answered! Such relief for everyone involved. The next few days and weeks I regularly thought about what Andrew had gone through and the very strange night I'd had, perched right on the edge of my bed while all the other events took place around us.

Julia Wall-Clarke, recounts;
At 02:34 I am a few moments away from the office, a message comes through from race director Justin Taylor. *'MOB recovered. Initial reports of shock and hypothermia. More detail to come as I receive it'.* I respond with just the words, *'Thank God'.* The feeling of relief was immense. It felt like a miracle, and I breathe a sense of relief for Andrew and his family. Jonathan and I would no longer be faced with writing the first death statement in the Clipper Race's nineteen year history. I've written one before during a marathon race and I had prayed never to have to do it again. I reach the office, Jonathan is already at his desk. He says nothing, he just gets up and gives me the hardest, longest hug. It says everything.

The lasting images many see around the world
Taken from Tristan's amazing on board footage

Top; The moment I am recovered

Centre; Conor making the 'mayday' calls

Bottom; Passed from deck to down below inside a sail bag

Photo Credits; Clipper Ventures PLC

Back on board

Now safely down below in the Saloon, I am laying on the floor only moments after being recovered. Michelle arrives and starts talking to me. *"Where the fuck have you been"* she says smiling, kissing my hands with tears rolling down her face. I smile but don't answer, I am bemused just returning blank stares. Later, she is asked by the media why she was blowing on my hands after pictures of this moment appear in the video news reports. *"Serious medical reasons"* she says with a smile. She stays with me all the time, talking to me, keeping me conscious as I start to drift in and out. Under Susie's clear direction, the others work hard to get my kit cut and out of the way as quick as they can.

Remarkably my base layers and thermals are dry! Everyone is astounded by this, at how well my Henri Lloyd dry suit has performed under these extreme conditions. I ask for a sick bag and hang onto it tightly. I never actually use it, but for next few hours I am pretty sure all of the time I will need to at some point. I feel constantly and violently sick. I start to reach a few times but nothing ever happens.

It takes a while to get everything away, as my shorts are removed Susie reaches over and places a balaclava over my privates. I joke with her that I'm so bloody cold there really can't be anything to see there anyway. Is a nice gesture and lightens the mood a little for us all. Once I am naked, I am transferred into a dry sleeping bag. Plastic crew drinking bottles filled with hot water and wrapped in clothes are placed all around inside with me. A few more sleeping bags are put over the top, and I am lifted up whilst a bunk mattress is slid in underneath. I start to drift in and out of consciousness again. Susie stays holding my head all the time, every time I drift off she jabs her fingers into behind my ears which hurts like hell. Each time I stir and wake up. She keeps on doing this, talking to me all the time for the next few hours as I start to warm back up to a safe temperature. I am so very cold again now, my whole body is hurting and shivering violently. I keep asking for a drink but Susie says no. I have a raging thirst, she gets some wet wipes and washes some of the crusted salt off my face, which hurts too as it has encrusted and scratches my face. My face is wind burnt, flaming bright red, my nose is badly wind burnt and weeping slightly with all the skin burnt off by the cold wind and salt.

Susie, Michelle, Wendy and Kristi all talk to me constantly to keep me awake. They ask what happened. In between drifting in and out of consciousness, I start to recount some of the ordeal to them. Kristi & Tristan take it in turns to film this. *"I ache all over, and I have a stonking head ache"* I say to Susie, *"it all happened so quickly"* I recount how quickly it all happened, and play some of it through. *"I didn't know if you were looking for me or not. I didn't know if you had seen me".* *"Did you not hear Sean's shout?"* asks Susie. *"No, nothing"* I reply. I talk about holding the spray vest up and that I put it down as I thought it was acting as a sail. Susie laughs and says *"now most people would be panicking at this point, but not Andrew, no, you're thinking about it acting as a sail".* Kristi says from behind the camera *"that's why you are our safety officer!"* I talk about the storm and Susie keeps asking me questions to keep me awake.

As I warm up slowly, I still can't feel my hands, and as I start to warm, everything starts to hurt, like a full body cramp, it is excruciatingly painful and I protest a lot and keep drifting off. Susie all the time supporting my head, talking to me, jabbing my cheeks and ears to wake me. Skipper comes down off deck a while later, the boat is now stable and sailing back in the right direction. He leans over. He looks wasted tired, I've never seen him look like this before. He says *"I don't remember giving you permission to leave the boat!"* And smiles. *"It's great to be back Skip"* I reply. *"oh yes, it's good to have you back mate"* he adds. *"thank you, thank you"* I say to him over and over again, and start to cry.

Susie passes my head to Wendy and goes to have a good look at my leg. *"Not critical"* she says, *"but it's starting to go a beautiful colour"*. She has no real way of checking for sure, but she agrees it is probably broken and says she will deal with it later. *"Let's just leave it for now and get you stable first."*

Every half an hour or so she takes another set of vitals, blood pressure, pulse, temperature etc. Then a few hours later she calls Praxes our expert shore based medical support team for further advice and some second opinion on drugs for the next rehabilitation stages. They agree with her diagnostics and drug suggestions, she comes back and gives me some really strong pain relief.

Susie and Wendy continue to rotate the hot water bottles to get me warm again, whilst all the time still talking to me and keeping me awake. A few hours later I am lifted and moved down towards the back of the boat, into a relatively accessible bunk. Wrapped into several sleeping bags. Susie still stays with me all the time and keeps me awake for another hour or so, then says she is going to let me sleep. She adds, *"I am going to wake you every hour though and take vitals, OK?"* I drift off straight away and don't remember answering her, or the next few times I am woken. She stays right there with me throughout the night. I remember stirring a few times and seeing her asleep, curled up on a bean bag on the floor next to me; she never ever leaves me.

Justin Taylor is at home from where he has been coordinating with the media teams and directors of Clipper race. He has resisted so far contacting my next of kin during the media blackout, deciding he did not wish to wake my parents in the middle of the night anyway. After receiving the news updates from Mark that I am back on board, he decides to now contact my brother Sean in Sydney. He thinks through carefully what to say, rehearses it a few times, then takes a deep breath and makes the call. *"Hello Sean, this is Justin Taylor, the Race Director of*

Clipper Ventures you are aware that your brother is competing in the Clipper Race?" Justin pauses, however only very briefly, and only just sufficient for an acknowledgement. *"Andrew is ok and in good spirits, he has however been recovered from the water after he fell overboard from the yacht".* He stops and pauses for breath, having got in there quickly that I am alive and well(ish).

The call comes through to Sean's mobile phone. Showing as from a UK phone number. Sean is used to Brits not remembering the time difference and calling him at odd hours but a quick mental calculation tells him that it is around 1:00 or 2:00am in the UK. *"This can't be good news"* He thinks, even before picking up. Sean describes the call as a *"polite, almost apologetic voice in a strong British accent which confirms initially that he is indeed Sean Taylor".* A massive rush of emotion washes over him, as he realises already that something is very badly wrong. *"This is Justin Taylor, I'm the Race Director of the Clipper Round the World Race. I'm calling to tell you that Andrew has been involved in an incident. He is fine but it is important that I tell you a few things about it",*

Justin goes on to explain that since my parents will likely be asleep for quite a while yet, he has called Sean first and hopes that it's OK to tell him what's going on as Andrew's next of kin. This again fills Sean with massive amounts of fear. There are enough clues in what Justin has already told him to make him more than a little bit concerned. Justin goes on to explain the events of the night and that I had been in the freezing waters, for what was thought to be an hour and 40 minutes! Sean recounts remembering a documentary he once saw, where sailors in the Falkland Islands describe how the body starts to shut down after 3 or 4 minutes without protection. Despite Justin's calming influence, Sean's heart is racing hard, and he feels cold, his hands shaking a little. Justin calmly explains that despite being alive, conscious and back on board, that we are very much not yet out of the woods. He explains it is believed I have broken my leg and maybe other bones, unknown at this stage. The chances of Hypothermia are still extremely high. Then there is a very real risk of secondary drowning. Justin goes on to explain what secondary drowning actually is. Given that Sean works in IT, he is already beginning to Google this at his desk, as Justin goes on to explain it. *"Shit, this doesn't sound good"* he thinks 'Secondary drowning is where ingested salt water draws liquid from the blood stream into the lung tissues slowly via osmosis. This slowly thickens the blood causing massive increase in the risk of full cardiac arrest. If left untreated the casualty would eventually drown in their own bodily fluids. Successful treatment would require hospital high dependency unit facilities and would not be possible on-board an ocean racing yacht.'

Trying to keep calm and gather his thoughts Sean begins to be apologetic & 'British' too. He even recalls asking if it was OK to ask a few more questions, given that it was the middle of the night in England? Sean is trying now to picture what everyone might need to know and asks *"what are the chances are of getting him off the boat to medical care if he goes downhill?"* The reality hits even harder when Justin begins to suggest that unless there is very luckily a naval boat nearby, the possibilities of rescue right now are non-existent. There simply are not rescue planes or helicopters that can fly that far. They politely finish the call, agreeing to speak again shortly.

Sean hangs up the phone, slumps back in his chair, stunned and lost for what to do next. When you have a news story, your first instinct is to tell someone. He really isn't sure if he should even share the information right now? He makes coffee and tells his boss what's going on, just to alert him to the fact that he might need to leave at short notice. He calls his wife and explains what's going on and then begins to plan for every scenario, without really actually knowing what he should be doing. He says afterwards *"For the first time in over 20 years I realise just how far away I am from my family at a time when potentially they may need me"*. He obtains flight quotes and leaves them open, set up on his computer to get him to LA or London at short notice.

Sean sends a text to Dad. *'Hi Dad, nothing to worry about but please call as soon as you pick this up'.* The hours pass slowly, seeming at times to be in slow motion. When the call comes from Dad, Sean pauses and takes a very deep breath before answering.

It's around 07:00 in Portugal, Mum & Dad have been away with an international bowls tour for three weeks and are preparing to head to the airport to travel home. *"Hi mate, everything OK?"* Asks Dad, in a chirpy but still serious manner. *"Yes, sort of"* says Sean. *"Listen, I've had a call from the Clipper Race Director, Andrew was washed overboard last night, he's back on board now, but he was in the water for a long time, we are waiting for more news from the boat, and I'm staying by the phone keeping it open to hear"*. Sean takes the same tactic as Justin and gets this all out in one go without a pause. *"How is he?"* Asks Dad straight away. *"Seriously, right now we don't know anymore. Justin says he's conscious, talking and in good hands. What's your schedule today so I can stay in touch?"* They exchange details and ring off. Dad pauses and stands fast and still for a few moments, Mum is staring at him questionably. The word 'conscious' is ringing in his ears; it is not a word you use in a minor incident. This is potentially more serious than Sean either knows or has just let on? They pause, looking at each other slightly shocked then he shares the news, sitting quietly for while in their hotel room together before going to join their colleagues for breakfast. They decide to keep the news to themselves for now, however within moments of getting to breakfast a close friend says to Dad "ok? *What's up?"* Realising something is wrong. They share the story with just these close friends and they feel like it helps a little to talk about it. They are both a little stunned and deep in thought. On the way to the airport, they chat about it and try hard not to speculate, which is difficult having so little news. Dad recounts several times that he knows I am in extremely good hands and knows well that Susie will have everything under perfect control. Dad spent time with Susie's family in London at race start and feels like he knows her a bit.

At the airport they call Sean again, he confirms the latest news *"conscious and talking, broken leg, possibly other bones, being treated for hypothermia and shock, race office concerned you knew and didn't hear it from anywhere else, there is a media blackout in place until we confirm all the family are aware so don't spread it too far for now, and make sure everyone knows please"*. *"Ok"* says Dad *"I'll contact family as soon as we land and call you later"*.

They board the three hour flight home. It's an age to be out of contact and seems to pass really slowly. As soon as they land Dad turns his phone back on and texts Sean. His reply reads, *'Have received some more updates from on-board via Justin. All news is, he is in good spirits, but still being treated by Susie, he's not out of the woods yet Dad. Call me when you get home'*. It's the middle of Sean's night now. Not able to sleep anyway, he continues to maintain regular contact with Justin. Dad calls my younger brother James, then Siobhan's Mum Jacquie to spread the news. Jacquie texts Siobhan and asks her to come home straight away. Dad has shared only brief highlights at this stage but is aware it is likely to appear on social media at some point really soon, so it's imperative family are aware as soon as possible.

Siobhan comes home and gets the news from her Mum, she is immediately concerned but not overly so, as she only has a brief encounter of the story so far. She has had many calls before to let her know I've fallen off a mountain bike, been hurt climbing or running. However, as the first Media story breaks, she is not prepared and becomes more concerned. Very quickly Jacquie stops all news exposure at home. After a couple of days Siobhan stops going out because the media story is fuelling interest. Everyone wants to talk about it to her and it's way too much for her for a few days.

On the way home from the Airport, Jules checks in with Mum & Dad. They are under pressure from the media to release a statement and Clipper race request Dad's blessing to do so. He agrees, Jules sends copies of the releases through each time before they are released, taking over all contact updates with Dad from this point.

A short while after arriving home, Dad texts Sean to see if he is still awake. Sean responds almost immediately, calling back on the house phone explaining *"I haven't had much more of an update but listen, he was in the cold water for an hour and forty minutes! Susie is treating him for hypothermia and secondary drowning. He's in very good hands, Justin talks highly of Susie and so do you. But they are a very long way out, there is no secondary rescue here. We are relying very heavily on the crew you know that right?"* Dad replies *"Yes, I know, he'll be fine mate. Sean (Skipper), Susie and the crew are excellent, I've met them all they are fabulous people and strong too, he'll be fine for sure"* Sean spares Dad the finer details of secondary drowning and for the moment feels like he carries the weight of this himself.

In the morning I am woken as normal again, Susie says I can have a drink now if I want one. She gets me a bottle of mixed juice, which I down virtually in one and a cup of hot, sweet tea which is wonderful. She asks if I want to eat, but I still feel really sick so decline. She makes me eat a couple of Ritz crackers with the tablets, and for a while I am pretty sure these are coming back up. I slip back off to sleep again and for most of the day we follow this routine every hour or so. I keep my liquid intake as high as I can and by midafternoon the inevitable happens, I am desperate to pee! I can't, Susie gets me a pee bottle, I can't do it laying down so she helps me up and I try sitting on the bunk edge for a while. This makes me feel even more nauseous and dizzy too. Still no luck either. Susie asks if maybe it is *"stage fright or mechanics?"* I am really not sure, but I am in a great deal of pain from this now and am desperate to go, but my body just won't. I try a few more times through the afternoon, eventually forcing some out, which is very painful and slow. It's hard work sitting up on the bunk too, trying to keep as much weight off my leg as possible. Feeling increasingly dizzy whilst balancing as the boat rocks and sways. I knock my leg a few times and swear with the pain. Susie helps and all the time gives me privacy too, this is a real skill and she is very good at it. When eventually I'm done she takes the pee bottle, empties and washes it before bringing it back. I feel totally embarrassed by this and really guilty. I apologise profusely. She asks me not to and says *"I know how you feel, but apologising isn't necessary mate"*. *"I know"* I tell her *"but this is above and beyond normal duties for a friend"*. It's not the same as a patient at work, when it's someone you know so well and are fond of it's quite different and difficult for us both. We laugh about it and make some jokes about taking the piss. She is required to do this a few more times through the next night as I gradually manage more and more. It's a couple of days before my body behaves anything like normal. I guess this is the body holding on to all its vitals and working it out for itself.

I continue to sleep a lot for the next 36 hours or so, then on the second morning I sit up and have some hot porridge. It's the first food for well over 48 hours, and it tastes really good! I could probably eat another bowl or perhaps even two or three maybe. But I resist, better to keep one down than eat two and throw them both back up I reckon. I feel pretty sick for the next couple of hours, but again manage to keep it down. At lunch time I am woken again and have some plain hot noodles, then sleep some more all afternoon. During the day each time I am awake crew members come by and say hello. It's great to see them and I thank them all. Hugs and hands held or kissed whenever I can manage throughout the day and the night too. Skipper comes and sits with me for a while and we talk about what happened. He gets quite emotional once or twice. This is not a side of Sean we ever see, he is always ice cool and keeps his feelings under control. He is however clearly moved by the experience and we hold hands for a moment with fixed eye contact, as I thank him so much for working so hard and finding me. It's a brief and privileged very close moment together with someone I owe a debt to which I shall never be able to repay. There is a call from deck for his advice. I think he is glad of the exit away from the emotion and he Skips away back to work. Such is the world of a racing yacht Skipper in the North Pacific. Sean does the most amazing job, his temperament and approach is as perfect as one could wish for. Always calm, always smiling, never chastises anyone. Only ever using positive advice and helping us grow and develop as a team. He has given us his confidence from very early on in the race and leaves us on deck to get on with the responsibility of sailing the boat for long periods of time. In turn he is confident we will call on him when we need to. This is such a two way thing and he has developed this leadership skill really well.

I drift off again and next time I wake it is night time. I open my eyes and from where I lay, I can see Susie. She is sleeping next to me, curled up on the bean bag again. Wearing her purple beanie hat, sailing boots and lots of warm layers. I lay still and just watch her for a while thinking about her commitment to looking after us all. I reflect upon just how much she has done for me and how great she is at doing so. Not to mention what an amazing person she is, bright and bubbly, always smiling. I am very fond of Susie and hope we will always be friends. As a team, we have all called on her expertise and medical knowledge quite a few times in the race so far. We have had broken ribs, a broken shoulder, dislocations, a really bad head injury and damaged tendons on board. It's not that long ago Michelle was in this bunk seriously injured with Susie & I reversed roles. Susie is quite frankly truly amazing, always calm and honest with her advice, always with a smile and an occasional joke, it's a privilege to have her on the team with us. It must be difficult treating people you know. Just not the same as treating an ambulance casualty. I lay still and wait for her to wake. When she opens her eyes she smiles and I say *"love you Sooz"*. We both have a little cry then she says, *"Right c'mon you fucking Muppet! Time you got up dressed and warm now"* she helps me get up and dress for the first time.

After having all my best base layers cut off, she gathers together sufficient layers, a fleece and some thick socks, plus a pair of combat trousers as a start at least from my kit bag. Keith lends me a pair of his thermal leggings, I am staying below decks for a while but it's still really cold on board, I really appreciate these to stay warm.

With some help from Susie & Keith to move along the boat, I join the watch teams for breakfast in the saloon, boy it's good to be back up and see everyone. It's so good to be dressed too. For the first time since being back on board I feel slightly more human and alive being dressed and warm. It's a strange feeling sitting up and I feel dizzy for a while. Loads of smiles and hugs all around. We have porridge, hot drinks and bread baked on board yesterday with Nutella & peanut butter.

We recount some of the stories of what happened and how I am feeling now. After a little less than an hour, I start to feel really tired, sick and quite tearful too. So with more assistance again, I go back to my bunk and get really upset, crying a lot. I can't stop it this time, there is nothing specific in my head which I am crying about it just keeps coming. Susie checks on me a few times, reassuring me but leaving me to it. When it eventually stops I wash myself off with baby wipes and fall back asleep again. Susie comes and wakes me up, checking me over and making sure I have had pain killers. We talk closely for a while and it really helps me feel better. I get back up and sit on the floor next to my bunk after lunch and start to write my diary. I want to capture as much as I can whilst it is still fresh. It helps me to write it down too, I can fill in the gaps as I go along and as it builds I fill in with stories from the boat which others talk through. I find the process quite cathartic and I think it helps with my recovery. After a few days I watch the on board footage back, so I know some of what was going on back on the deck whilst I was in the water. It's horrible to watch, and it takes me a few attempts to do so.

I telephone my brother Sean in Sydney, he had been the main point of contact between Clipper race team and my family during the events of the last few days. It is really good to speak with him and great to hear that he has spoken to Mum & Dad. Even more so that they subsequently spoke to Siobhan before the news story broke in the media back home. I had been really worried about this and that any of them might have heard it from another source. This puts my mind at ease a lot. We have a good talk through what happened. He massively praises Justin Taylor, the Race Director for the way he handled the communications. He cannot speak highly enough of him and repeats this. He gets quite emotional talking about it. I ask him to let everyone know I am ok and he promises to spread the word. He says *"brace yourself, it is a massive global news story already. Lead story on all channels in Sydney for the last 24 hours"*. He has seen some footage of the rescue and recovery which was quite dramatic and emotional to watch. I ask if the boys are ok, he says they are pretty upset by the story, but excited at all the news coverage. More so, just relieved I am OK, and following it all closely. I ask him to let Mum & Dad know we have spoken, pass on that I am sort of ok, and to tell them I will try and call them in the morning their time, he sends them a text and email to expect my call.

Next morning UTC, quite late evening on the boat, I call my parents, I get through first time. Mum answers. *"Hi Mum, it's Andrew, I am OK. I am calling from the boat, it's a satellite phone so there might be a delay, and we could be cut off, if we are I will try and call you straight back"*. I blurt all of this out in one go, without a pause, without a breath. I wait for a response, I can feel my heart beating and am starting to get upset.

Mum manages *"hello"* back and just about gets through *"how are you?"* It is clearly way too much for her and I can hear her crying, she is upset and breaks off. I can feel myself welling up and I try and take a breath to pull myself back together. *"Hold it together for this one"* I say to myself in my head, *"you need to show them you are OK"*

Dad takes over the conversation. *"Hello mate'* he says, as if we just met at home after a day at work. *"How are you doing?"* I repeat satellite telephone warning and ask *"is Mum OK"? "She is fine mate, we are all fine, tell us how you are?"* I tell them I am relatively OK, bruised and beaten, but OK. I tell them I am sure my leg is broken but other than that I'll be OK. I ask how they heard and where they were to reconfirm they got it from my brother Sean and at a good time. They were about to fly home from Portugal when he called them, and had time on the plane to reflect, albeit they say this was really hard. Being out of touch, not knowing the latest news whilst in the air. By the time they land back in the UK, it is all over the world news. Dad confirms he has spoken to Siobhan, this is even better news. I really dreaded her seeing it on TV or hearing from a friend first. My worst nightmare. He says she is ok, a little overwhelmed by it all, but doing well. I tell them again and again I am ok, if it wasn't for my broken leg I would be thinking about going back to work on deck. I praise the team and how well I have been treated and looked after. Dad says he would expect nothing less, knowing the team. He knows I am in good hands and says *"knowing you are back on board and being looked after by Susie, we know you will be OK, you're in great hands"*. He says they have had several thousand messages of support already, many from people they don't even know and from all over the world too. They have had a really nice email from Skipper Sean's Dad Andy McCarter. I spent a lot of time with Andy & Paddy his partner, in both London and Rio, they are such genuinely proper nice people. We sign off and I say I will fill in the gaps in the story from San Francisco.

I ask them in turn to let Siobhan know I will call her that evening. Dad reconfirms he has been keeping her updated and will speak to her and let her know straight away. Dad promises to post on my Facebook he has spoken with me and tell friends and family I am ok too. I thank him, and we say farewell for now. It's a hard conversation, a call I had hoped I would never have to make. I stay in the Nav station for ages thinking it over. It all seems like a dream and the time passes in a sort of slow motion blur. I don't know how long I sat there, but Susie arrives and says *"time for bed mate, c'mon shift your fat arse back to your bunk please"*.

Later that evening I crawl back to the nav station again, to call Siobhan. I haven't relaxed all afternoon, I can feel the nerves and tension and am struggling to think straight. I call her and get through straight away, she is loud and clear on the line. It is so good to hear her voice and I nearly loose it at first. I really need to hold it together for her sake and try really hard not to show her I am upset and crying just now. I tell her I am ok apart from my leg. She says she has heard from my Dad and knew how I was. She says shame about the leg, but tells *"you are a really lucky boy Dad, if you get away with this with only a broken leg"*. Which is so true but I am still having trouble coming to full terms with this myself. I don't tell her this. Siobhan says she has seen a little of the news, but doesn't want to watch the videos, she is finding it all a little difficult and hard to take in. She is keeping a low profile for now too. Everywhere she goes people talk to her about it and it's really hard for her. Her Mum is keeping the news stories recorded and they are going to watch it together when she is ready. I change the subject and ask her for her news and for the rest of the call we concentrate on this.

236

First her driving lessons and then great news & progress on her apprenticeship work to supplement her college. All really good news and she sounds really positive about her world and life which is really good to hear. She chats for ages and we sort of avoid the topic of my incident. We eventually sign off and agree to speak much more as soon I land in San Francisco. She pauses and says *'love you loads Dad'*. I pause, choke hard, and say the same back. She closes off with *'love you bye, love you bye, love you bye, love you bye'* and keeps repeating it until we hang up. After the call, I sit in the nav station on my own totally choked for a while, I can still hear her in my head. It takes me a while to compose myself before exiting and crawling back to my bunk.

By now, the media attention following the incident has increased, we are getting lots of email requests through to the boat from the race office for interviews, video and stills. Tristan has some really great footage from on deck and has already started interviewing crew. He sends off straight away an interview with Skipper and a short montage of all the best bits of footage. This seems to fuel the media focus and the requests flood in thick & fast.

I return to Julia Wall-Clarke, PR Manager for Clipper Ventures;

As it was still before 3:00am, we had the benefit of a few hours before people started waking up and realising something was wrong via the Race Tracker, which clearly showed *Derry~Londonderry~Doire* circling in a search pattern, with *OneDLL* turning back to assist. Race supporters are glued to the tracker and don't miss anything. It wouldn't be long before questions come.

Justin continued to find out the facts and Jonathan and I started to draft a media statement. Sir Robin was answering emails from the very start of the incident and had been about to head to the office when we got the word that Andrew had been retrieved. He remained on email all morning, joining Jonathan and I in the office before 5am. He was a very big part of the communication and response in this situation, entirely reflective of his hands-on approach to the race in all respects. He has obviously seen and experienced pretty much everything in ocean racing and offers huge guidance to the team in all manners. Safety and training are an integral part of the Clipper Race at every level and that is largely thanks to Sir Robin who has ensured this ever since he founded the Clipper Race almost 20 years ago.

Once the statement went out, the expected barrage of media calls began. Everyone wanted to talk to Andrew, Skipper Sean or his team mates. Early on there was never a hesitation from our perspective. We would not be arranging interviews direct with the boat. They had just gone through a massively traumatic experience, and had now resumed racing. That, and providing round the clock care and recovery support to Andrew was their absolute priority. Andrew must be allowed to concentrate on getting better. The initial statement was detailed and factual. All interview requests were passed to Sir Robin and Justin Taylor to elaborate further.

This was a story that could have had such a tragic, painful ending. All circumstances considered however, we were able to provide incredibly powerful, high quality video footage of a miraculous rescue. The footage not only gave reassurance that Andrew was safe, but also satisfied the media demand for further updates, and interviews. Before the footage went out, I spoke with Andrew's father, Tony, who agreed it all and was thankful for the update. I remember him seeming surprisingly calm and relaxed as he told me stories about Andrew, and how he knew he was holding up well from being able to speak with him on board.

As the boats continued on their way to San Francisco, the US media soaked up the footage, broadcasting it on every national and regional TV show across the USA. We had calls from NBC, CNN, CBS, ABC, FOX, WYTV (Ohio), WKMG

(Orlando), KXAN (Texas), just about every letter in the alphabet was covered stateside! The biggest national morning news programme, NBC's 'The Today Show' ran two lengthy features on it that week, as well as 'CBS This Morning'. Our media monitoring service could barely keep up. As well as every major UK outlet, the video had made headlines and features everywhere from Australia, to New Zealand, France, Norway, Poland, the Ukraine and Russia. My sister even emailed saying she saw it where she lives in Buenos Aires, Argentina.

The MOB took place in the early hours of March 31st but I even had an email from a Spanish journalist on April 1st asking me if the whole thing was an April Fools prank. I remember being quite angered by this at the time as I couldn't believe someone would consider we would joke at the idea of the life and safety of one of our crew. He apologised immediately but explained he had just never heard of such a rescue before, someone being found after being alone in the water for so long. It sounded so impossible.

Neither Sean or Andrew, or anyone else on the team were asked to do any media interviews during those first few crucial days. Andrew needed to concentrate on getting better, so we continued to decline all requests, no matter who they were. We also wanted to get the balance right, and not appear to be sensationalising the story unnecessarily, but we were still getting a huge amount of enquiries, including from supporters of the race, who wanted to know how Andrew was doing.

Later that week, word was that Andrew was up and about and recovering well. With Andrew's blessing, and with interview requests continuing to flood in, we decided he would sit down with Tristan and film one short piece to camera update that we would then issue on wide release to press to calm the demand and show how well he was doing. Again, the first people I shared this with was Andrew's parents.

Sean did his first phone interview, with BBC 5Live's Victoria Derbyshire. Sean spoke fantastically about the team's effort and the way in which everyone responded in process of getting him back on board. By Friday, most of the press had used Andrew's video comments and attention has begun to calm down for now. The only people continuing to request an interview at this point were BBC 5Live. They called me every morning at 5.30am since it happened. Victoria had handled Sean very well and promised to do the same with Andrew. Andrew had the final decision and agreed. Again, I let his parents know so they could listen in. Andrew stayed calm as he recollected the moments, and spoke well. The producers then called back and asked if they could speak to his parents 30 minutes later about how they had dealt with it all. His Dad was happy to do this. Unknown to his Dad though, they also planned to bring Andrew back on the call to speak with them.

Aside from the initial nauseous feeling when we got the news, I had been too busy to really process much that week. It is a small team in our office and as soon as the statement went out we had been overwhelmed by media requests and enquiries. Working on UK breakfast media time from from 5.30am, to the end of the day on the US west coast timezone, approximately 1:00am our time.

That moment, on BBC 5Live when Andrew spoke to his parents live on air and they both got emotional was the moment it all hit home for me that week. My eyes grew wet and I blinked back tears, as I heard them break down in utter joy and relief. They had been so strong all week. I felt guilty at first, should I have given them the heads up that Andrew would join the call? I called Tony afterwards and he told me not to worry, that they were just so happy they had gotten to talk to him again. He also thanked me for keeping them informed and updated all week. That they had felt so well supported by the Clipper Race team, which had given them strength. It was really warming to hear that we had been any help to them during this incredibly difficult week.

Back onboard Derry LondonDerry. The race office arrange a sat phone interview with associated press for me; this can be networked and cuts down the amount of interviews I might need to do. After I do this, we get loads more subsequent requests for telephone interviews, Skipper does a live interview with BBC radio 5Live and Foyle radio. The next day 5Live do another live interview with me. They introduce this as 'exclusive to 5Live', promote it as my 'first and only live interview from the boat'. We interview live with Victoria Derbyshire for around 10-12 minutes talking about what happened, how I felt and what it was like being in the water for 1hour & 40minutes. Later in the morning they call us back and ask if I'll go back on air live again later. When I call in and get put through to the studio they are already in the process of interviewing my parents and I get to listen in to their interview, then I get put through to talk to them at the end of the interview live on air. It's all quite emotional and Mum gets really properly upset this time. The previous interview included me saying I had remembered it was Mums birthday and didn't want to die on her birthday. The radio interviewer is quite sympathetic, but I am sure the media and BBC love this emotional connection. They milk it out a little as it makes a good radio story and adds to the drama and personal touch. It's a nice touch to have joined the interview with Mum and Dad. During the interview, they also read out a tweet from my cousin Steven, who has been listening in. It's another really nice piece and rounds the family angle further.

By the middle of the afternoon, I am absolutely wasted tired and extremely tearful again. I slip away to my bunk for a couple of hours peace. I set out to listen to some of my favourite music and drift off to sleep for a while, I am feeling really very fragile.

Back home Jules arranges for ITV to interview my parents, they send a crew from London to their home in Newmarket. Jules has confirmed with the ITV crew to be kind to my parents and is sending some media material with the crew for Mum & Dad to see. The two man media team arrive at the house and

Mum makes them tea. The interviewer says he has some footage from the boat for them to see, setting up his laptop for them to watch this. He shows them the first footage from Tristan on board. Including shots of me in the water, being recovered and first few words when back on board. It includes some of the more dramatic shots which have not been released to the world yet. Mum & Dad are shocked. The scale and enormity of the incident had net really hit home yet until they see this. It's a lot for them to take in and it takes them a while to recompose for the interview.

Back in Gosport, training had already commenced for 15/16 race, with some refresher training for crew joining towards the end of this one also taking place. Dave Warwick, Clipper training Skipper, has a group of 15 or so crew on board preparing to head out for their training week. Many of them have questions and concerns about the MOB incident. Sir Robin arrives and joins them on board, providing much needed reassurances and confidence to them. He emphasises the critical level of importance race training had played in both my survival and successful recovery. He spends a good while with them on board answering questions and supporting them. Throughout the many weeks and months that follow. Sir Robin, Justin and Mark continue to do so with training crews, providing much reassurance to them.

Next day I am up and around early before breakfast, I stay around and have breakfast with both watches at watch change over. Breakfast on board is a good social time with all the crew. We convene around the galley and help ourselves to bread with Nutella or peanut butter, cereals, dried fruit, honey, maple syrup and anything else that happens to get put out on the counter. It creates a great sense of sharing and social eating. Much more so than we do at lunch and dinner, when getting passed a bowl of hot steaming food and a spork is just not the same.

During the morning on deck, the crew hoist and drop two spinnakers, then back to white sails again, so there is a lot of work to do with wooling and repacking the spinnakers down below. I put my lightweight foulies on, with knee armour in them. They are perfect to crawl around on the floor and wool the spinnakers which I just get down and get on with. It hurts like hell when I have finished and I go and lie down for a while and elevate my leg. For the first time however it really felt like I was back contributing to the race again. It's been a frustrating few days. If it wasn't for my leg I would have been planning a return to deck work and would have certainly already been back up at some point by now. I feel stronger too. Not back to full strength yet for sure and I occasionally still feel tearful and fragile. But I am feeling good about myself. At least I do until Susie removes the splints & checks my leg over again. It is incredibly swollen almost twice the size, bruised and jet black from the calf down. The area around the impact is severely bruised and extremely tender to touch. My foot is completely black and very swollen. I can't move my toes, Susie concludes this is fluids and trauma from the injury above on the lower leg, draining down into the foot as I move around on the boat. She gives me anti-inflammatory drugs and strict orders right back to my bunk. *"Stay there, elevate the leg for the next few days to allow the swelling to subside and allow it to heal quicker".* My brief return to work on board is halted again. I appreciate in the short term this is important and valuable healing time, but boy it's frustrating not being able to assist with the team. All of whom are working so hard in extreme conditions to get us to San Francisco as quickly as possible.

For the rest of the run into San Francisco I am confined to either bunk or Saloon with my leg elevated and resting on a bean bag. It is immensely difficult for me to accept this. As the boat heels around there are times when it is almost impossible for me to move about, I still need to use a bed bottle to pee in and am not leaving my bunk any more than occasionally rolling out onto a bean bag and making myself as comfortable as I can. Many of the crew are helpful and come to chat when they have a chance. The mothers send me food parcels down.

I try and make the best use of this time, profusely writing my diary. Scribing huge amounts of new dairy stuff, upon which this book is now based. I use my iPad to make a new Derry team video promoting us heading home into Derry. Whenever I can evade Susie and make it to the Nav station, I check out what I can assist with, but as we head east across miles of open ocean, there isn't much navigation to do. As we approach closer to San Francisco, the team starts to go through the usual prep for arrival. Getting bags and kit ready for arrival and getting off the boat. We have some lengthy discussions with the Race Office team and arrange my hospital checks and media press conferences for when we first arrive. I start to prepare a short statement in my head, ready for the media when we get in. Despite my best efforts, I am not emotionally prepared for what greets us as we arrived in San Francisco.

Photo Credit; Clipper Venture Plc

San Francisco
Beaten but not broken

As we make our final approach into San Francisco, the wind hole catches us and we sit bobbing around overnight. We had a 02:00 arrival eta, which becomes 04:00 then 07:00 then 10:00. I start to get anxious; the wait for arrival & getting away to my medical checks is painfully long. Susie has helped me pack up some kit. Chris has a small bag for me he is going to take straight to a hotel we are going to share, and I have a rucksack of kit to take with me straight to hospital. Eventually we make our final approach, Susie & Chris help me get dressed into my team kit and up onto deck. We pass under the golden gate bridge at around 14:30 local time. The views on the final approach are amazing, the coastline & bridge quite spectacular in the early afternoon sunshine. I start to feel really nervous, apprehensive about arrival and the attention I might face. I know there are going to be media here. I have been warned about being asked questions when we land, although the feelings of having arrived are a massive relief and a huge sense of achievement too. Leg six across the North Pacific has always been the race I was least looking forward to and the one which made me the most nervous. I am so glad it is now over, and I can see around me many others whom are pretty glad to have arrived at the end of this epic part of our adventure together too. Emotions on board are clearly running very high.

I never considered it would ever be quite such an eventful & epic a journey and story. I can feel the relief of having arrived, together with the stress of what's about to follow mixing up and stirring my stomach. I struggle with the tears and have to hold it together pretty hard to stop myself breaking down. The team are great, many of them hug me or just smile. A few actually say nothing as they do this, enough is said by eye, we all know each other well enough by now, with what we have been through together and how much it means to now be here safe. The very best things are sometimes those not said

At one point it is all a bit too much, Michele gives me a massive hug on deck, I break down, crying deeply, both of us blissfully unaware that the media helicopter has already captured this moment and it's gone out live on TV. It is now one of the big headline still photos that ends up around the world's media over the next few days. It's a great picture which evokes many very deep memories for me even now. There is a media RIB out following us, I feel horribly like I am being watched from every direction now. I become aware of media taking photos of my leg and foot, I pull my foulies down over it and sit with it tucked underneath me for a while. It all gets a bit much so I go below deck for a while and sit quietly. Wendy passes by and gives me a hug, we don't speak, which is rare for Wendy who normally never stops speaking!

As we enter the dock, there are thousands of people lining the upper board walk, looking down on us. I spot some friendly faces in the crowd. Round the world crew member Charlie's wife and daughter, Wendy's Mum, Anthony, a good friend from Mission Performance and his fiancé. Then, alongside these and at the front of the big crowd are all the crew from Qingdao and OneDLL. Lined up together, all in their branded team colour crew kit, applauding and cheering all of us as we pull in and moor up. It's a fantastic gesture from the other teams and really means a lot to all of the crew onboard Derry, this applause is for all of us. The race is jammed full of truly great people and this moment absolutely captures the spirit of the whole race for me. One big family. It is one I shall remember and cherish forevermore.

Along the pontoon the Clipper race crew are preparing to receive us. They are struggling amongst the media who have broken ranks now and are follow us along the pontoon as we approach our mooring. Sir Robin and Mark bark at them to move away to make some room, it falls on deaf ears as they snap and roll cameras aimed at us. It feels like they are mostly aimed at me, but I know they are filming the whole arrival spectacle. I can see amongst them, reporters doing pieces to camera with us in the background. Some of this is being broadcast live across the US and beyond. My brother and his family in Sydney watch this live on their main Australian news channel.

I try and stay calm, thinking carefully about everything I am doing, where and how I sit and stand. At one point, for a few moments, I back away and stand behind the boom with some of the other crew. I know the cameras can only see my feet from there. As I come back around, I can feel it all start over again and the cameras snap away with added vigour.

Once we dock, I sit quietly and talk to the crew. Boy, it is so good to be here. I go over in my head what I am going to say to the media. We have agreed to make a statement before I go off to hospital. I run through it in my mind over and over, creating some sound bites I know will be used later. I greet from the deck the race office crew, Gillian, Race Manager, Mark, Deputy Race Director, Justin, Race Director and Sir Robin, all of whom give me a hug and share a few moments together. Sir Robin asks after my family and if I need anything which is really nice. I have come to know him well over the race so far; he is such a genuinely nice bloke, always stops and passes the time, engaging with you. The British Consulate representative introduces herself and asks if I need anything, insisting I can contact her 24/7 whilst here for any support I might need.

After immigration have cleared us I am free to go to hospital, I gather my overnight bag which I prepared a few days earlier and get ready to leave. I move across and sit on the edge of the boat. Marina from our press office has a tough few moments controlling the media scrum. I sit quietly whilst they jostle around for a bit. Then I calmly say I will make a statement before leaving for hospital. They quieten down and settle. I take a deep breath and calmly speak as best I can.

I thank Skipper and the crew for their hard work during the search and rescue. I thank Ollie and the crew of OneDLL for ceasing racing and coming to assist so quickly, the race office for their support to my family and to everyone around the world who has sent messages of support to all of us. I say my leg is very painful and needs medical care which I am leaving for as soon as I have finished this statement. Other than this I am fine, but really looking forward to spending a few days on land, before continuing with the race if I can and am allowed to.

I remind everyone we have been racing hard since it happened and none of us has yet had time to process and understand it properly, we all need some time and support whilst in San Francisco to do this. Finally I remind everyone this is stressful and emotionally difficult for all of us, not just me and we need to support everyone. I thank them for their time and say farewell.

Questions are fired quickly from all directions in a rain storm of voices. I pick out the one about whether I will continue with the race, and say *"absolutely I will, as long as I am able to"*. The blast of questions comes again and I pick out one about how my family are, I say they are fine, I have spoken to them once from the boat, and I now am really looking forward to catching up properly with them. I really struggle with this one and can only just hold it together. I am sure this shows in my voice and face as the cameras rattle and scream pictures whilst I struggle over the words. It may have been a mistake to pick out that one to answer, but it's how I felt and family are so important to me it felt like a good opportunity to mention them. I try to get out to leave and the cameras and questions keep flying, but I'm not going back for more this time. Marina staves them off and insists I will be available tomorrow for interviews and questions, no more today please whilst I go for medical care.

The medical team have arrived, they have a stretcher and several guys in smart uniforms waiting. It all feels a little over the top, but at least it gets me out of the crowds and away from

the media. Once I am strapped into the stretcher, we are off.
Marina from our media team and Tristan our camera man both
travel with me to the hospital. A few close friends hug and high
five me as we make our way out to the waiting ambulance. Just
as I am being loaded in, Sofia and Wendy jump out of a cab,
Skipper Sean and round the world crew member Andy's wives.
They both come over for a hug before I am slid into the
ambulance, with more picture of this broadcast again. Marina,
Tristan and the medical team jump in and the doors close. I
immediately and completely break down. That was such a
stressful couple of hours, I am so relieved of the moment's
privacy. It takes me a few moments to pull it together again, and
we talk all the way to hospital with the med team who make
themselves busy doing their vitals and checks on me. They talk
to Tristan about camera work and he keeps them amused, I am
really grateful for this as I don't need to converse for a while.
Occasionally they dry up and I throw in something
conversational about filming to start them up again.

We arrive at St Francis hospital straight into check in.
Tristan gets his shots of me checking in, then I quietly ask him
to leave, he asks to stay but I say *"enough already mate, I really
have had enough, sorry, not now, please just leave me alone for
this bit now"*. He is gracious and does not argue at all, *"no
problem, I get it. To be honest I am struggling with filming this
anyway, it doesn't feel right to be doing it."* He says, checking
some timings with Marina for tomorrow before leaving.

I am taken down a short corridor to a private room to be
checked in and wait a few moments for the doctors to arrive.
One by one, a number of polite and efficient hospital staff arrive
and do little things. Each appears to have a specific role in
getting me comfortable and checking me in. After each bed
straighten or cover check I am given various forms to sign and
asked if I am satisfied with their service and ok to proceed. Like
a massive check list, I am passed along until a doctor arrives, he
had a quick look at my leg, asks some questions, then signs a

form and I'm off to X-ray, processed again along the line of specific people with specific roles. One gets me ready to leave, one checks the papers are in order for me to leave, one makes the call for a 'transporter' then the transporter himself arrives with an assistant to open and close doors for him. All very efficient and probably extremely expensive private medical too!

After the X-Ray, which mirrors the process on arrival for the amount of people involved, I am returned back to my room to await the doctors again. When he returns, it's great news, my leg is not in fact broken, just very very badly bruised. He suggests they cast it anyway to allow the bruising to settle, and I see an orthopedist and a sports injury rehabilitation specialist on Monday. All sounds good to me. They form a plastic cast around my leg and instruct me on the use of crutches in graphic detail.

With some super strong pain killers, I am discharged and allowed to leave. First however the most important forms arrive, who's paying, when and how, who is responsible for me now, and am I completely satisfied and not going to take action against the hospital for any mismanagement? *'Please sign here sir'*. All very bureaucratic but super-efficient and extremely caring too. I make it back to a hotel for the night and spend some time alone for a while reflecting on the surreality of the last couple of weeks. It's the first time I have been alone since I was in the water. I Skype call Sean, my elder brother as he was the primary contact for news from the boat. Clipper race office liaised with him directly and he cascaded information to family; a really difficult task for him. This is why he was my nominated contact; strong and reliable to communicate best with family, and do the right thing in the right order. I have however now burdened him with this task, and am aware of a debt I owe him for this.

I talk through the whole experience with him, it is really interesting to hear his side of events, which turns out to be pretty much exactly as I expected it to be and mirrors everything that happened, which further reinforces what a great job the race office did in updating him and keeping him informed. Diana his wife and Patrick & Jack my nephews join the call, it's great to see them and catch up. I miss the boys a lot too; we had such a great time over Christmas and spent some really good quality time together, can't wait to see them again. It's a great call and cheers me up quite a bit chatting with them and praising the fact I am so lucky. I am super grateful to Sean for the efforts he gave towards this and thank him a great deal before sign off.

After the call, I log on to the internet. My email, Facebook, Twitter and LinkedIn accounts are mental busy, with hundreds of messages and posts all over them. I read over them and brake down a few times, the messages are far reaching and really touching. The news stories even more so, I had no idea just how far the story has reached, it's a humbling experience. I really miss my family and friends and realise deeply just how lucky I am and what a big event it has been, I am really glad of the time alone this evening to reflect. One of the break downs is proper huge and wipes me out, probably quite cleansing, and I probably really needed it. The crew have been deep cleaning the boat as normal and I've had several invites to go join them in the yacht club for drinks later, which I politely decline. When Chris arrives back from the deep clean and yacht club, it's late, I am already sound asleep and do not hear him come in.

Next morning we have breakfast together and I start a few calls home. I have a long chat with my parents and daughter. They are well, but everyone is clearly touched and upset about the experience. The calls are very different. For Mum & Dad I fill in the details of what happens and how it all played out, how I am feeling now and what my plans and options are. If my leg is not fit enough, I am off the race for sure, probably until New York in a months' time, in which case I'll either go home or go to Sydney for some R&R time to get fit again. Alternatively I still have the option to get off for some head cleansing time and get back on in Panama or Jamaica in a few weeks. No one will question this if I do, it will for sure be perfectly accepted. I am really not sure yet what I want to happen, it's all a bit of a dream and until I know my full medical status and fitness I won't be able to decide. Part of me hopes the decision will be made for me, broken leg, or not fit, it might be easier. The call with my parents is tempered slightly. One of my father's lifelong friends and companions has died, it's a massive shock to him and Mum too, it is clearly a difficult time for them. I feel selfish again putting them through this at such a time. I talk to them about how they are and Dad fills me in with the tasks ahead of him sorting out his friend's estate and belongings, including emptying his house and sorting his stuff. This will be very difficult for him. He will have the support of his own group of close friends back home, whom will undoubtedly help, but as always they too will look towards my mother & father for strength and support. They are super strong people and respected as such at times like this. It does however burden them and adds stress to their lives. I hope it goes without too much fuss and bureaucracy.

For Siobhan it's much quicker and all about me being ok now, she fills me in with all her news and I concentrate on this for most of the call. It is so great to hear her news and I am in truth much more interested in that anyway. She has had a really tough time through her exams and the last few months at school. Things are at last settling down for her now and I am really pleased, it has been a worrying few months and not being there for her has been really hard for me, there have been moments when I really considered stopping and going back home to be there for her. After speaking with her, I just sit and contemplate how lucky I am to have her. And to have her with me, quietly on my shoulder all the time, I am self-conscious of this and it's a warm feeling knowing she is with me.

I make my way back to the race office early morning. I spend an hour or so with Gillian & Justin, discussing what happened and how I am feeling about getting back on. It's pretty early days and there is much speculation about whether I can or not. Even though its great news the leg is not broken, I am still yet to weight bare on it. Gillian is caring and understanding, offering me huge amounts of pastoral care, Justin however is slightly more formal and matter of fact about my fitness to race. I am already thinking he is going to stop me racing the next one.

I do a couple of press interviews in between. Then during the afternoon, I spend several hours with Sir Robin discussing what happened. We talk it through in minute detail and pick out some cracking items we can use and learn from the experience. The helicopter strop clasp is a big one, neither Jason nor I could operate it with cold hands. Jason's lifejacket inflating restricted his ability to work, so in training now the auto-inflate charge will be removed as standard practice. The pull pitts are way too narrow and this emphasises the fact, there is a new design underway for refit now as a result. AIS beacons and Drysuits require much further consideration and advice. They both undoubtedly contributed to the story outcome. As I always put it: "my *dry suit kept me alive, the AIS saved my life"*. Together with the excellent training and my own ability to stay calm and focused. Finally, such a cool Skipper and professional capable crew to conduct the search and rescue in the way in which they did.

I take a really early night and on Sunday I have a late breakfast with Keith, Chris & Conor. We meet up with Michelle and her mate Jen from Canada and buy tickets on the gate for the Giants baseball. A great way to wind down we spend the afternoon in the sun watching the game. There is an Irish bar outlet behind our seats and we drink Guinness and Irish coffee, in between nachos and hot dogs. It's a fabulous afternoon, very relaxing and an opportunity to try and get away from the circus. Throughout the day, I realise further how far the story has reached. Everywhere we go I am recognised and people want to say hello, shake hands or have their picture taken with me. In the apple store, Chris ends up getting a really great deal on a new phone after spending a while talking to staff and customers about the incident. In the yacht club and the restaurant, as we have breakfast, people recognise me and say hello one lady wants to touch me for luck, another is desperate for a picture with me, and it's all a bit surreal.

On Monday, I return to the hospital and immediately get stuck into a massive bureaucratic muddle. The desk don't have my information and won't see me until they know who is paying. They contact the ER who say they have already sent the information to them, the insurance company say the same. I contact the race office for support, the hospital allow me to use a telephone. The race office contact the insurance company and so the loop goes around. Mission Performance are just arriving so the race office are now occupied and out of touch for the next few hours. The specialists are only around for another hour and they want me to make an appointment for later in the week. I get frustrated, I really need to get on with this today if I stand any chance of getting back on. I try and assist further but the hospital telephones won't dial internationally. Eventually after a massive credit top up on my Australian mobile, I make some calls myself and arrange for the details to be faxed through to the front desk directly. They come through in a few minutes and all looks good. Then the desk request the doctor's name specifically be added to the forms so we go around the loop once more before everything is finally in order. It's been a really testing morning and whilst I may have held my cool throughout, inside am intensely frustrated with the overly bureaucratic nature of it all. It makes me think about the stresses of going back to work and dealing with these formalities again. I am going to find this incredibly difficult after being in the environment of the yacht where things just get done and everything happens efficiently and without any fuss, drama or hierarchy.

The osteopath and sports injury rehabilitation specialists spend a good deal of time with me assessing the damage. They provide me much clarity of how it's traumatised and what to do to help it repair. We discuss the environment of the boat and how I can best do physio whilst aboard. It's a really useful session with some great advice and close attention. I leave around mid-afternoon really satisfied with the outcomes, and with only one crutch to assist walking. I make my way back down to the race office and discuss getting back on, walking as best I can to prove a point, whilst actually still in very much pain. I discuss with Gillian and Justin and we agree I will do the corporate sail in a few days' time and see how I feel, making no decisions until afterwards. Justin is clearly still sceptical. I do some more media interviews and agree to a live link up to BBC breakfast at 23:00, which gives me an opportunity to close out the loop at home and say thank you to as many people publicly as I can. It's a really difficult one to do. I have a laptop set up with a Skype call to BBC, they can see me but I can see them. We set up a Clipper race poster as a backdrop and I wear my team colours. I can hear the studio and wait patiently until they come to me. The interviewers introduce me and ask about the experience, they fill in the gaps and tell me what they are watching and I try and match the answers to what they are watching. It's really difficult not being able to see them. I overrun my time and keep talking to get in the thanks to everyone around the world for their support. Next day there are tweets and Facebook posts of the BBC breakfast studio with my face on the screen behind them.

At prize giving, Henri Lloyd arrive with a new dry suit for me, they want to present it to me on stage as part of the prize giving. I politely ask if they might not; I don't like the idea of doing this in front of all the other crew members. They accept this and we do it quietly in a corner. They take lots of photographs and I tell them how pleased I am with their gift and how very well the original one performed. Happy to give them a quote or endorsement if they wish for one. It's an awesome gesture from them. I know they got a lot of mileage from the media coverage, but it's still a very generous gesture to offer a new replacement to me, I am quite touched by this.

So the day arrives for the corporate sail and I awake feeling pretty apprehensive and nervous. I take a light breakfast in the hotel and make my way down to the boat early. There is no one around and I start to prep for sail. I stop and pause for a while, just sitting on deck taking in being on board. It makes me feel sick again, and I can feel the tension, I wonder if I am doing the right thing or not. I come very close to getting off and gather my things together at one point ready to leave. I stop and think about my motivations. Circumnavigation is everything for me, I have to get back on board and as soon as possible. If I wait until Panama I will almost certainly feel worse when I get back on after time to think and stew about it. Today is only a day in the bay; worse case I can go below and wait it out if it's bad. Susie & Michelle arrive and together we prep sails and tidy up. Skipper & Ali arrive soon afterwards and we are soon ready to greet our guests who arrive bang on time. It's a selection of senior team and customers from ARM one of the GREAT Britain sponsors, many of whom have sailed before. After a short briefing we slip lines and motor out into the bay. All the time I can feel myself getting tense and nervous, no turning back now though.

After a simple and uneventful main sail and stay sail hoist, we do final checks for Yankee hoist. As we start to hoist, the sheets are caught, quickly I can see the lazy is incorrectly run and Susie is wrestling with it to free it up and untie it. Instinctively, I run up to the foredeck to help, I duck under the stay sail and am quickly sitting below the stay sail leaning over the rail, with one arm around the sheet I am untying it with the other one, the wind beats the stay sail hard against my back and the Yankee flaps heavily around us. I pause & look up. Susie spots me immediately *"you're not happy there are you matey?"* She shouts at me, *"nope! Not really"* I reply, *"ok"* she says *"listen very carefully and do as I say, put that down right now,*

I'll get it from here. Now you fuck off back to the cockpit right now, right?" With a big smile she points aft wards. I do as I am told right away and sigh a small sense of relief and large sense of failure too when I get back there. It's been a big tester for me and I ponder for the rest of the day if I should get back on or not. The rest of the days sailing is uneventful and fun, from my place firmly stationed in the cockpit. We race around the bridge and Alcatraz against four other Clipper race boats, the sun shines all afternoon and many of the guys on board get stuck right in and do all the work, with us just overseeing them. We lose the race by a long way. But the corporate guests have a great time and cheer us as we slip back into the marina.

After they leave, we tidy up, then join them in the yacht club for free food and drink. I stick to soft drinks and enjoy a plate or two of mixed food. As before, everyone in the yacht club wants to say hello, have their picture taken with me or ask questions about what happened. I politely oblige, but it feels like a real chore this time, probably as I am really tired now. Lots of people ask me what I am going to do, and I reply *"absolutely get straight back on"*. I still consider this might be step too far, my leg really hurts now too and I couldn't walk back to the hotel if I tried. For a while, I wonder if I could even walk to a taxi. I grab a seat on the balcony away from the crowd and chat & rest with some of the crew for a short while, before making a quiet exit, excusing myself for an early night. All the while, wondering about whether to get back on or not. Underneath, all the pain and mental struggle about getting back on. Actually, I am just very very tired. It's been a torrid few months. All the round the world crew are feeling it, many on other boats are getting off and taking breaks to recover. It would be really easy for me to sit out the next race and get back on in Panama in three weeks' time. However it is only three weeks, and should be a relatively easy sail. And with 22 crew on board for the next race, I should be able to hold back. I really struggle to sleep, wondering about what to do for the best.

In the morning I awake with a clear head and a clear decision. I signed up to circumnavigate and that's what I intend to do, no second measures, no second place, time to get straight back on. I think about the challenge I set out to achieve. I think about the gate at St Katts, the journey I set out to complete and how easy it would be to get off right now, this journey was never about doing easy. I get up and go for a shower.

On the way to the boat to join in with maintenance and repairs, I pass by the race office and confirm with Gillian & Justin this is what I plan to do. Gillian is really pleased, Justin is happy but sceptical and gives me a serious face of reason. I tell him I am fine and good to go. He is clearly not in support of this and, for a moment, I am convinced he will still overrule me. But he gives me his blessing and tells me to be careful, *"yeah righto!"* I say. I meet up with Sean in a cafe and we have coffee together and de brief how we feel, what has happened and approach to the next race. It's a tough one for me, I am still really nervous about getting on. I absolutely must do this though and am going to dig in and get back on. He supports me and says he is sure I'll be fine. He asks how I feel about watch leading. Not this time I reply, one step at a time I reckon, let's see how I feel once we are under way. It's a good session together and gives me lots of strength and confidence.

After some shopping to replace the clothes cut off and my camera which got smashed in the recovery, I pack and get myself ready to sail. I put my kit back on board a couple of days before race start and make sure I am absolutely more ready than ever. I don't want any last minute struggles or panics to unsettle anything. At race briefing, both Justin and Sir Robin make reference to the incident and update the crews on what's coming out of our discussions. Sir Robin praises Sean, the crew and myself, whilst outlining the importance of safety and looking out for each other. He talks about what happened and recounts the story. I really struggle with this and I sit quietly, with tears rolling down my face. At the end of the briefing there are a couple of questions which I didn't expect. I am put right on the spot a little and have to take a deep breath to recover and answer them. Which I do as best I can. The benefit of all the media work we have done this week, is that I do have many short and pre-rehearsed sound bites I can now use to easily answer stuff with confidence quickly.

We have our team brief with Sean, who again praises the team and talks about safety on board. We exit back to the yacht club once more and I exit there really quickly, heading out for a quiet dinner with some of the crew, then straight back to the hotel for a last minute pack of my final stuff and texts home. I am in bed for around 22:00 and sleep reasonably soundly all things considered, through to a 05:30 alarm call to get ready to leave.

I wake up, just make it to the bathroom and throw up. I feel really sick about getting back on! After a quick final shower, I grab my few bits I have left at the hotel together and head outside for a cab, I grab one easily and get dropped off a block or so away from the marina to walk the last bit. It's still early and there are very few people around. I walk down to the boat and put my stuff away. A couple of crew who stayed on board last night are just starting to get up and about. There is a fair bit to do still, and we set to it reasonably quickly as other crew slowly start to arrive. It gets really congested very quickly with 22 crew trying to sort their kit out down below. I go and grab some quick breakfast at the small cafe over the road from the marina, on race start day we often don't get to eat until very late, so always good to get something if you can.

When I get back to the boat, Clipper race media team have arrived and want to interview me about how I feel. I hadn't prepared for this one and find it quite hard to do without appearing upset. Up to this point I had just kept myself busy and not thought too much about it, a bad plan with hindsight. The interview almost tips me over and I need a little while alone afterwards to recover. I go below and grab my shore bag, sitting on my bunk for a while, I come very close to getting off. After throwing up again I put my shore bag away and take a walk around the dock to say goodbye to friends.

As I get back to our boat CBS news have now arrived and want an interview, bugger! Deep breaths and straight into it, he fires questions at me, some of them a little silly. I stick to my script, thanking people for support and emphasising how important it is for me to get back on and finish the race, partly convincing myself.

I sweep around the friends and family saying goodbyes, all the while conscious it feels like there are cameras everywhere again, and climb aboard. First stop down below for a while to escape the circus. We have a final brief from Sean and slip lines to reverse out of the marina. It's low tide and as we reverse we dig and scrape the bottom with the keel, it takes a bit of wriggling to get free and escape out into the bay.

I stay up on deck for the media sweeps and parade of sail, then head down below and take up my regular position in the Nav station for race start. We carry out a man overboard drill. All the boats have been asked to do so before departure as a refresher for all crew. I hear the calls from up on deck and press the button on the plotter as procedure calls for. Then I call distance and direction until Sean comes around to make his final approach. All the while I am thinking about Conor and Michelle who did this for real only a few weeks ago. It makes me cold and I am really glad I am not up on deck. I can hear the media helicopter and in addition to just not wanting to be up there, I don't want to be photographed doing the drill. As I hear the boat coming around to make the final approach for recovery I can see on the plotter we are 300m away from the mark, strong tides in the San Francisco Bay! After the drill, the crew settle down quickly into race mode as we make final preparations for race start.

A media welcoming scrum in San Francisco.
Photo Credit; Clipper Ventures PLC

Above;
Michelle & I during
the final approach into
San Francisco

Left;
Heartfelt greetings in
San Francisco from
Sir Robin and Justin

Photo Credits;
Clipper Ventures PLC

San Francisco to Jamaica
Panama Canal

We tack around, back and forth, preparing to line up for the start line. Skipper has a good start in his sights today and is right on his game calling the shots. We interact briefly to discuss the angles for the bridge and away out past the lighthouse, then I settle and await the start countdown. It's a beautiful day and the fleet looks magnificent against the back drop of the San Francisco skyline.

I can see the rest of the fleet on AIS and watch as they all circle around and around. Ten minute countdown mark and we circle past the line. Four minute countdown mark, we turn and run in. At the one minute mark we are traversing the line and turn to cross just as the final 5-4-3-2-1 is called. Sean is a pure genius at race starts, we are first over the line, and after a couple of tacks, first under the bridge too. Awesome spectacle for those watching us, friends & family especially. We head out into the outer bay and tack around the lighthouse, at one point we get confused by the navigation systems which have been reset and have different readings on them. It makes me really nervous and I call a tack right at the very last minute, Sean obeys quickly, we tack once more and head out onto the rum line still in the lead. Brilliant race start, we are away south, leading the fleet, it's a great feeling.

We settle onto our line south and hoist the first of many spinnakers, it's quite beautiful sailing. Calm seas, bright skies and slightly off a dead downwind run. Sailing along at a consistent 12 ktts. Over the next few days we peel spinnakers up and down the gears 3-2-1-2-3 as the winds change around us. On one day we change five times. Peeling spinnakers is one of our secret weapons on Derry, one of the things we are very good at. It holds our speed and maintains course. Below deck becomes a spinnaker wooling factory, which varies from 35 minutes to two and a half hours to complete a fully wooled sail.

35 minutes when we needed it back up fairly quickly and two and a half hours when there was little else going on and we chat throughout the process, with at least one cup of tea and a break twice to write a ships log.

Skipper praises our spinnaker work and the crew working together so early on. He reminds us we are one of the few boats in the fleet whom have not dropped one in the water yet and, despite our major trashing of the code two, on the last race, the repair appears to be working really well and the sail performing excellently. His words are barely echoed when that evening we hear a crash and the spinnaker halyard lets go. Code two over the side and in the water. 'All hands on deck' called and together we man haul it back in board, which takes a full crew and all their strength. Once a spinnaker hits the water, it sticks like glue and is amazingly hard to lift back up. I find myself a couple of times leaning out over the rail, pulling against the sail. I really don't like this and as we start to move forward along the sail, I shift back and stay aft of the mast and work from there. We get the sail back in board, remarkably without any fuss and even more remarkably without any damage.

The events of the kitemare ring through my head all night and keep me thinking hard. I have not helmed yet and have not been on the foredeck either, keeping myself busy in the cockpit and Nav station. Each day I have been drawing maps on the white board and posting scheds for the crew to read. It's a good contribution to the crew on board and is well received, but in truth it is keeping me busy away from the deck. In between deck work, I am getting some well-earned really good rest too. Not having a watch lead responsibility is really nice and quite freeing too. I have been assistant watch leader since Albany and am enjoying the brief respite away from responsibility. All of the round the world crew are pretty tired and this leg of champagne sailing and a high number of enthusiastic new crew is giving us our first break from full on sail work. I am still really nervous about being on board and am only very slowly settling back into it. I am however being seriously over cautious and probably need to accelerate this now whilst the conditions are still good.

On the next watch I helm for half an hour and on the next 40 minutes, I continue to helm for short sessions and ease myself back in gradually. It hurts my leg like hell but makes me feel better pushing myself back into it. I have always been really hard on myself, my own worst critic and self-motivator, perhaps sometimes to my detriment. Years ago, I would have pushed myself much harder and been slightly OCD about achievement. I have mellowed a little as I age, but I am still really hard on myself, if I run, cycle or swim, I'll always push for that little bit more, an extra length, or set out for a run and add another longer route around something, cycle into the wind by choice. I've never been an athlete and never will, but the satisfaction of pushing and achieving is a drug I do crave. It's something more than anything I really miss whilst sailing around the world actually. The lack of exercise is really hard on the body. It's a surprise to me, that after seven months at sea, I am now probably less fit than I have ever been in my life. The muscle wastage around bum and thighs is palpable and cardio vascular fitness is relatively nonexistent now. I am really looking forward to getting back to regular exercise when the race is over and have started looking for the first challenge, probably a 10k, closely followed by a half marathon and a triathlon, hopefully before the end of spring 2015. Could be a tough challenge whilst getting back into life on land and holding down a new job, whatever that might be?

After only four days out, we start our final approach to the scoring gate. OneDLL and Invest Africa are right behind us, and have been for a while. GREAT Britain are out west as are Garmin, Switzerland and Jamaica, we are all converging on a narrow point just of the Baja peninsula. We stay as long as we possibly can on our starboard tack, we won't quite make the gate and will need to tack right at the last minute to slide across the line, but it's much faster and makes us more south mileage. GREAT Britain appear from the west and slip over the line about seven miles ahead of us, disappointing for us, we really dislike loosing anything to GREAT Britain. Looks like we have OneDLL and Invest Africa pinned, but Team Garmin have tacked around and are approaching fast from our starboard side, we hold as long as we can and tack round behind them at the very very last minute. We squeeze everything we can for the last run in, at times we think we have cut it too fine and won't make the gate. Sean and I calling distance and angle back & forth constantly on the final run in. We squeeze in right behind Garmin who beat us over by a few seconds only after 1,000 miles. We have cut it as fine as we possibly can, only 50m inside the mark, in thousands of miles of ocean. We celebrate a provisional third place and the fact Garmin get the points not Henri Lloyd or OneDLL which is good for us in the overall points table.

The day after the gate finish, life on board quietens down, the wind eases, the temperature rises and we settle into the next stage of the race. On this day for some reason I think of Siobhan all day and miss her dearly. I don't know why this day in particular. Perhaps I am a little bored, perhaps it's the quiet, tiredness, emotional stability returning as I get comfortable on board. I really don't know and stop trying to work it out. I think about the good times we have spent together. I am really lucky to have had so much quality time with her. The holidays, weekends and festival times together were awesome. We also had some really cool holiday trips around the world, skiing, visiting friends, Disney in LA, Christmas in Sydney. We have been really lucky to have had these opportunity, the time was so very precious. I feel old too in these thoughts. She has her own life developing now, I don't figure quite so much as I did and it's time to accept this more. It was part of my decision making process to take part in the race, giving her space and time as she gets older. I wonder if this is a good thing, or if I am just justifying the possible selfishness of doing the race. Either way, I really miss her and spend the day smiling behind some tears as I think of the good times we spent together. Remembering she is with me on my shoulder every step of the way.

The weather progressively improves and temperatures start to rise. Each day gets increasingly warmer, then the nights warm up too. Foulies and sleeping bags are packed away, high factor sun cream becomes the norm every day, and watch wake up times are made later as we just need shorts and tee shirts now so can arrive on deck quicker at watch change over. We erect a shade cover over the helm for some escape from the heat. The deck becomes almost too warm to sit on and we have to wear shoes as it's too hot to walk on during the day. It is so nice to have a dry boat, we have not been wet down below once on this leg so far.

After leg 6, it is such a relief to be dry for a change. Life below on this leg is however made more difficult by having 23 people on board. After a while, we settle into moving around together, but at first it's clumsy and difficult. Everything takes marginally longer. Meal times are longer, cooking takes on a greater challenge, heads are more often engaged and watch changeover takes ages. On leg six, at times we had only four people on watch, now we have miniMum ten, at times eleven. It's a big culture change, one we will need to get used to as we are at this level of crew now all the way back to London. It's great to hear however from the leggers recently joining how welcome we have made them feel, and how quickly they felt like part of the team.

After nearly 2,000 miles of racing, we are less than 300m from Team Garmin and only half a mile from OneDLL & Switzerland. Garmin call us and request our AIS be switched on so they can track our course, reluctantly we agree and switch it on. It gives us a very slight upper advantage if the opposition cannot see our course and speed. We can just see GREAT Britain out on the horizon, we are around 8 miles behind them on the scheds, but have a much better angle at the moment. As the wind starts to ease off further, we tack towards land to see how the sea and land breezes might work out for us. Team Garmin and Switzerland have the same idea. Time for windseeker as the winds die down to virtually nothing and the sea starts to turn oily and flat calm. We can see some of the other boats farther north, using the coastline, and as we monitor them closely it appears they are not getting the benefit, so we tack back out again and abandon this idea for now.

As we approach the second finish line we have GREAT Britain ahead of us already across it and Jamaica about to cross. We are fast approaching from the north and have Garmin out to our west on a much harder angle. As we start to harden up and close in, Garmin take advantage of the steeper angle and pip us across the line. We celebrate a minor victory over Henri Lloyd and OneDLL then set about heading for the third of the finish lines. The race feels like a bit of a lottery, not knowing which finish line will be used is frustrating and confusing to us all, but it's how it is, so we get down to work.

Another 400 miles to the third finish line. The race office email and confirm they will not be shortening the race any time before 3 days' time at 06:00UTC. We hope to be over the third line by then. We shift back to Yankee again and beat hard into the wind for two more days, crossing the line third behind, Jamaica Get All Right and GREAT Britain. Around a day or so later we receive the final finish line news. It's a new line around 130 miles south of our current position, GREAT Britain and Henri Lloyd are already 35+ miles closer and we are still out west on a perfect course for the fourth and final finish line, which is now no longer in play; bugger!

We catch a few squalls intermittently and it's great to shower and freshen up on deck. In one of these we catch a massive lift in speed and drop the rail down into the water. The code two and wind-seeker are both still on deck, packed into their bags and resting just in front of the mast, neither are tied down. They both slide over to the shrouds and get picked up by up the water rushing along under the guard rails which are now under water. For a moment, we are sure we will lose them over the side, as they float up towards the open water. Skipper drops the boat back level and Jason & I jump up and recover them onto the high side, where we tie them down. Approaching the final finish line we receive an email from Andy's wife confirming GREAT Britain have won. We can see a few boats ahead so we know we have now missed out. As the boats start to show themselves our worst fears are realised, ninth place. Our joint worst result so far on the race, and last time we got ninth, it was a big celebration, after coming back from a 650 mile detour, when we medivac'd Michelle into port Elizabeth and still made a ninth into Albany with a sprint finish against four other boats.

With a little over 850 miles to Panama, we plan a route into Golfito bay in Costa Rica for a re-fuel, the mood on the boat is lifted by the possibility of fresh food, smokes and beer in a few days' time. We set course and motor on as soon as we pass the line. Next day Clipper race team request we collect jerry cans from Old Pulteney and motor straight to Panama, we have sufficient fuel, if we sail 150miles to supplement it. The dock & fuel fees in Costa Rica are really high, and the race decide to minimise the amount of boats who dock. So GREAT Britain, Mission Performance, Switzerland and we go straight ahead.

With a few days to make the mileage, we set about winch servicing and deep clean, by the time we reach Panama we are all set with very little work to do. The last 40 miles, Ali & I helm and spot with Skipper in the Nav station calling the shots. It rains solid the whole time, at times so heavy we cannot see. Ali & I have just shorts and bare feet, with life jackets on, for the first few hours it's really refreshing and fun, but as it gets dark and starts to cool down it becomes a bit of a chore. We have a laugh together just us on deck, occasionally someone pops their head out has a look and goes back down below. Even Skip rarely opens the hatch for Nav, staying dry down below. We dock around 23:00 and head straight for the bar, where rum is the order of the evening for many hours. Next day after a refuel and canal audit, a group of seven of us head into Panama City by cab for a tour of the old town. Our taxi acts as guide for the day, he shows us around the canal museum, the fish markets, state parliament buildings and Placa Francia viewpoints. We head back to the boat around 22:00, ready for a 05:00 departure though the canal.

We slip lines around 05:30 and motor out to the bay where we wait for several hours for our canal pilot. Once he arrives we follow, Old Pulteney & Henri Lloyd until close into the Canal where we raft up three boats abreast.

The canal transit takes the rest of the day. It's an awesome experience, a truly magnificent engineering project spectacle and getting up close and personal with massive cargo ships and tugs. In each loch, the operators throw lines down to us with bags of bolts on the end, they seem to play 'who can get it closest to your head' with these each time! The heat builds as the day progresses and most of sleep for a few hours as we cross the lake. Arriving into Shelter Bay marina around 21:00. The club house has arranged a buffet dinner and between the three boats we clear it away pretty quickly, empty the bar of rum and take over the swimming pool for most of the night. It's a relaxing night and everyone lets their hair down. There is nowhere to go and nothing to see here, we have no work to do and a free day tomorrow. We all absolutely max out this rare opportunity out! Next day is quiet again, in the afternoon, boredom gets the better of us, and we go and clean the boat, giving her a really good polish.

We slip lines at 19:00, no ceremony or music, just getting out and heading out to sea. We motor in formation through the night, waiting for the last three boats to clear the canal. They are still in the lake when we slip out, and don't exit until after 22:00. Our motor slows down to 3ktts to let them catch up. They eventually arrive with us around 06:00 and we set about a Le Mans start for 07:30. The start goes well and we set out second into a deep fast reach. It's a short sprint race and really close sail racing all the way, with many boats in sight. After around 3.5 days we converge on the folly lighthouse on the eastern tip of Jamaica.

As we turn the corner the boats stall in the shadow of the island, it takes an age to get across to the entrance to the bay, we stop and start, stall and bob along, all the time watching other boats slip past, then catch them again. At one point we manage 3-4ktts whilst Qingdao next to us are going backwards, then the situation is reversed! Around 01:00 we slide into the outer harbour at Errol Flynn marina. The bars are still lit up and reggae music is blaring out across the water. We eye up a place at the bar from a distance and edge forward, putting pressure on the shore team to get us moored up quickly. After the usual immigration and race office check, we head for the bar and spend the rest of the night there, most of it in and out of the pool, not all by choice! Next morning it's deep clean, it gets done quickly before the sun gets hot and we all leave by lunchtime to our respective accommodations. I jump in a cab and head to my apartment, when I get there Anthony has already set dinner and wine on our terrace. I shower and join him, after a fantastic dinner and wine, we join next door's apartment for cocktails and music on the beach with a bonfire until the early hours. A quite fantastic evening. For the next two days I don't leave the apartment, unless you count the balcony!

I have an open boat to manage and a half day work and maintenance, apart from this it's down time, a welcome break and rest. By the time prep day and briefings arrive I feel great and can't wait to get back on.

Jamaica to New York
"It is an honour and a pleasure to be in your club"

On the morning of race start we meet in a restaurant overlooking the marina for breakfast and our final briefing. Skipper takes us through race tactics and the watch teams. We review the parade of sail details and slipping orders for a final check, then it's onto the boat for final stow and pre-race checks.

We slip in order and circle the bay together raising our head sails. Once all are formed up we circle in formation fly past the dock where friends and family are waving. The spectator boats and beaches are all full and reggae is blaring out again as we head out to sea. It rains tropical storm rain for most of the fly past, we stalwartly stand proud and take it in formation, stopping to change into our wet gear only once it's all over.

All twelve boats get full sails ready and take practice line up around the start line area and towards the windward mark. As we approach the line each time there are several other boats in very close quarters. The start line is only 300m long and even with four or five boats around its incredibly tight, this is going to be a very exciting start line.

We set up our tacking angles, check the final approaches, as ever, Skipper on the helm and me checking and rechecking angles and distances down below in the Nav station. We establish together how close in to shore we dare go and where the real 'no-go' areas are and where we just don't have enough navigation detail to be sure. The charts for this area are ancient, needing a good pinch of salt and some instinct to adapt for our use today. Once we are happy, we head back around and practice one final line up. After the ten minute gun, we make our way around and set about claiming our space. The boats are almost on top of each other tacking around, there is virtually no space at all and we wait each time calling for water to tack. As we make our way back towards the line, with two minutes to go, Conor is calling the time from a stop watch, me calling distance and angles, Kristi calling distance from right up on the bow. We have Switzerland right underneath us and Old Pulteney ahead. We skirt right in the edge of the line, across as shallow as we dare right on the edge of the lighthouse. I am convinced we are too close, but Sean stays with it. Right at the last minute we sharpen up to wind, catch some speed and we are away, second across the line to Old Pulteney. It's a real close dog fight all the way down to the windward mark, tacking back and forth in close quarter. As we make our final tack, we get caught underneath Mission Performance, we have to bail out and tack around again, it costs us dearly and we round the mark in fifth place, setting course to the north east. It takes us around 36 hours to catch them and get back into the lead group.

The first couple of days are match racing with six or seven boats all jostling for position, at times right next to each other and close enough to talk to the other crews. As we head north towards Cuba & Haiti, the sun continues and the temperature eases to a more comfortable level; beautiful sunshine without the extreme heat is really pleasant. Passing between the islands of Cuba & Haiti we pass a theoretical port way point marker to leave Cuba at least 12 miles away, we are not allowed into their waters.

Heading toward the scoring gate, we lose out to Henri Lloyd & OneDLL, also fighting Old Pulteney for third place. Less than a mile from the gate a squall hits us but misses Old Pulteney, taking us out of the running and we miss out on the points. The winds ease off as we head further north, and for the last sixty miles we are fighting for either first or fifth with GREAT Britain, Old Pulteney, Henri Lloyd and Switzerland. We have taken the inside track and it's serving us well all the way, eventually we miss out by no less than a few miles, settling for fifth place into New York.

We drop sails and motor up the Hudson into the city. Everyone on board is excited and really looking forward to this stopover. Kristi is like a cat on a hot roof; it's her home town and she has lots of people meeting her. Heading in up the river is awesome, the city and Liberty statue lit up and looking truly magnificent. It's a really long night, Conor on the helm and me in the Nav station all the way in again. Most of the crew and Skipper too grab a few hours' sleep, or rest at least. The welcome is excellent as we enter Liberty Landing marina, on the Jersey side, lots of friends and family here to meet us, we refuel first then move over into our berth by around 3am. We stay up all night drinking and the sunrise over Manhattan is absolutely fantastic. As ever, straight into deep clean and maintenance all day, with some radio and newspaper interviews for me in-between.

Next morning it's a full media day, with British Channel5 and NBC filming interviews with us all day. Jason, Kristi, Conor & I all have sessions with them, and in between we finish boat maintenance and I look for accommodation, eventually finding a really nice apartment for the week just off 5th avenue in Manhattan. Team Garmin arrive early evening and a few friends and I head over to Manhattan, meeting up with some others in the awesome rooftop bar in the Conrad hotel. Next morning it's a full day of media again, interviews and filming on board too with NBC. They are making a 90minute documentary about the MOB and complete 2-3 hour full studio interviews with Sean, Jason, Kristi, Michelle & myself. Then we sail out in the bay with them and film on board, including an interview with Kristi whilst halfway up the mast! We finish the sail docking into North Cove Marina, which is less than a block from ground zero and the new World Trade Centre. I visit both which is quite moving. As we prepare to leave the boat, Sean calls me to one side. *"How do you fancy stepping back into watch lead"* he asks, *"your confidence is improving all the time and I'd really like you back on the lead team"*. *"Wow, do you think so?"* I reply, *"c'mon mate, step up, get back in to it fully?"* *"Alright, OK, but how about maybe assistant?"* He agrees and we discuss the watch teams briefly and settle on me working with Nick, with

Kristi & Conor leading the other team. I am proper chuffed he has asked me and thank him for the opportunity again. I have thought before about getting out what you put in. I also like to challenge myself as ever, so I am really looking forward to pushing myself and to working with Nick again on our home race leg.

Next day, I spend the morning with Henri Lloyd discussing their equipment and feeding back suggestions from the crew, then back to the apartment for a shower and change before heading off to the Royal New York Yacht Club. Arriving at the yacht club, dressed in brand new chinos, pressed new white shirt, a borrowed tie from Jonathan, head of Clipper race PR, and a blazer borrowed from Patrick, Skipper of Old Pulteney. I feel almost human. It's the first 'non boat' style clothes I have worn in over a year.

As I arrive at the yacht club, I cannot help but be impressed by the place. Outside it's a three story historic and imposing stone building, with massive upstairs windows carved out in relief in the style of Spanish Galleon windows. There are enormous flags flying, stars & stripes plus the NYYC flag. A canopied doorway with massive solid double mahogany doors and frosted glass gives a hint of the opulence ahead as you enter inside. If it were not for a small brass plaque on one side of the building you would not know what it was. Looking out of place amongst the downtown high rise glass and steel buildings, the yacht club has been here since 1858, which in American terms is really old.

Inside, once past reception, more akin to a five star hotel concierge desk, I made my way up the massive stone stair case laid centrally with a red carpet, off to the left is the model room, where the yacht club staff are setting up for our dinner. Two and half stories high, with stained glass roof and a balcony all the way around looking in from above. A huge stone open fireplace centres the room, which is filled with yacht models on the walls and in enormous glass cases, which have been rolled back to the edges of the room, the leather chesterfields stored neatly underneath them. Dinner is laid in round tables of ten for around 140 people, beautiful flags as centre pieces and gold blocked menus with Sean and my name on. A stage and lectern, sits next to a massive back projected video screen.

Towards the rear of the building is a club style bar with more artefacts and massive artefact national treasure trophies all around. Leather and mahogany everywhere, massive fireplaces and beautiful paintings. Guests for the evening start to gather here from around 16:30 onwards and by 18:00 when cocktails are served in the model room, most people are already here. There are a few crew from the Derry team here too, which is great to see, especially as the $85 ticket was not waived for anyone. Most of Sean's family are here and loads of people Sean knows from previous round the world sailing.

The room sits bang on 19:00 and the club commodore speaks introductions and a short welcome speech, then he introduces Sean who speaks for just under an hour. He talks about his early career, then makes some comparisons between Clipper racing yachts and the swan 66 he sailed around the world on with many people who are now in this room. It's an amusing comparison with pictures of the wood panelled en suite on the swan, compared to our racing heads, and linen draped tables for lunch compared to our racing bowls and sporks. He goes on to talk about our race, the route, adding stories along the way, he talks about our knock down in southern ocean and winning our division of the Sydney Hobart, showing some great videos in between to add to the interest. Then he talks about the man over board incident and introduces me with video of the search and recovery.

I had been pretty nervous sitting through his talk, waiting my turn. It's an incredibly imposing venue and the first time I have talked publicly, other than to media, about the incident. Right up until the video, I think I am ok and am looking forward to the experience. Although always nervous, I do really enjoy speaking publicly. The video almost sends me out though, it brings some of it back home again, it's really tough watching it on a massive screen, and I take a deep breath before stepping up to the stage. Knowing in advance I would probably need some time to settle into this speech, I had a scripted and well-rehearsed opening piece, I have memorised this and I try hard to pull it off as though it is not scripted. I open with:

"When I signed up for the Clipper race, I never dreamed I might be invited to the New York Yacht Club, let alone be invited to a dinner, let alone have my name on the menu and be asked to speak. A very good evening to you ladies and gentlemen. It is a genuine honour and pleasure to be in your company and in your club, thank you"

I pause and take a breath. To my amazement it gets a big round of applause, which buys me some more time to brace myself. I lighten the mood then with an anecdote about filming the story with NBC yesterday and getting through it in just over nine hours, and how I expect to trim that down a bit this evening!

I go on, recounting the story and some of the drama and feeling, I stumble over a few bits and pause when I need to. I had added in some of Sean's great lines from the events. *"Fancy a lift"* and *"I don't remember giving you permission to leave the boat"*. Each of which gets and laugh and lightens off the end of a serious piece of the story. I praise Kristi for her bravery. She has attended the dinner with an old college friend from New York. I talk freely about her selfless bravery up the mast during the search, which I am really pleased to have had the opportunity to do in public and in front of her. I can see Kristi not far away in-front of me, close to the centre of the room. I glance across and can see tears streaming down her face. I pause again and nearly lose it when I see her. Continuing on with the story after a deep breath, speaking in all for around 45 minutes. At the end of the story I close out with some more pre-rehearsed and scripted closure:

"There are some fantastic lessons to learn from this unique experience, which I am very happy to share. My dry suit kept me alive, but my AIS saved my life. Some new equipment is already on board the Clipper race fleet as a direct result of our feedback, there are some changes to training procedures and development work has started on a possible new AIS system for the race. I genuinely believe as a direct result of some of this learning and feedback, lives will be saved in future. One thing is for sure, it gives each and every one of us a big drama story to tell our friends and family for generations to come. Each will be slightly different, viewed from a different perspective. The drama will surely be exaggerated in places and the excitement enhanced. Waves may get bigger and wind perhaps stronger as the years pass. But each and every story will always end the same way. I shall be back on board safely in the end and we shall all arrive in San Francisco safe and sound with all of our Derry crew in good shape, ready for a drink and to tell a great adventure story with a happy ending for ever.

The Clipper race office team, and Sir Robin himself have been truly fantastic throughout. The way they have communicated with my family, supported us and offered me pastoral care has been phenomenal, and I owe them all a huge debt of gratitude. The crew of Derry LondonDerry, OneDLL and all the other boats equally so.

My story is dramatic and epic, but I have to say, I wouldn't want to be Skipper on a boat who lost a crew member, looking for them! I am told by the crew, Sean stayed calm, collected and professional throughout. We all believe on team Derry, that in Sean we have the very best Skipper in the fleet. Sean does the most amazing job, his temperament and approach are as perfect as one could wish for. Always calm, always smiling, never chastises anyone, only ever using positive advice and helping us grow and develop as a team. He has given us his confidence & trust from very early stage on in the race, he leaves us on deck to get on with the responsibility of sailing the boat for long

*periods of time, which at times must be very difficult for him.
However, in turn from doing this he is confident we will call on
him quickly when we need to. This is such a two way thing and
he has developed this extremely well. We all love him!*

*I am done speaking for the evening now, thank you for
listening. I am a very very lucky boy. But please, right now join
me together in a round of applause. Not for me, but please for
the legend that is Sean McCarter"*

The whole room stands in an instant, applauds and cheers
for many minutes, I step down, shake hands and hug with Sean,
a hug and kiss from Sophia his wife, and I join the applause for
him. I can see Sean's mother and family, Sophia, Derry crew,
Kristi and a few other guests crying too. It's a fabulous moment
I shall remember for a very long time. As the room quietens
down the club Commodore steps up and commends us both to
the club, presenting us with the most amazing framed scrolls
from the club, thanking us for the evening.

I could not resist the opportunity to praise and commend
Sean, and given the amount of people he knew that evening, it
was a perfect opportunity. The evening will stay in my memory
as one of the most amazing evenings, and a very very special
memory. The scroll has already found a very special pride of
place at my home. Many of the guests compliment Sean and I
on our speaking and several recount it is the first time for a very
long time they have heard the model room silent and attentive
during a speech. This is probably more the topic than the
presenter. I am however humbled by the gratitude and truly
honoured to have been asked to do this.

Next morning, a car arrives to pick me up at my apartment
at 04:45, it's a sharp wake up call, having been at the yacht club
the night before until the small hours. It takes me straight to the
Fox AM TV studios, where I am joined by Julia our press
officer. We are me by the concierge and taken through to the
breakfast news studios green room, they whisk me off to make

up, then into sound to get mic'd up. When I get back to the green room, Jules compliments me on the makeup. She says it *"helps me not look so shiny"*. Then she back tracks and says *"no, no, that's not what I meant!"* She stumbles around the words apologising and just digging a deeper whole. I tell her to stop, we have a hug and big laugh about it.

I go back outside, Fox shoot a small teaser of me re-arriving at the studios as a *'coming up next'* piece. Then it's in to the studio, on set and introduced to the presenters, they quickly run through how they are going to play the story, then the studio goes back live. They introduce me and show video clips of me in the water and being recovered. They ask a few questions about how it was and I get to thank people for their support. The only question they stop me with is the one about my mother's birthday. I pause and take a breath then turn it into a positive about how it gave me strength. I have used this tactic before and it gets me out of talking about it in some ways, but also makes a great story line. In just a few moments it's all over and they exit with a link to the next story about a rap artist who developed dancing hamsters for his videos and they now make more money than him! I joke with the presenter as they cut to a news story and he comes back to me, I have found my place now, straight from me to the dancing hamsters!

Less than an hour after arriving at the studios, we are done, out walking through Times Square and out to get breakfast. We have a New York style, pancakes, bacon and sausage breakfast. Then I take a cab back to the apartment, where they are all still asleep! It feels weird, like I've done a full day already, like being on night shift. I make fresh coffee and write my diary.

New York to Derry
Home port celebrations

The day before departure we have our crew briefing at a local sports center in the gymnasium. We talk about ice warnings and limits, the possible weather conditions over the Flemish cap and the Grand Banks. Scenes from the perfect storm played out right where we are about to race. The race will pass within less than 100 miles of the Titanic last resting place. All this adds to the drama of our last ocean crossing, which, whilst only two weeks, is 2,800 miles and really not one to be taken lightly. After the briefing I head back to the apartment, via ground zero, where I pay some respects and take in the scenes as people mill around slightly dazed and confused by the experience.

Next morning we grab coffee and breakfast early before making our way to the marina. It's a small and intimate setting for race departure and as friends and family gather, it's a great atmosphere. The Mayor of Derry comes along for a photo call with us, and we all say our goodbyes. It feels like a jolly and joyous fun occasion for a change, everyone seems really happy, and looking forward to the race to Derry.

We slip bang on time to much cheering and applause from the gathered masses. We motor out into the Hudson and form up in parade order with the other yachts, main sails, flags and banners flying high and proud. The parade looks fantastic around past the Manhattan skyline and along in front of the Statue of Liberty, the resulting photos looked amazing. As we turn and head east out to sea, OneDLL call us and offer us a subway lunch. One of their sponsor contributors delivered subway to their boat in the morning and delivered way too much, so we gratefully accept a free lunch opportunity. They also give us their massive outdoor music speakers which have been temperamental and subsequently replaced on OneDLL, however after a full strip down and service I get them both working, install them at the back of the boat, our music upgrade is excellent and works fine for us.

Lining up just offshore for a Le Mans start, the countdown loud and clear on VHF. Once again Derry get the gun and we are first away. After ten minutes we peel to a code two kite and are first to do this, which gives us an extended lead. OneDLL, Switzerland and GREAT Britain follow suit and we pull away from the fleet slowly, making a steady 9ktts. We sail together, match racing, right next to each other almost touching at times for the first 15-18hours. We gybe back and forth a couple of times and by next morning we are alone again.

We didn't expect it to be quite so hot as we head offshore and for the first two days we are still in shorts and t shirts, doing a steady 10ktts under kites. The boat is level and, for the first few off watches, I get some great sleep, which is much appreciated after the hectic few days in New York. Ironic that one gets back on the boat for a rest! It's emotionally less stressful at least. We have a handful of new crew, and some previous leggers returning for leg 8, 'the glory leg' as we have called it, heading for home, three races back to London via Derry and Den Helder. On the third day, we start to layer up and within 24 hours we are back into full foulies and base layers again. The sea temperature drops 14 degrees in 36 hours. We make 60 miles VMG on one shed, racing along under the code two in a deep reach, with the nearest boat behind us making 30, and some only 11. We are starting to pull out a lead in first place, and everyone begins to hold their breath.

On day five, just after watch change at 12:00 midday, we are tidying the deck and plan to jam off a spinnaker halyard and move it across to a winch the other side of the cockpit. I jam it off and ease it out the winch. As I am flaking the halyard 'BANG' it let's go and the spinnaker falls a few feet as the halyard runs through. At first I am confused as to what happened, the kite is still flying and the halyard still tight. Then I can see the problem, the outer sheath of the halyard has sheared away, the spectra core has pulled through, milking the outer core into a ball against the jammers. I try to free it but it is stuck fast, I try to winch it, but no chance with it in this state. We call below for extra hands and prepare for a drop, once ready we cut the halyard free. A drastic measure and the first time we have ever been required to cut one away. As it drops fast we lose it over the side into the water, it is momentarily out of control and we drop the sheets away to protect it from shredding on the guard rails. Now the whole kite is in the water dragging behind the boat. We pull up to wind to keep it away from the rudders and start a retrieval. It's extreme proper hard graft to even move it. We set about organising the deck team and working as one, with calls of *'two six heave'*. Slowly we get it back on board, and rest for few moments before trying to get it down below. Meanwhile, a separate team have rigged a Yankee for hoist and get us back underway and racing again. We wool the kite as quickly as we can and get it straight back up onto deck. Prepared and ready for re-hoisting and set about a peel back to the code two. Once back up and flying we get a brew on and reflect on the last five hours hard work, all starting with a split second in time and an innocent halyard move. I feel guilty about the fallout from this manoeuvre. Albeit a routine job, it was me that was doing it. The crew play it back down and are gracious about it being just one of those things, but I still feel guilty just the same.

Next day the wind comes around and heads us, so it's back to Yankee. Within hours we are surfing at 12-15ktts, each time a new high speed is set we call it out to cheers from around the boat. The speeds get progressively higher, midafternoon there's a 19.6ktts to much oooorah! We hold the Yankee through the night and helming is proper hard work, it's a full upper body workout. Nick & I split the two four hour watches between us and helm through the night, in between, I am exhausted and sleep solid for three hours still in my foulies. It's the first time for a while we have had a proper workout on the helm and its great fun. Although dog tired, I feel really alive and settle into a groove. Comfortable with the feel of the boat, helming to the heel and wind on my face. I am pretty sure I could do this blindfolded now as Sean had suggested back in the Southern Ocean six months ago. The scheds roll in, three times in a row we are fastest boat in the fleet and the fourth sched GREAT Britain are the only boat faster and only by one mile. Morale on board is extremely high and we are in a really good place, whilst everyone is still holding their breath.

Sean is starting to get fidgety and jumpy, he sleeps for only an hour or so at a time and is up and down on deck like a Jack in the box, smoking way more than usual. I feel his pressure and tension, home port race, family, friends, media all watching him. It's an all or nothing race this one, probably the most important race of his career.

We change down from Yankee one to Yankee two, Charlie & I lead the team to un-hank the one and bring it back for flaking. About two thirds of the way through this manoeuvre I start to feel really uncomfortable on the foredeck, it's only mildly rough by comparison to what we have experienced before, but it's still pretty tasty and we are getting bashed around and pretty wet all the time. I slip back to the cockpit and change places with Niall who goes and finishes the job. Later Charlie comes and enquiries why I left him, I admit to feeling bad and he gives me a rare hug and sympathy; Charlie doesn't show his emotions very often and I am humbled by this. A few days later we change back to Yankee one, Charlie & Jason both encourage me to help and get in amongst it, with some initial trepidation I do. It's still tasty conditions and we get thrown around quite a bit. I get the sense they both have my back covered and it gives me some confidence to stay with it. I feel pretty sick and uncomfortable a few times but stay with it and once we are done I feel pleased with myself for sticking it out. Jay & Charlie pat me on the back and pass a *"well done mate"*. I smile in return and thank them. It's enough conversation about it. As Worlders we don't need to discuss everything, we really know each other very well inside and out now, we know what each other is thinking most of the time. As part of the getting back on board process it makes me feel good about myself and my confidence on deck continues to improve as a result.

The ice gates are moved south by 50 miles following an ice berg sighting, we double our ice watch and add a radar watch 24hours a day. A nervy time as we head around and only just clip the edge of the ice gate which is now directly in our path.

50 miles out from the scoring gate, we are second to Jamaica, fighting another light wind patch. We push as hard as we can with the wind available, changing sails round and round, but never quite catch them and pass through in second place. Second place gate points to Jamaica is ok, at least we take a margin on OneDLL & GREAT Britain on the gate at least.

Michelle & Charlie take up mother duties. It's their last ever mother watch on the race, and there is much discussion and hilarity around this. Talk of race finish and life after Clipper race is regular occurrence now for everyone. Interestingly there are varying degrees of clarity on what's next, some of us have really clear plans, some go back to previous jobs and houses, most are looking for something new, and very few of those have hard and fast plans. My own plans are at a bit of a hiatus now, I won't really know for sure until after race finish we can try and force a final job offer. I hope to have this confirmed by late August, move by early September and settle in by end of September. For now I can only hope this comes together and keep some options open elsewhere just in case. Whilst we sit together over lunch, someone wishes me a happy Father's Day. I didn't realise it was. I stop in my tracks and pause for moment thinking of my father, then thoughts of Siobhan. I haven't seen either of them for nearly a year now and miss them both a lot. Emotional thoughts fill me and in a moment I am totally overwhelmed. Michelle gives me a hug and we talk about Siobhan briefly. I go to my bunk for a little while for some peace. Racing around the world is an emotional experience, it's been a pretty full on few weeks, and I'm still tired from MOB, media and racing too.

The scheds roll in each day regular as clockwork on time, we are aiming straight at the mark still and we hold our position nicely. We watch the weather reports closely each day, there is a massive high pressure off the coast of Ireland which we are trying to avoid. It starts moving south. Immediate change of plans, we tack back and head north, the comfortable lead we have built up crashes down around us. We knew this would happen, but it's still hard to watch. We have to head north to skirt around the high pressure between us and Derry. The other boats will have to do the same, so we are not overly worried, but it's so hard to see a 150mile lead fall away to barely 20 miles.

The race office call and ask what we are doing, as they are considering a course alteration and need to be clear it will not be overtly advantageous to us. Sean discussed it with the team and later that morning we get the official notice. Course change, the race will finish at 12:00 midday UTC on 22nd June, all distance to finish positions will stand at that point. This fits with our strategy and we hold to the current plan. Our only real concern now is getting over the top of the high, and whether GREAT Britain will make it round the south side of it, which it looks like they are doing.

24 hrs to go and Jamaica are now only 20 miles away, Team Garmin, PSP Logistics and GREAT Britain are even closer and Old Pulteney are coming up fast. We look at the weather around where they are coming from, none of them 'should' be able to sail this fast! But they are and we can see it. We squeeze every last ounce of speed out of our CV30 hull. 12 hrs out, Jamaica now only 15 miles, Garmin 10 and Old Pulteney closing very fast from the south. 6 hrs out Garmin only 7 miles away, Jamaica 22 miles and Old Pulteney 20 now in third place. 2 hrs to go to the finish and they all appear on our AIS systems onboard, now we can see exactly what they are doing. We are holding station on Garmin, around 7-9 miles maybe. Jamaica appear to be

dropping away and Old Pulteney are catching us. Sean gets and email from his Dad, *"8 mile lead, two hours to go" "hold it out for just a short while longer"*. It's really tense on deck now; no one is talking, no eating or drinking, everyone down below is in the saloon. It feels a little like a wake on board it's so quiet everywhere. Sean is still helming, he has done most of the last 6 hours, he passes over to me for a short while, whilst he checks his email and makes a few calls, and then he is back on and focused again.

12:00 comes and we count down the seconds giving out a small potted cheer at the hour. We don't know where we have come as the other boats are all over the place on our systems, we need to wait for the official race office measurement. We hold our breath and await the email. At around 19minutes past the hour it comes through on our sat email. Provisional first place, to Garmin by 7 miles with Old Pulteney about 10 miles behind. Less than 10 miles separates the boats in fourth to ninth place after 3,000 miles. It's been an amazing race, so closely fought by all of the fleet.

A massive cheer goes up on deck and below as soon as we hear, the boats in range all call us up on VHF and congratulate us, we are really pleased for Garmin too, their first podium on the race so far. Old Pulteney too, it's the perfect podium for us. OneDLL finish eighth, which is also great news and closes our point's table gap to them down to only five points with two races left to go, all to play for still. It's only the third ever home win in 9 Clipper round the world races.

We have a 150 mile motor now to Derry and we set about getting as much work done as we can, servicing winches and deep cleaning. As we approach offshore Derry, boats start to come out to join us in flotilla. The first boat to join us is the lifeboat, with Sean's sisters and wife on board, they bring us Guinness, Champagne and bacon rolls at 01:30 about 40 miles out. The second boat is a Clipper'60 with friends and family on board. The third is a local yacht with Derry team on board from the last race, dressed in their original team kit with bottles of champagne for us. As we approach the mouth of the Foyle, the flotilla grows as more and more boats come out to join us. Along the banks, all the way in, there are crowds of people out waving and cheering. We pass schools where all the pupils are outside or down by the river. At the docks, all the workers have stopped working and line the dock waving their hard hats. A line of JCB with flashing lights on top, raise and lower their buckets in unison whilst blowing their horns. Gradually, the noise increases as we approach our moorings which are right in the city centre by the peace bridge. The Mayor is here on the dock to welcome us in. We talk Sean into standing on the bow with a red flare, he is slightly reluctant too, but we insist. I hand him the flare and say *"C'mon matey, when will you ever have this opportunity again?"* Music blaring, fireworks banging and a massive purple confetti cannon to welcome us home. It's been and emotional journey up the Foyle. We get immigration and media photos done as quickly as possible and exit the pontoons to greet family.

Heading up the pontoons, I am really excited about seeing my family, I can see them right by the gate, with lots of media standing close by. When I reach the gate I can see the media jumping in and stopping anyone else getting out. So I drop back and come out last. Massive hug from my mother who's crying as well, followed by Dad, and Shauna, my niece. My younger brother and his Irish wife are here too; it's great to see them all. Media form a scrum around us and jump in for photos and interviews. We oblige and make some statements, then once they start to jostle and push we close out and ask for some privacy. Taking official photos only then with Clipper race media.

We spend some time together chatting and reflecting, greeting other friends and family around. Everyone who passes stops to say hello and shake hands. There are some media commitments already and together for a few hours we interview with BBC and NI radio & TV taking photos along the way. As soon as we can we make a sharp exit, heading back to the cottage Mum & Dad have rented for the week, joined later by the same great friends from Scotland who were in Brest all those months before. We have a fabulous evening, even if I do fall asleep at the table during dinner!

Above; Triumphant team arrival in Derry
Below; Reunited with Mum, Dad & Shauna
Photo Credits; Clipper Ventures PLC

Derry to London, Via Den Helder
Heading home

The six day stopover in Derry is fantastic, it's all about the people, spontaneously grateful and celebratory with us. At prize giving in the guildhall, on stage Brenda Stevenson, the Mayor of Derry makes a short speech about my incident and how it may have spoilt my mother's birthday, then she presents my mother with a massive birthday cake in front of all the crews. Mum is put right on the spot and makes a response speech, gratefully thanking the crews who worked to recover me, and wishing the whole race safe passage. She does a fantastic job, Mum is a great public speaker and captivates the audience. We hug and share a big moment with the Mayor too, I don't think I have ever seen a mayor cry before!

The reception and cheers we get as a team as we collect our prize is enormous, a very popular win for Derry, in Derry.

A few evenings later we are invited on stage with the beach boys, Sean is interviewed and presents the team to the audience individually. Throughout the week, we are treated like kings everywhere we go. Free drinks in pubs, discount in restaurants, lots of smiles and hugs everywhere, sometimes from random people who just love the race. I am regularly recognised from MOB media and people stop and talk about the incident, many ask for photos to be taken together. Much of this is genuine and it's a pleasure to stop and talk to people. It takes up huge amounts of time and often interferes with what I am doing, but I cannot ignore this support and always make time to stop and talk. The MD of McMurdo, who made the AIS beacon I used, has flown in especially from Southampton to present me with it mounted on a presentation plinth. They have examined it after use. AIS technology has never ever been used to recover a man overboard before and they are very excited to hear more feedback. On the last evening there is a massive fireworks display on the river, a spectacular end to a spectacular week.

On race morning we are onboard by just after seven o'clock, the council provide us with breakfast in a marquee close by and we parade back to the boats all the teams together. The resulting photo of us lined up on the dock is excellent. The fleet slips lines to boat songs, with us slipping last. Then parade, flags and banners flying proud, around past the Peace Bridge and the assembled mass crowds. The sendoff is amazing. I get to see Mum & Dad, Shauna, James and Jackie briefly just before we slip lines. It's an emotional farewell, I play it down with a nonchalant *"bye for now, see you in two weeks in London"*. We get to go around again a second time to wave to the crowds, with our team song blaring out. As we pass the dock, we are blasted with a purple confetti cannon, the highlight of the day for some! At one point we conga around the deck and Mexican wave to the masses, much to everyone's cheering delight. It's a fantastic send off and we milk every minute of it.

We motor out to the start line and try to hold formation with all the other boats for 'the money shot' with the Red Arrows in the background. The media guys tell us they have it, and the results are amazing. Then it's down to work for race start, a straight drag for the line, tacking back & forth against as many of the other boats as we can.

Sean absolutely nails the start once again, first to GREAT Britain and Qingdao, it's the perfect way to leave Derry, in the lead as we head out to sea, awesome! I take up my position in the Nav station and call to Sean on the helm distance and bearing for shallows, rocks and other boats for the next five hours, whilst we settle into the race.

We make reasonable progress for the first 24 hours staying with the lead group of Jamaica Get All Right, Switzerland, Old Pulteney and PSP. The winds lighten, Invest Africa & Mission Performance get caught in the tidal gate and stall for several hours, costing them around 40 miles on the lead group. 24 hours into the race, we are in third place to Old Pulteney & Switzerland, but less than a mile separates all three of us.

I have my last mother duty with Mike on day two, chicken pie, mash & gravy for lunch, and curry for dinner. I am glad of the extra sleep it gives me after a full on week in Derry. Only 13 days now until we get back to London, I can't believe it's nearly race finish and so close now. I am really looking forward to seeing Siobhan in London. I think about the gate at St Katts and hope we pass back out of it. Most of all, I really hope we now all stay safe until we finish.

As we head further north and round the north coast of the Hebrides, we are back in ninth position. Turning east around the north westerly tip of Scotland we head in land and pick up the currents. Traveling through the Pentland Firth is stunningly beautiful. I am familiar with the coastline and have been there many times, with very many fond memories of great times living in the Highlands to recount to myself as we sail across. We catch the tides at the turn and heading towards the last few miles we gather speed as they sweep us along faster and faster. Heading out to sea away from John O'Groats we can see the boats ahead of us and set our sights on catching them. One by one we pick them off, PSP & Team Garmin first, but they are still very close, then OneDLL & GREAT Britain but equally there is not much in it. The North Sea takes hold and it gets proper tasty rough for a few days, wet, cold and grey exactly as you might imagine the North Sea to be. The Worlders are suffering now, everyone is really tired after the racing to this point and a pretty heavy week in Derry too. As we start to head towards race finish, the adrenaline occasionally wains and tiredness catches you. Most of us are carrying injuries too, everyone has suffered something, somehow. Half way across the North Sea, Michelle falls and hurts her hand really badly, missing a few days on deck. It's another sharp reminder to all of us just how quickly and easily one can get injured on board. The winds hold and we race fast onwards towards Den Helder.

A few days out we suffer a major steering issue, the rudders will hardly move and the helm feels as though they are locked tight. We have had many issues with steering and rudders all the way round the world, but this is by far the worst. We cross our fingers for the wind to stay on the nose as we would never be able to fly a spinnaker with steering this bad. Approaching the finish line we chase down Switzerland and get the gap down to a mile and half. Crossing the last of the TSS offshore, they have to bear away massively to navigate past a big ship crossing in front, we hold our course and get through without fuss. It costs them dear and we close right up to less than half a mile, with five miles to go. Skipper takes the helm and we all get up onto the rail for a little extra speed. Crossing the line no more than 250 meters back from them. Less than 10 miles separates the first six boats. It's been a great race and it's so great to sail across a finish line, instead of having a shortened race or time lapse finish this time. We celebrate on board and get to work cleaning the boat down for arrival. Only three points now separate us from overall third place behind OneDLL. That's a really tough call for the last race, but it is still possible for sure.

Many of the crew head off into Amsterdam for a few days. Some of us however decide to stay in Den Helder and enjoy the local hospitality, we rent cycles and tour around, kayak through the canals and enjoy a magnificent evening watching Holland in the semifinals of the world cup with the locals. In all, it's a great few days and I feel good as we start to prepare for the last race. Purposely taking it a little easier here, I want to be really fresh and fit when I see Siobhan and my family in only a few days' time in London. The excitement is building and I can feel myself getting anxious about it already.

Our exit and parade from the dock on race start day is reasonably quiet, but there are many people along the canals as we exit to cheer us off. We get down to race start mode very quickly and take up our places on deck. It's mental on the start line and really close, we think we are third, maybe fourth to OneDLL and Old Pulteney as we exit the bay and turn out into the North Sea for the last time. It's a straight drag race across and as we make good time, the race office extend the course twice to take us north again, then back around a loop before we enter the Thames estuary and head for Southend pier. The winds lighten and we can see the other boats ahead of us. OneDLL have covered us on every move across the North Sea, and as we approach the Southend Pier finish line, we are around 75 meters behind them, which gives them third place overall. Well-deserved for them, they have raced very hard and worked hard too for that. It is so fantastic to have fought with them right to the wire all the way around the world. We make a swift flypast and applaud & cheer them as we pass. They swing back around and do the same for us.

Mum's surprise birthday cake at prize giving in Derry from Brenda Stevenson, The Mayor of Derry

Photo Credit;
Clipper Ventures PLC

Return to London
Homecoming

We spend the night off Southend, cleaning and preparing the boat for the parade next morning, grabbing a few hours' sleep each where we can. Next morning around 06:30 we muster all 12 boats together and prepare for the parade. By 07:30 we have our flags and banners proudly flying, fall into formation, line astern and set off up the Thames estuary. It is way longer than you might imagine and takes us several hours just to get to the city boundary. As we approach the Thames barrier we can see the beginnings of the flotilla coming out to join us. One by one the sail boats, RIBs and cruisers pass by, circle around behind us and join the parade. A short while later the spectator boats arrive. Our own friends & family spectator boat, arranged by our team shore support team, passes by the fleet and settles alongside us. It's absolutely covered in purple, with massive Derry flags everywhere and our team song, 'Hall of Fame', by the Script blaring out in the background. The crowds onboard are cheering and waving madly. Everywhere we look there are faces we recognise, crew from earlier legs of the race, friends, family, even the Brenda, the Mayor of Derry and her entourage. I can see my parents at the front of the top deck and wave & blow kisses to them. We get ourselves together as a team for photos and we all wave for ages. It's a fantastic welcome and one we should all be really proud of.

After a while of waving and cheering, I am watching Mum & Dad mingling with the crowds, I am sure I recognise the lady next to my Mum. She looks exactly like Diana, my brother's wife. They live in Sydney, so it can't be her. She is waving now and blows me a kiss, I look again, bloody hell it 'IS' her! I look again and there's my brother, and his two sons, my nephews. Oh my god! I can't believe it, what a massive surprise. They realise now I have seen them, the boys are laughing and waving madly. I try and call over to them, something like *'what are you doing here'* or *'when was this planned'* but they can't hear me over the music and cheering. I am overcome with seeing them, I try and tell Michelle but I well up and cry before I can finish telling her. *'I know'* she says *'we all know!'* she gestures around the crew, one or two others have seen this and smile back. *"How did you all keep that a secret?"* I ask. *"Bloody hard"* says Michelle, *"I've known for months! Now go and enjoy it!"*

It's an amazing sight and I am really touched they are here! We spend the next couple of hours staring and waving at each other as we traverse the Thames all the way up to Tower Bridge. As the rest of the day progresses, and even well into tomorrow I recount this surprise to people. *'Guess what?'* I say, and almost all of them reply with a smile *"yes, we know!"* Most of the team, the crew, our friends & family, the race office, the media team, even Sir Robin himself, all knew they were coming from Sydney to London, many of them have known for months! It's a proper awesome and very very special and touching surprise.

Approaching Tower Bridge we peel off, the first three boats go under the bridge, we go around again. I speak to Siobhan on the phone and she explains exactly where she is standing. As we round the Thames and head back out I catch a fleeting glimpse of her massive smile and wave. She is standing on top of a bench behind the crowds bouncing up and down with excitement. We text each other over the next hour or so and I let her know timings and positions for when we are due in. We eventually get our radio call from the race office team to make our final approach. We turn around for the short motor up, then swing around into the dock. Slowly we pass through the dock and I stand proud on the starboard side waving to Siobhan, blowing each other kisses with massive smiles. I get a few hugs from crew members who see this and it's getting too much for me already. We spin around and make our reverse into the dock in one manoeuvre. Not a time to get this one wrong! Sean makes it look easy and we slide into the dock perfectly. I have an aft going spring mooring line in my hand, I lean out and pass it over as we reverse in. On the dock is Hannah White, the TV compere for the live event, keeping the crowds up to date with what's going on and being filmed for the massive TV screens all around the dock. She turns and says *'I've got Andrew Taylor here with me'* the camera points straight into my face *'what's it like to be home Andrew, you have had a more traumatic experience than most?'* She recounts some man overboard details and asks me to comment. I say *"it's been traumatic for everyone not just me"* I go on to thank Skipper and crew and everyone who has supported us as team. She asks if *"it's good to be back"* and I say it's all going to be about family time now. She asks what I am looking forward to the most and I say without hesitation seeing my daughter, I can't wait to see her, I am really struggling with the words now, I look straight down the camera and say *'love you Siobhan'*.

All the time whilst I have been interviewed, unbeknown to me, Siobhan is standing right in front of the big screen, with her Mum and my Dad. When I say *'love you Siobhan'* she completely melts and breaks down big time. All three of them together have a massive hug and it takes Siobhan a good long while to recover herself. Later she makes her way around to the walkway above the boats and we chat briefly across the 3-4 meters which is now all that separates us after a year apart. As we await the final formal proceedings. The teams are called to the stage in reverse order, when we get our chance, we all parade up together, too much clapping & cheering all around us. Sir Robin greets us all center stage, shaking hands and smiling with each and every one of the crew as they step up to the stage. As I step up, we both pause together looking at each other, with fixed eye contact for a short pause with a big smile, then we embrace into a massive hug together. *"Good to see you safe and sound back home mate, well done you, bloody well done you"* says Sir Robin into my ear. *"Boy it feels good to be home"* I respond *"thank you so much for your support matey"*. Sir Robin asks *"have you seen your daughter yet?"* *"No not yet"* I say, *"but she's just up there"* pointing away to the crowds above us. *"Enjoy the moment Andrew, this one is very very special, you enjoy it mate"* he says. After some brief interviews with Skipper on stage, more media photos and special presentations for our overall fourth place, we are free to go. We exit slowly in almost single file via a raised walkway from the pontoons.

As I look up along the walkway I see 'the gate'. This is our gate, it's where we started, it's the image I have carried with me around the world, the moment I have looked forward to so much. I remember some of the times I have thought about this. Now here we are about to exit it. Out through the same gate where we left almost a year ago to join the race.

My heart starts to race and I can feel myself becoming emotional and filling up. As we exit the gate we are swamped into massive crowds. It's a lot to take in, I am feeling even more overwhelmed now, not sure where to go, I feel scared and short of breath, my heart is beating heavy in my chest. The crowd seems to clear slightly. Right there only a few feet away is Siobhan, she is standing right there in front of me now. It seems to go quiet, almost like I have gone deaf. I forget about the moment, forget about the crowds, like it's just me and her. She looks absolutely fabulous, the most massive smile I have ever seen on her beautiful face, we both step forward, she jumps up as we grab hold of each other, embrace tightly, hugging for ages, both crying really hard. I can think of nothing to say, other than *'love you'* over and over again. When we eventually release each other we just stare at each other with massive smiles.

"Boy oh boy! It is so unbelievably good to see Siobhan again, to hold her and to talk to her, to finally be home. Alive, safe & sound"

Back together again
Photo Credit; Warren Sutton

Left to right above;
Jack, Siobhan, Andrew, and
Patrick
Photo Credit; Warren Sutton

Post Script

I am under no illusions, I fully appreciate and will never ever take life for granted. I am an incredibly lucky boy.

To have returned fit and well, after 1 hour & 40 minutes in the freezing North Pacific with a possibly broken leg, in icy sea waters of below 9degC, over 1,500 miles from land, about as remote as one could ever possibly be on this planet.

I am eternally grateful to our Derry Skipper Sean McCarter, to all of the crew who worked so hard on that day, to Olly Cotterell and the crew of OneDLL, and to the race office teams on land. All of whom were so incredibly professional during the search and rescue operations.

I am extremely humbled by the level of support shown to the crew, to my family back home and the race as a whole from people all over the world. The amazing messages of moral support we all received really did help us through the remainder of that fateful day and some of the really dark ones that followed. There are many elements to this chapter of my life which could have turned out differently. However, the whole episode has been extremely traumatic for all of those involved; not just me. Writing this book has been quite therapeutic for me. I have had some very dark days whilst writing this but I hope that perhaps one or two others may find some therapy in reading it.

There are some fantastic lessons to learn from this unique experience, which I am very happy to share. I genuinely believe as a direct result of some of this adventure lives will be saved in future.

One thing is for sure, it gives each and every one of us a big drama story to tell friends and family for generations to come. Each will be slightly different, viewed from a different angle and perspective. Over time, I have no doubt the drama will be exaggerated in places. Waves may get bigger, the wind may get stronger as the years pass by. But each and every story will always end in the same way. The normal, ordinary and now lucky guy who fell off a racing yacht, in possibly one of the very remotest parts of the world, shall be recovered back on board safely by a team of true superstar legends, who never ever give up hope of finding him. We shall all arrive in San Francisco safe and sound, ready to each go on to tell their own version of a great adventure story with a truly happy ending. I genuinely truly and openly hope you have enjoyed my version of this story.

To all those involved in my safe recovery
"Thank You"

To everyone else around the world;
"Fair winds, safe sailing and good luck."

Andrew Taylor

Tributes

As a family we are deeply indebted to the patience and expertise, of Skipper Sean McCarter, and his wonderful crew of dedicated amateur sailors, who on that night, truly showed all the team spirit and skills, they had learned throughout their Clipper training, which no doubt played a major part in the successful rescue of a beloved son.

Anthony & Eileen Taylor

For the first time in over 20 years I realise just how far away I am from my family at a time when potentially they may need me Later, we were able to plot a wonderful surprise to meet Andrew as he sailed back up the Thames and I don't recall ever being so happy to see someone in my whole life.

I was also able to shake Justin's hand and thank him sincerely for the care and professionalism in dealing with what must have been one of the most difficult phone calls he'll ever have to make. I'd like to again thank him, and publically this time, for the care and attention he gave my whole family at a harrowing and difficult time. Andrew was in good hands on board. Justin made sure we were in good hands too and we will all be forever grateful for that.

Sean Taylor; Andrews's older brother

Watching Andrew slip over the side and the subsequent hour and forty minutes it took us to recover him was the most terrifying ordeal of our race. The manner in which the crew reacted was textbook; a testament to the rigorous training provided by Clipper. Andrew's sheer determination and also the fact he remembered his Sea Survival training were crucial with such a long time spent in the water. The knowledge that our friends on OneDLL were diverting to help us search was another huge source of comfort for which we were all grateful.

Sean McCarter, Race Skipper, Derry LondonDerry Doire

Nobody wants to hear a Mayday call, however this call was made all the more pertinent as it came from some of our best friends. I certainly will remember that radio call for the rest of my life. I am exceedingly proud of how the crew of OneDLL handled themselves, performing complex evolutions in cold and extremely challenging conditions to get the yacht stopped, turned around and heading back towards Andrew's position. They achieved this with an efficiency that would be the envy of many professional crews.

Progress back upwind towards Derry's last position was slow due to the large seas, strong wind and powerful squalls but the OneDLL crew did a great job as on scene support and communications, thus enabling Derry to concentrate on their search pattern.

It can't be understated just how challenging the conditions were. All credit must be given to Sean McCarter and his entire crew for their successful recovery of Andrew. It was a source of massive relief and joy when we heard that he had been recovered successfully and was alive".
Oliver Cotterell, Race Skipper OneDLL

It was probably the longest night of my life. I was alone in my house that night not as alone as Andrew was, but nonetheless I had to keep my emotions in check so that I could perform my job well and do what was necessary. My grimness turned to elation when he was recovered alive, I could not sleep for the rest of the night.
Justin Taylor, Race Director, Clipper Ventures PLC

All in all, a quite unexpected series of events, initiated with absolutely the worst phone call of my life. But like all good fairy stories, a happy ending and as with all situations of this nature, some huge lessons to be learnt and developed further for the future safety of all Clipper race crews.

I would like to say how proud I am personally of all the people involved in this entire situation. They acted with total professionalism and ultimate commitment to the cause and those are exactly the values that we promote at Clipper Ventures and the Clipper Round the World Race.

Mark Light, Deputy Race Director, Clipper Ventures Plc

One of the bleakest experiences of my life to date, hearing the shout "Man overboard" when you are in the middle of one of the world's harshest oceans is something no crew should have to hear. That said, no-one panicked, the team had just one focus, to recover Andrew. What so many of us forget, is that the crew are just ordinary people, and although timely, the recovery was flawless. For this we must remember, we as a whole crew achieved something truly extraordinary that day.

Michelle Porter, Crew Member, Derry LondonDerry Doire

It is only upon reflection that the magnitude of the event truly hits home. At the time there was no pause for thought, everybody just assumed their respective roles as trained. For the very longest hours we collectively focused on one thing only, locating and getting Andrew back!

Jason Middleton, Crew Member, Derry LondonDerry Doire

For some crazy reason when Sean shouted out 'man overboard' I honestly thought how strange it was to have a MOB drill in the middle of the North Pacific, but how very thorough of Clipper race to ask the Skippers to run a drill! For the next hour and a half on deck searching the huge waves for an orange speck I thought about all the reasons why Andrew couldn't have turned on his AIS beacon.
Once the beacon came on I only had one thought, that Andrew was well enough to turn it on and that we were going to find our friend alive.
Susie Redhouse, Crew Member Derry LondonDerry Doire

The events of the night of 30th March 2013 were relayed to us at home in Derry through the then Mayor Martin Reilly we were shocked but elated in equal measures. To have someone go overboard our own Derry Londonderry Doire Clipper race yacht wasn't what we envisaged at any stage throughout the race. We were just glad that the outcome was positive and that Andrew would make a full recovery. The whole crew made the City of Derry Londonderry so proud and I was especially pleased to meet Andrew in New York and hear first-hand of his experience of MOB and that of his skipper Sean McCarter who successfully led the team to saving Andrews' life.
Brenda Stevenson, Mayor Derry LondonDerry

My prayers were answered! Such relief for everyone involved. The next few days and weeks I regularly thought about what Andrew had gone through and the very strange night I'd had, perched entirely on the edge of my bed while all the other events took place.
Helen Staniford, Partner of Mark Light, Deputy Race Director

A message came through from our race director Justin Taylor. 'MOB recovered. Initial reports of shock and hypothermia. More detail to come as I receive it'. I remember responding with just, 'THANK GOD'. The feeling of relief was immense. It felt like a miracle, and I breathed a sense of relief for Andrew and his family, and that Jonathan and I would no longer be faced with writing the first death statement in the Clipper Race's nineteen year history.

I reached the office and Jonathan was already at his desk. He didn't say anything. He just got up and gave me the hardest, longest hug. It said everything.

Julia Wall-Clarke, PR Manager, Clipper Ventures PLC

I knew Andrew was a strong chap, but this was a quite amazing survival in some of the most extreme conditions on the planet. I was amazed at the calm and composed manner in which Andrew recounted his experience whilst wrapped in a cocoon of sleeping bags and hot water bottles to regain his body temperature. I was mindful of the impact of the search to find Andrew had upon the crew as a whole. As part of our race training we undertook sea survival training. But suddenly the reality of what we had been trained to contend with was grounded with the images of Andrews rescue that now seemed ever present in the worlds media.

Nial Heally, Crew Member, Derry LondonDerry Doire

Shock evolves into action in a split second. I raise my arm to point to our crewmate floating far too quickly towards a choppy horizon. For me, the noise all around us has become merely a background murmur. I have one job to do. Don't lose sight of Andrew. Three massive rolling waves later, I did!
Later I am told over 90 minutes has passed. They were very long minutes. Ones I am in no hurry ever to repeat. And the lesson? Don't ever give up. No matter what.
Chris Matthew, Crew Member, Derry LondonDerry Doire

We got an unusual signal from the skipper that he wanted to talk to everyone, kind of out of the blue at an odd time for chit chat. We get the message that a crew member on another boat has been lost over board, total silence! "who"? someone asks, "we don't know at this point". Other boats are helping to look. I get a heavy sinking feeling knowing this is very bad. We numbly return to our tasks someone shouts Clip on. We all think 'yes I will clip on this time' for sure, and we all do. Watch ends and off to bed with nothing said. Sometime later we learn that the man over board has been recovered. It was not till we got to port that I learned that it was Andrew who went over board and that if it had not been for his dry suit and AIS he would never have made it back alive. We met on shore, shake hands, embrace & talk. I can see he is a changed man, little wonder!
James Dick, Crew Member, Henri Lloyd

Extract from the Derry LondonDerry Doire log book:

Sunday 30th March 2014 - (Local times)

MOB called @ position 41:43:213N 179:11:451W
11:32 MOB called
11:35 1st Mayday call broadcast
11:37 search pattern in place and underway lost visual contact with casualty
11:40 DLL respond to mayday call, making best speed to join the search
11:45 2nd Mayday call broadcast, nothing heard
11:50 Search pattern widening, search continues
11:55 3rd Mayday call broadcast, nothing heard
12:50 DLL arrive on scene and join the search
12:57 AIS activation connection made: 2.5nm away, drifting at a speed of 4.5kts, position bearing 082deg from the boat
13:15 Casualty recovered and back on board
Recovery: 41 42 89N / 179 08 84W - exactly two miles from point of entry
13:20 Casualty below deck receiving emergency medical care
13:30 DLL continue to escort with medical support if required
13:50 DLL stand down and return to the race, but the crew & Skipper of OneDLL elect to stay with Derry for the next 24 hours offing moral support.

Extract from the OneDLL log book.
All times UTC

30 March
Situation prior to first transmission from CV30:

Skipper on helm. Sail plan: poled out Yankee 3, 2 reefs in the main. Watch changeover, deck crew preparing to gybe prior to lunch on deck.

Weather: westerly wind 40 ktts true, pressure rising 1010, moderate to rough sea state, 4/8 cloud, fair weather and good visibility.

2340; First VHF transmission from CV30 on Channel 16 call to "OneDLL" moved to M1. Informed on M1 of M.O.B Position of CV20: 41 48.302N, 178 56.996W

Skipper called all hands on deck, directing two crew to the nav station to contact CV30 to get their position, the time of the MOB and give them our position.

2342; Call to CV30 on VHF Channel M1. Received position of MOB: 41 43.213N, 179 11.451W. Nav station crew plotted position in SeaPro and position and course in Garmin, relaying new course to Skipper on deck.

N.B. All further position updates were plotted in Garmin only as SeaPro repeatedly froze and crashed several times during first position plot due to proximity to International Date Line.

2345; Crew gybed Y3 to port, got pole down and secured on deck.

2349; Call to CV30 on Channel 16 to inform them of our position, situation and ETA.

2350; Foredeck crew dropped Y3 and secured it on deck. Checked that staysail and pole were well   secured.

During Y3 drop, wind picked up to 70-80 ktts true and sea state became very rough. Pit and mast crew put third reef in main. Skipper asked nav station crew to contact CV30 to find out whether the race office and Falmouth coast guard had been informed. CV30 informed us that they had not yet contacted the race office or Falmouth CG, so we confirmed that we would do so on their behalf. Throughout the incident CV20 relayed information between CV30 and the race office.

2351; Call to Mark Light via Fleet Broadband to inform him of the situation, give the time of the MOB, the positions of both vessels and the weather. ML confirmed that he would contact Falmouth CG.

2352; Call from CV30 to inform us that the MOB was not the Skipper, and that they did not have a visual on the casualty.

2354; Mayday on Channel 16 from CV30.

2356; Call to CV30 to confirm that ML would contact Falmouth CG.

2357; Comms lockdown instigated.

Deck crew tacked to return to last position of MOB and pinned in the main ready to motor sail back to CV30, who were directly upwind of our position.

Position of CV20: 41 49.714N, 178 54.073W

2359; Nav station crew tried to contact CV22 Qingdao on VHF Channel 16 as next closest Clipper vessel but without success.

31 March

0000; Crew opened wet exhaust outlet to engine and checked that day tank was topped up in preparation for starting engine. (Engine was last wobbled at 0455 on 30 March 2014.)

Call to CV30 but lost transmission.

0001; Tried again to contact CV22 without success.

0002; Call from CV30. Received new position of MOB: 41 43.227N, 179 11.449W. Confirmed that still no visual on the casualty.

0003; Nav station crew plotted new position and course in Garmin and relayed information on deck.

0006; Mayday on Channel 16 from CV30.

0012; Call from ML for update on situation. ML confirmed that CV22 was not in VHF range, requested that we ask CV30 to call

ML when convenient and also asked for confirmation that both vessels were in comms lockdown. ML asked us to call back in 30 minutes or when we next had an update from CV30.

0016; Started engine.

Position of CV20: 41 48.035N, 178 53.924W

0019; Call to CV30 to ask them to contact ML and confirm the comms lockdown, and give an update on our situation, position and ETA to last MOB position.

0020; Rotated crew on and off deck to eat lunch, keep warm and therefore be fresh and ready to search when needed. Helm plus three crew remained on deck at all times.

Medic retrieved IV fluids in case they would be needed and placed them in the engine room to warm up.

Weather: squally conditions including hail.

0043; Call from CV30 to inform us that they had picked up an MOB (AIS) beacon and give us the new position: 41 42.917N, 179 09.067W. CV30 was 2.8nm from this position and proceeding there to restart search.

Nav station crew plotted new position and course in Garmin and relayed information on deck.

0046; Call to ML to give update. No response so left a message.

0049; Call to CV30 to ask for a description of the MOB.

Casualty wearing a yellow dry suit. Relayed information on deck.

0050; Call to ML to give update. While on phone received 0051 call from CV30 and gave ML updated position for MOB beacon.

0051; Call from CV30 to give new position for MOB beacon: 41 42.892N, 179 08.846W, travelling at 1.6 knots on a bearing from CV30 of 56'T.

0055; Call from CV30 to inform us that they had a visual on the casualty and were instigating recovery procedures.

Nav station crew confirmed that we would inform ML.

0056; Call to ML. No response so left a message.

0059; Call to ML to relay latest from CV30.

0101; Call from CV30 to inform us that the casualty had been retrieved and that they would call back to let us know their condition.

0103; Call to ML to relay latest.

Call from CV30 to tell us to disregard the last. The casualty had not yet been retrieved.

Nav station crew informed ML.

0113; Call from CV30 to inform us that the casualty was on deck and their condition was being assessed.

Call to ML to relay latest. While on phone received 0114 call from CV30. Relayed news to ML.

ML asked that CV30 call him as soon as possible.

0114; Call from CV30 to confirm that the casualty was alive.

Nav station crew confirmed that ML was aware and asked that they call ML ASAP.

0117; CV30 appeared on AIS on a bearing of 256', distance 6.45nm.

Plotted new course in Garmin to their position and relayed information on deck.

0120; Call from CV30 to inform us that the casualty was cold and shaken but OK.

Nav station crew informed them that we were slowing down but maintaining our heading until informed otherwise.

0130; Skipper off helm and replaced by rotation of three crew members.

0150; All crew on deck and numbered off for debrief, review of events and update on situation prior to resuming racing.

179W One Seven Nine West